Julian of Norwich's *Showings*

✳

Julian of Norwich's *Showings*

FROM VISION TO BOOK

*

DENISE NOWAKOWSKI BAKER

PRINCETON UNIVERSITY PRESS

PRINCETON, NEW JERSEY

Library of Congress Cataloging-in-Publication Data
Baker, Denise Nowakowski, 1946–
Julian of Norwich's Showings : from vision to book /
Denise Nowakowski Baker
p. cm.
Includes bibliographical references and index.
ISBN 0-691-03631-4 (alk. paper)
1. Julian, of Norwich, b. 1343.
Revelations of divine love. I. Title.
BV4831.J83B34   1994
242—dc20   94–4399

This book has been composed in Caslon

Princeton University Press books are
printed on acid-free paper and meet the guidelines
for permanence and durability of the Committee
on Production Guidelines for Book Longevity
of the Council on Library Resources
Printed in the United States of America   •

1 3 5 7 9 10 8 6 4 2

TO MY MOTHER, ELEANOR,

AND IN MEMORY OF

MY FATHER, EDMUND

✳

✳ *Contents* ✳

✳ *Illustrations* ✳

✳ *Acknowledgments* ✳

ALTHOUGH many friends and colleagues have encouraged my work, I can mention only a few. I learned much from Jodi Bilinkoff as we taught a class on medieval and Renaissance women writers and in our subsequent conversations. Charles Orzech spurred the writing of chapter 3 by referring me to works on theodicies. Mary Bullington commented extensively on the first four chapters and discussed with me her own research on the medieval practice of meditation. Caroline Walker Bynum made valuable suggestions for improving chapter 5. Nicholas Watson offered me new perspectives by sharing his own work on Julian of Norwich. The final version of this study owes much to both of the readers for Princeton University Press; it is a better book because of their requests for revision.

I wish to thank the University of North Carolina at Greensboro for supporting my work on this book with an Excellence Fellowship for the summer of 1987 and a research assignment in fall 1988. The staff of Jackson Library made it a pleasure to work there; Sigrid Walker of Acquisitions and Gaylor Callahan of Interlibrary Loan cheerfully responded to my numerous requests. I am also grateful to Duke Divinity School and Cambridge University for allowing me to use their libraries.

Finally, throughout the years, my husband, Lee, and my daughter, Andy, have sustained me with joy.

Julian of Norwich's *Showings*

✳

IN THE last quarter of the fourteenth century, while Chaucer wrote vernacular poetry in London, some one hundred miles to the northeast in Norwich, the first English woman identified as an author was composing a book in prose. Impelled by a visionary experience in May 1373, she completed two different versions of her *Book of Showings*, the short and the long texts, over the course of at least the next two decades.

Little more is known about this woman beyond what she herself relates. A scribal note introduces the only extant copy of the short text as "a visionn schewed be the goodenes of god to a deuoute womann, and hir name es Julyan, that is recluse atte Norwyche and ʒitt ys onn lyfe, anno domini millesimo CCCC xiij" ["a vision shown by the goodness of God to a devout woman, and her name is Julian, who is a recluse at Norwich and still alive, A.D. 1413" (125)].[1] This woman is probably called Julian after the church in whose anchorhold she was enclosed from at least 1393/4. The fact that a female recluse occupied the cell during the last decade of the fourteenth century is verified by bequests to "'Julian' anakorite" in several wills dating from this time until 1416.[2] Although her state of life at the time she composed the two versions is unknown, these bequests indicate that the author of *A Book of Showings* was recognized regionally as an anchorite by the end of the century.

The evidence of the wills is corroborated by Margery Kempe's account of her consultation with "Dame Ielyan" early in the second decade of the fifteenth century. Margery reports that she was divinely directed to go to Norwich from nearby King's Lynn to seek spiritual guidance from Julian, "for þe ankres was expert in swech thyngys & good cownsel cowd ʒeuyn" ["for the anchoress was expert in such things and could give good advice"].[3] Since the advice that the anchorite gives Margery echoes ideas articulated in the long text, there is no reason to doubt that this Julian is the one who wrote *A Book of Showings*.

Despite her regional reputation as a holy woman, Julian of Norwich was probably not well known as an author during her lifetime. The small number of extant manuscripts and the late date of most of them indicate that *A Book of Showings* did not circulate widely. Furthermore, the differences among the texts in the early and later manuscripts raise questions about the process of their composition.

Only two of the six extant manuscripts are pre-Dissolution: British Library Additional 37790 (referred to as "Amherst" after a previous owner) is mid-fifteenth-century, and the Westminster Archdiocesan Archives MS was produced around 1500. Four later manuscripts were copied at religious houses on the Continent around 1650: Bibliothèque Nationale Fonds anglais 40, British Library Sloane 2499 and Sloane 3705, and St. Joseph's College, Upholland (Lancashire, England).[4] Although both early manuscripts contain versions of the *Showings* much shorter than that in the Continental manuscripts, they differ from each other. Westminster provides excerpts found only in the seventeenth-century manuscripts, demonstrating that the longer version was available as early as 1500. Since a scribal note at the beginning of the Amherst MS states that it was copied from an ancestor produced in 1413—while Julian was still alive, but probably only a year or two before her death—one might conclude that its short text, like Westminster's, was also abbreviated from the long by the author herself or someone else. On the other hand, the short text found in the Amherst manuscript corresponds roughly to Revelations One through Twelve despite some rearrangement and much elaboration in the long text.[5] The fourteen chapters that constitute Revelation Thirteen of the long version expand the material appearing in five and a half chapters (mid-13 through 18) of the short text. And only rudimentary traces of Revelations Fourteen through Sixteen exist in the final seven chapters of the Amherst version; there is no hint of the parable of the lord and servant or of the Jesus-as-Mother analogy so significant to the long text.

What, then, is the relationship between these two different forms of *A Book of Showings*, designated by scholars as the short and long texts? Is the short text in Amherst, the earliest extant manuscript, an abridgment of or an antecedent to the long text witnessed by the remaining five manuscripts? Indeed, were both versions composed by Julian herself, and if so, when did she write them? Since the answers I offer to these questions form crucial assumptions underlying my interpretation of *A Book of Showings*, I had best articulate them before I embark on my argument.

I agree with the standard explanation, presented most thoroughly by Edmund Colledge and James Walsh in the introduction to their Middle English edition of the *Showings*, that Julian herself composed both versions and that the short text preceded the long by twenty or more years. This interpretation of the puzzling manuscript evidence is based on additional information about the chronology of composition provided by Julian herself. Although she never says when she composed the short text, she gives the date of her visionary experience as May 1373 in chapter 2 of the long text. She also confesses that she did not completely understand the revelations when she first received them. In chapter 86 she admits that she reflected on her showings for fifteen years before she understood God's meaning (16.86.732–33). And in chapter 51, just before she relates the parable of the lord and servant, she acknowledges that she pondered this enigmatic example "for twenty yere after the tyme of the shewyng saue thre monthys" (14.51.520) ["for twenty years after the time of the revelation except for three months" (270)]. Julian thus implies that she was not able to complete the long version of her *Showings* until at least two decades after her visionary experience in 1373.

The omission from the short text of all the material in Revelation Fourteen except the discussion of prayer in the first three chapters appears to confirm Julian's confession of her initial perplexity about this showing and to corroborate the assumption that the short text preceded the long. Because only these chapters on prayer are referred to in the summary of the revelations that opens the long text, Colledge and Walsh argue that Julian composed two "editions" of this later version: an intermediate one without the expansion that constitutes most of Revelation Fourteen started around 1388 and the final, complete version some time shortly after she achieved her insight into the example of the lord and servant in 1393. Based on this theory about the two stages of the long text's composition, Colledge and Walsh conclude that Julian must have begun the short text soon after the visionary experience of 1373.[6] That a scribe copied the short text as late as 1413, according to this theory, only indicates its continuing popularity or his independence from Julian's supervision. Although it remains possible that someone else may have abridged Julian's long text around 1413 to produce the short text, the scribe's identification of her as the author renders it unlikely.

The priority of the short text to the long is crucial to my study of *A Book of Showings* because I endeavor, in the chapters that follow, to delineate Julian's maturation, in the process of composing these two different versions, from a visionary into a theologian. Analyzing the differences between her conceptualizations in these two texts, I hope to show that this devout woman's near-death experience provided the catalyst for her growth into an erudite and original religious thinker, familiar with the traditions of late medieval theology and creative in adapting them to her own purposes.

The portrait of Julian of Norwich that I will present, however, contradicts the evidence about how severely educational opportunities for women were restricted in medieval society. Because the degree of learning that she exhibits is so extraordinary, the lack of information about her life poses a particular challenge. As the first known English woman writer, Julian provokes fascinating questions about her motivation and preparation for authorship. As a visionary and mystic, however, she writes in a genre that seems to elude critical investigation.

Julian recognizes her uniqueness as a woman writer. In contrast to the Continent, where accounts of visionary experiences by women were prominent, England manifested a conservative spirituality that discouraged such a tradition of women's writing.[7] Realizing that she may be accused of violating the church's prohibition against women's teaching, Julian forestalls such criticism in the short text by representing herself as the messenger of God.

> Botte god for bede that ȝe schulde saye or take it so that I am a techere, for I meene nouȝt soo, no I mente nevere so; for I am a womann, leued, febille and freylle. Botte I wate wele, this that I saye, I hafe it of the schewynge of hym tha(t) es souerayne techare. Botte sothelye charyte styrres me to telle ȝowe it, for I wolde god ware knawenn, and mynn evynn crystene spede, as I wolde be my selfe to the mare hatynge of synne and lovynge of god. Botte for I am a womann, schulde I therfore leve that I schulde nouȝt telle ȝowe the goodenes of god, syne that I sawe in that same tyme that is his wille, that it be knawenn? And that schalle ȝe welle see in the same matere that folowes aftyr, if itte be welle and trewlye takynn. Thane schalle ȝe sone forgette me that am a wrecche, and dose so that I lette ȝowe nought, and behalde Jhesu that ys techare of alle. (1:222)

[But God forbid that you should say or assume that I am a teacher, for that is not and never was my intention; for I am a woman, ignorant, weak and frail. But I know very well that what I am saying I have received by the revelation of him who is the sovereign teacher. But it is truly love which moves me to tell you, for I want God to be known and my fellow Christians to prosper, as I hope to prosper myself, by hating sin more and loving God more. But because I am a woman, ought I therefore to believe that I should not tell you of the goodness of God, when I saw at that same time that it is his will that it be known? You will see this clearly in what follows, if it be well and truly accepted. Then will you soon forget me who am a wretch, and do this, so that I am no hindrance to you, and you will contemplate Jesus, who is every man's teacher. (135)]

Like the Continental women mystics, Julian initially authorizes herself as an intermediary between the sovereign teacher, Jesus, and her fellow Christians; as a woman, she can minister to them only because she is the medium for a divine lesson.[8]

Although she undoubtedly believed it, Julian's claim to be an intermediary between her audience and God seems to preclude an investigation of her role as author and to foreclose critical examination of *A Book of Showings*. The rhetoric of visionary or mystical discourse typically denies the contingency of its production; in proclaiming their authors as recipients of supernatural truth, these texts attempt to transcend historical and cultural contextualization. Such claims have, until recently, limited the study of mystical writings to two camps: believers who wish to elucidate and assess the orthodoxy of the mystic's message, and skeptics who hope to explain the physical or psychological pathology that produced it.[9]

Nonetheless, visionary and mystical phenomena, like all other kinds of experience, occur within particular cultural frames of reference. An investigation of the belief system incorporated into accounts of these experiences does not, therefore, imply a judgment on their ontological or epistemological validity, but simply acknowledges the impossibility of having any experience devoid of preconceptions. As philosopher Peter Moore observes,

> while it is undoubtedly the case that a mystic's beliefs and expectations are likely to affect the nature both of his experience and his report of his experience, this influence constitutes no more of a problem in the case of mysticism than it does in the case of any other form of experience. The mystic's doctrinal background should, therefore, be seen as a key to his experience rather than a door which shuts us off from it.[10]

In Julian's case such doctrinal background is the only key available not only to understanding her visionary and mystical experience but also to ascertaining her mental and emotional preparation for such an experience. Without assuming the stance of either a believer or a skeptic, I hope to provide the cultural frames of reference for *A Book of Showings* by investigating the affinity of Julian's texts with various traditions of medieval spirituality and theology. I also consider her predicament as a woman writer within a discursive field dominated, at least in England, by men, and I examine the ways in which she elucidates these traditions to better suit the demands of her gender and her personal values.[11]

Because Julian of Norwich was a woman, however, it is difficult to determine which cultural frames of reference will provide an appropriate context for *A Book of Showings*. As a woman, how familiar might she have been with devotional or theological traditions, and how might she have gained such knowledge? On the one hand, the scant information available about schools during this period of English history indicates that girls received little formal education beyond basic literacy. Aristocratic and middle-class daughters were usually taught Latin pronunciation, but not grammar, either at home or in convent schools;[12] and they were prohibited from receiving university training. On the other hand, considerable evidence attests that women read or listened to various kinds of texts. During Julian's lifetime both Richard Rolle and Walter Hilton wrote vernacular books of guidance for women friends who were nuns or anchorites.[13] Extant wills, primarily from the fifteenth century, document bequests of manuscripts by both religious and lay women, often to other women.[14] Even those who were not able to read had access to a wealth of religious instruction through sermons, conversations, and the practice of reading aloud. The illiterate Margery Kempe, for example, was very familiar with the currents of late medieval spirituality and mentions hearing such texts as Bridget of Sweden's *Revelations*, Richard Rolle's *Incendium amoris*, and *The Prickynge of Love*, a translation of James of Milan's *Stimulus amoris* possibly made by Walter Hilton.[15]

At the beginning of the long text Julian seems to provide a clue to her learning—or lack thereof—by identifying herself as "a symple creature vnlettyrde" (2.285) ["a simple, unlettered creature" (177)]. Scholars have debated the meaning of this phrase; their positions range between two extremes, one that denies her learning and another that maximizes it.[16] Some critics claim that Julian is declaring her inability to read or write. If she were indeed illiterate in this modern sense, the argument goes, then the effort to interpret her *Book* in relation to other medieval texts makes little sense; she is best approached as a unique, perhaps even eccentric, visionary.[17] Other scholars, most notably her editors Colledge and Walsh, cite the allusive and rhetorical texture of *A Book of Showings* to contend that "Julian had received an exceptionally good grounding in Latin, in Scripture and in the liberal arts, and that thereafter she was able and permitted to read widely in Latin and vernacular spiritual classics."[18] According to their argument, Julian's assertion that she is unlettered may be attributed to the conventional modesty of authors, particularly women, and to her fear of antagonizing critics. Colledge and Walsh's extensive annotations demonstrate one possible consequence of this position, for in their efforts to prove her learning, they seem to deny Julian's originality.

This debate about Julian's learning is complicated by the fact that the fourteenth century is a transitional period in the history of literacy. As M. T. Clanchy has demonstrated, the medieval terms *litteratus* and *illiteratus* do not correspond to modern notions of literacy and illiteracy. "Medieval assessments concentrate on cases of maximum ability, the skills of the most learned scholars (*litterati*) and the most elegant scribes, whereas modern assessors measure the diffusion of minimal skills among the masses."[19] Moreover, the meaning of the term *illiteratus* shifted throughout the Middle Ages, so that the phrase "a symple creature vnlettyrde," used out of context, might denote either a lack of erudition or the inability to read. "Roughly down to the mid-thirteenth century," Alexander Murray observes, "*litteratus* meant 'able to read and write Latin'. From then on it implied the acquaintance with Latin literature which a student might expect to acquire at a serious school or at university. It became much like our 'lettered', or even our 'educated'."[20] However, the modern meaning of *literate* began to emerge in the fourteenth century with the rising prestige of vernacular languages. After 1300, Clanchy remarks, *litteratus* was increasingly used to refer to a person with a minimal ability to read in Latin.[21]

The range of contemporary meanings implicit in Julian's reference to herself as "a symple creature vnlettyrde" is clarified by two works of spiritual guidance composed within a few decades of the long text of *A Book of Showings*, Richard Rolle's *Incendium amoris* (*Fire of Love*) and Nicholas Love's *Myrrour of the Blessed Lyf of Jesu Christ*. Writing in Latin around 1340, Rolle offers his *Incendium amoris* "for the attention, not of the philosophers and sages of this world, not of the great theologians bogged down in their interminable questionings, but of the simple and unlearned, who are seeking rather to love God than to amass knowledge."[22] But Rolle does not exclude the "experts" from his audience if "they have forgotten and put behind them all those things that belong to the world . . . [and] are eager to surrender to a longing for God." Surprisingly, he concludes, "The more learned they are, the more ability they naturally have for loving, always provided of course that they both despise themselves, and rejoice to be despised by others." For Rolle, then, the phrase "the simple and unlearned" refers not to the literacy or learning of his audience, but to their purpose in reading. He identifies as "simple and unlearned" those who, regardless of their expertise in theology, are approaching his text with a spirit of humble devotion. The fact that Rolle writes to his intended audience in Latin indicates a high degree of education among them and suggests that many were clerics.

Within two decades after Julian's completion of the long text of *A Book of Showings*, however, Nicholas Love uses the word *symple* to refer to an audience not schooled in theology and able to read only the vernacular. In the proem to his English adaptation of the very popular thirteenth-century *Meditationes vitae Christi* (*Meditations on the Life of Christ*), Love discusses the purpose of his translation. He begins by observing that a number of books and treatises have been composed "not onelich to clerkes in latyne, but also in Englyshe to lewde men & women & hem þat bene of symple vndirstondyng" [not only for clerks in Latin, but also in English for lewd men and women and those who are of simple understanding]. He then praises the *Meditationes*, written in Latin for a woman religious, as appropriate for "symple creatures" because of its affective power and the clarity of its teaching.

> Wherfore at þe instance & þe prayer of some deuoute soules to edification of suche men or women is þis drawynge oute of þe forseide boke of cristes lyfe wryten in englysche with more putte to in certeyn partes & wiþdrawyng of diuerse auctoritis [and] maters as it semeth to þe wryter herof most spedefull & edifyng to hem þat bene [of] symple vndirstondyng.[23]

> [Therefore, at the solicitation and the prayers of some devout souls and for the edification of such men or women is this translated out of the aforesaid book of Christ's life and written in English, with more added in certain parts and with the omission of diverse authorities and matters as it seems to this writer most advantageous and edifying to them who are of simple understanding.]

Because his intended audience is not scholarly, Love not only translates the *Meditationes* into English; he also adapts the text, omitting the citations of authority and adding more edifying material. Nonetheless, this audience of "symple vndirstondyng" includes both women and men who can read the vernacular.

These examples from her near contemporaries demonstrate the range of meanings Julian's reference to herself as "a symple creature vnlettyrde" would have had during the fourteenth century. Both Rolle and Love use similar phrases to indicate that their texts are affective rather than intellective. Both also refer to their literate audiences as *simple*, although Rolle's readers were proficient in Latin, and Love's in the vernacular. Phrases similar to Julian's "symple creature vnlettyrde" thus seem to be conventional signals of devotional discourse rather than descriptions of the educational achievements of their readers.[24] Even though this evidence does not resolve the question of whether she could read Latin or only English, it does undermine the view that Julian of Norwich was unable to read or write in any language. Her silence about an amanuensis, in contrast to the illiterate Margery Kempe's report of difficulty in finding someone to transcribe her autobiographical *Book* a half-century later, gives further warrant to the conclusion that Julian not only composed but also inscribed and revised her own text.

Although scholars will probably never be able to ascertain the facts about Julian's formal education, it is nonetheless crucial to an understanding of *A Book of Showings* to identify the cultural traditions contributing to her intellectual and emotional formation.[25] Both Julian's initial showings and her retrospective interpretation of them during the twenty or more years of reflection preceding the long text's completion must be analyzed in terms of the doctrines, practices, and institutions in which they are embedded. In this regard, Moore's distinction between the *incorporated interpretation* and the *raw experience* within the mystical phenomenon itself proves a very useful heuristic in analyzing *A Book of Showings*. The former includes "features of experience which have been caused or conditioned by a mystic's prior beliefs, expectations and intentions."[26] In contrast, all aspects of the experience unrelated to the mystic's previous horizon constitute the raw experience.

Moore divides the *incorporated interpretation* into two categories: (1) *reflected interpretation* or "ideas and images reflected in an experience in the form of visions and locutions and so forth"; and (2) *assimilated interpretation* or "features of experience moulded into what might be termed phenomenological analogues of some belief or doctrine."[27] Reflected interpretation Moore attributes to the practice of meditation, defined as "the disciplined but creative application of the imagination and discursive thought to an often complex religious theme or subject-matter." Assimilated interpretation he associates with contemplation, a devotional practice that develops from meditation but "attempts to transcend the activities of imagination and intellect through an intuitive concentration on some simple object, image, or idea."[28] The two categories of incorporated interpretation that Moore identifies correspond to the three different kinds of phenomena that Julian says she experienced: "Alle this blyssede techynge of oure lorde god was schewyd to me in thre partyes, that is be bodylye syght, and be worde formede in myne vndyrstandynge, and be gastelye syght" (1:224); ["All this blessed teaching of our Lord was shown to me in three parts, that is by bodily vision and by words formed in my understanding and by spiritual vision" (135)].[29] Julian's visions and locutions are examples of what Moore terms reflected interpretation; her more abstract ghostly sights, of assimilated interpretation.

Since I am not interested in assessing the ontological or epistemological validity of Julian's showings, I will not attempt to describe or evaluate her raw experience. Rather, I will concentrate on the interpretation that Julian incorporates into her account of the revelations.[30] By examining her reflected interpretation of the near-death experience and the assimilated interpretation she derives from it, I hope to situate the two texts of *A Book of Showings* within medieval religious culture and to chart Julian's transformation, over a quarter-century, from a visionary into a theologian.

The first two chapters of this book trace the reflected interpretation incorporated into Julian's showings to late medieval affective spirituality. Concentrating on the genesis of the short text, chapter 1 demonstrates that her youthful request for three gifts provides the key to her extraordinary experience at the age of thirty. The visions and locutions she receives attest to her prior familiarity with the tenets and practices of affective piety, particularly as they are articulated in her desire for the third gift, the three "wounds" of compassion, contrition, and longing for God. Chapter 2 examines Julian's description of her visions in both texts in order to show their resemblance to the late medieval visualizations of the suffering Savior encouraged by meditation on the life of Christ and by religious art.

In the next three chapters I focus on the assimilated interpretation informing Julian's most significant additions in the long text of the *Showings*. Despite the prohibition against women's formal education in cathedral schools and universities, by the time Julian completed the final version sometime after 1393, she had acquired an understanding of moral and mystical theology that enabled her to use this discipline's terminology and adapt its concepts with subtle creativity. Chapters 3 through 5 analyze her original response to a question that has persistently puzzled Christians: Why does a God who is all-good, all-knowing, and all-powerful allow evil in the cosmos? In developing her theodicy, her solution to this problem of evil, she combines concepts from the late medieval theology of salvation (soteriology) and the teachings of mystics about the nature of humankind (anthropology) in order to explain that "alle shalle be wele" despite human sinfulness. Chapter 3 demonstrates how Revelation Thirteen transforms the usually distressing doctrine of predestination into a theodicy addressed not only to the elect but also to those apparently not yet chosen. Chapter 4 examines Julian's challenge to the medieval ideology of sin, particularly in her revision of the prevailing interpretation of Adam's fall in the parable of the lord and servant. Julian's assurance that "alle shalle be wele" ultimately rests, as I show in chapter 5, on her radical understanding of the concept of the *imago Dei*, central to mystical anthropology; in the last part of Revelation Fourteen, she concludes her theodicy by comparing the ontological connections between the three persons of the Trinity and humankind to familial relationships, stressing Jesus' role as a mother.

These first five chapters are organized thematically and analyze Julian's ideas in a straightforward manner admittedly very different from the way she presents them in her two texts. The final chapter therefore adopts a literary perspective to examine the recursive structure of *A Book of Showings* that renders these revelations both so enticing and so elusive. By exploring Julian's strategy of revision and her artistry in bringing readers to reenact her own struggle to understand the revelations, this chapter intimates Julian's development and achievement as a writer.

Finally, I wish to acknowledge that I can only speculate about the means by which Julian acquired the erudition I claim she exhibits in the long version of *A Book of Showings*. Although I quote extensively from devotional and theological texts, I cannot prove that she knew these works firsthand. I cite these texts as analogues rather than sources for her ideas. All of them, I believe, circulated widely in England during her lifetime. Given the vibrant religious culture of late medieval Norwich, Julian would have had ample opportunity to learn about these texts, or at least about the currents of thought they represent, through a variety of means ranging from sermons to conversations to reading.[31] From the sophistication with which she expounds concepts from moral and mystical theology, particularly in Revelations Thirteen and Fourteen, I hope to prove that she was conversant with the issues and assumptions informing such discourse, though not necessarily the specific texts I cite.

More significant than her erudition, though, is Julian of Norwich's remarkable creativity in synthesizing these traditional concepts into theological insights uniquely her own. This study attempts to reveal her intellectual transformation from a devout young woman, familiar with the conventions of affective spirituality, into a mature thinker of subtle perceptiveness. Compelled by her visionary experience, Julian of Nowich devotes twenty years or more to exploring the problem of evil, and she resurrects from the fragmented corpus of medieval theology an orthodox yet original theodicy reflecting and refracting her experience as a woman.

Affective Spirituality
and the Genesis of
A Book of Showings

ON 13 May 1373, a thirty-year-old woman lay near death in Norwich, England. She was being cared for by several people, including her mother. Though she had received the last rites of the church four days earlier, the curate was called again on the eighth day of her illness because she seemed in danger of imminent death. Taking the cross from the young boy who accompanied him, the priest held it before the dying woman.[1] Gazing upon it, she saw the room dim around her as the cross grew radiant. Suddenly the woman's pain diminished. Through the rest of that day and again that night, she experienced a series of revelations that she recounts in the earliest extant English text known to have been written by a woman, *A Book of Showings to the Anchoress Julian of Norwich*.

Julian's visionary experience commences when the figure of Christ on the crucifix that the priest holds before her eyes starts to reenact the sufferings of the Passion. In graphic detail she describes her corporeal visions of the body of Jesus grotesquely disfigured as he is crowned with thorns, is scourged, and dies. She begins the account of the revelations in the short text, for example, with a vivid verbal portrait of the bleeding head of Jesus: "And in this sodaynlye I sawe the rede blode trekylle downe fro vndyr the garlande, alle hate, freschlye, plentefully and lyvelye, ryght as me thought that it was in that tyme that the garlonde of thornys was thyrstede on his blessede heede" (1:210); ["And at this, suddenly I saw the red blood trickling down from under the crown, all hot, flowing freely and copiously, a living stream, just as it seemed to me that it was at the time when the crown of thorns was thrust down upon his blessed head" (129)]. This concentration on the suffering of Christ's humanity situates Julian of Norwich within the culture of affective spirituality that pervaded popular religious life during the late Middle Ages.[2]

To ascertain the characteristics of affective spirituality, one need only contrast Julian's vision of the animated crucifix with the Anglo-Saxon version of a similar situation in "The Dream of the Rood."[3] The poem, probably composed by the early eighth century, records the experience of a narrator as he beholds a cross come to life. Although this event resembles Julian's experience, the poem is a literary dream vision rather than an account of a literal visionary event. Moreover, the object before the narrator's eyes is not a crucifix but an ornamental cross that does not bear a figure of the dying Christ. "I saw the glorious tree joyfully gleaming, adorned with garments, decked with gold: jewels had fitly covered the tree of the Lord." Nonetheless, the narrator dimly recognizes the same physical evidence of pain that Julian does. "Yet through that gold I could perceive the former strife of wretched men, that it had once bled on the right side. . . . at times it was bedewed with moisture, stained with the flowing of blood, at times adorned with treasure."[4] As the personified cross addresses the poem's narrator, however, it ascribes the bodily suffering of the crucifixion to itself and portrays Christ as the triumphant warrior victorious over sin and death.

These differences between the Anglo-Saxon dream vision and Julian of Norwich's actual vision parallel the contrast in the visual arts between the Romanesque *Christus triumphans* and the Gothic *Christus patiens*. Around A.D. 1000, the figure of the majestic Christ on the crucifix is gradually displaced by the suffering Christ: the calm features of the regal Son of God distorted to express the anguish of the tortured Son of Man, the royal crown replaced by a crown of thorns, and the erect body of the victor twisted into the battered torso of the victim.[5] An increased interest in the emotional reactions of those witnessing the Crucifixion accompanies this greater naturalism in the representation of the dying Christ. Mary and John stand beneath the cross not as abstract types but as grieving human beings. They are joined by numerous other figures, including Mary Magdalen, who reflects the penitential program informing affective spirituality, for she laments not only for the dying Jesus but also for her own sins, the cause of his death.[6]

These contrasting images of the Crucifixion in the verbal and visual arts strikingly attest to the transformation of Western religious consciousness that occurred between about 1050 and 1200. As R. W. Southern and Colin Morris, among others, have shown, this period marked a turning point in medieval culture as an unprecedented interest in individual experience and introspective analysis developed.[7]

One of the catalysts for this change was the satisfaction theory of salvation proposed by Anselm of Canterbury at the end of the eleventh century. In his *Cur Deus homo* (*Why God Became Man*, 1098), Anselm rejected the prevailing model of redemption, the so-called Devil's rights theory. Anselm's summary identifies the main premises of this theory:

> We also commonly say that God was bound to strive with the devil by justice, rather than by force, in order to set man free. On this showing, when the devil killed Him in whom there was no reason for death, and who was God, he would justly lose his power over sinners. Otherwise God would have done unjust violence to him, since he was justly in possession of man; after all, he did not seize man by violence, but man handed himself over to him freely.[8]

According to this model, based on an analogy with the feudal custom of *diffidatio*, the Devil had certain rights over humankind because they had repudiated their fealty to God through original sin. Humankind could be released from the Devil's dominion only if they voluntarily returned to God or if Satan violated the rules governing his legitimate claim over them. The former course was impossible, but the latter was achieved when Satan unlawfully extended his authority by taking the life of the sinless Christ. As Southern aptly observes, the Devil's rights theory conceptualized redemption as a legal contest in which humankind plays a minor and static role. "The war was one between God and the Devil, and God won because he proved himself the master-strategist."[9]

In *Cur Deus homo* Anselm rejects this model of the Devil's rights by placing the humanity of Christ at the center of the salvific drama. Contending that only a human being could make amends for the offense the species had committed against God, but that no sinful individual was capable of satisfying this debt of honor, Anselm concludes that the Son of God assumed a human nature in order to atone for humanity's sins. By suffering pain and death, the God-man made the necessary reparation to the Father and redressed each breach of divine honor with a countervailing indemnity.

> For when death had entered into the human race through man's disobedience, it was fitting that life should be restored through the obedience of man. When the sin which was the cause of our condemnation had its beginning from a woman, it was fitting for the author of our justice and

17

salvation to be born of a woman. Since the devil, when he tempted man, conquered him by the tasting of a tree, it was fitting for him to be conquered by man's bearing of suffering on a tree.[10]

The elegance of this satisfaction theory of salvation ensues, as Anselm realizes, from its focus on the humanity of the Redeemer.

Such an emphasis on Christ's solidarity with humankind also pervades Anselm's prayers. As influential as his theology, they express a new interest in the reality of Jesus' human experiences and a more emotional response to them. In his "Prayer to Christ," for example, Anselm imagines himself on Calvary and envisions the pain of the Savior's physical suffering.

> So, as much as I can, though not as much as I ought,
> > I am mindful of your passion,
> your buffeting, your scourging, your cross, your wounds,
> > how you were slain for me,
> > how prepared for burial and buried.

Anselm concentrates on the passion of Christ in order to elicit his own compassion.

> Why, O my soul, were you not there
> > to be pierced by a sword of bitter sorrow
> > > when you could not bear
> the piercing of the side of your Saviour with a lance?
> > Why could you not bear to see
> the nails violate the hands and feet of your Creator?[11]

Anselm's desire to suffer with Jesus, at least in spirit, signals a change in medieval religious consciousness. Just as his satisfaction theory transformed soteriology by emphasizing the humanity of Christ, so his prayers altered the devotional practices of Christendom by responding emotionally to that humanity. In succeeding centuries, Anselm's dual contribution to Western spirituality developed in two related discursive fields, the theological and the devotional.

During the next two hundred years theologies of salvation concentrated on the love the incarnate God demonstrated for humankind by submitting to torture and death in his human nature. In the twelfth century the most radical expression of this new soteriology is Peter Abelard's statement that salvation hinges on the mutuality of love between the Redeemer and the redeemed.

It seems to us that *this* is the way in which we have been justified in the blood of Christ, and reconciled to God: that by this singular favour shown to us (that his Son took our nature, and persevered until death, providing us with both teaching and example) he bound us more fully to himself by love. . . . And so our redemption is that great love awoken in us by the passion of Christ, which not only frees us from the slavery of sin, but acquires for us the true liberty of the sons of God, that we may fulfil all things more by love of him than by fear.[12]

Although Thomas Aquinas acknowledges a century later that Christ might have redeemed humankind without suffering, he recognizes the affective value of the Savior's passion: for "man could thus see how much God loved him, and so would be aroused to love him. In this the perfection of his salvation consists."[13] Bonaventure concurs with his Dominican counterpart about the significance of Christ's suffering: "In order to show you how much he loved you, [Christ] even died to liberate you from death, so that he could confer on you not only the benefit of pious regard, but also show his feelings of love."[14] This loving and suffering God-man of late medieval soteriology strikingly contrasts with the clever, dispassionate Redeemer of the earlier Devil's rights theory.

This theological emphasis on the love Christ expressed for humanity in his passion was complemented by a devotional emphasis on humanity's duty to reciprocate this love through compassion for Christ.[15] One of the few similarities bridging the enmity between Peter Abelard and Bernard of Clairvaux, for example, is their agreement on the value of suffering with Christ in spirit. A sequence of hymns composed by Abelard between 1128 and 1140 voices the sentiments that would become commonplaces of the next century. This verse, for instance, articulates both the satisfaction soteriology and the affective rhetoric characteristic of late medieval devotions:

> For they are ours, O Lord, our deeds, our deeds;
> Why must thou suffer torture for our sin?
> Let our hearts suffer for thy passion, Lord,
> That sheer compassion may thy mercy win.[16]

Compassion for the suffering Christ is also the foundation of Bernard's spiritual program. Like his contemporaries, Bernard believed that God assumed a human nature in order to elicit humankind's love.

19

I think this is the principal reason why the invisible God willed to be seen in the flesh and to converse with men as a man. He wanted to recapture the affections of carnal men who were unable to love in any other way, by first drawing them to the salutary love of his own humanity, and then gradually to raise them to a spiritual love.[17]

Although Bernard acknowledges that this attraction to the humanity of Christ only initiates the individual's progress toward the most perfect spiritual love, such carnal affection is valuable and necessary, he insists, because it displaces other sensual loves from the soul. "Your affection for your Lord Jesus should be both tender and intimate, to oppose the sweet enticements of sensual life. Sweetness conquers sweetness as one nail drives out another."[18] Using Bernard of Clairvaux as her example, Julia Kristeva describes this revolution in Western consciousness during the twelfth century: "Saints and troubadours seem to proclaim, *Ego affectus est*, thus glorifying what, in the light of Reason, will appear to be base irrationality. They impart willpower to their love, enlighten it with reason, tinge it with wisdom, in order to raise it to the dignity of a divine essence. . . . For God is love."[19] This emotive concentration on the passion of the Redeemer and the compassion of the redeemed informs the range of later medieval devotional attitudes, practices, and rhetoric collectively referred to as affective spirituality.

I

Julian of Norwich provides a clue to her familiarity with the tenets of affective spirituality in her statement about the three gifts or graces for which she prayed at some unspecified time prior to the events of 13 May 1373. "I desyrede thre graces be the gyfte of god. The fyrst was to have mynde of Cryste es passionn. The seconnde was bodelye syeknes, and the thryd was to haue of goddys gyfte thre wonndys" (1:201); ["I desired three graces by the gift of God. The first was to have recollection of Christ's Passion. The second was a bodily sickness, and the third was to have, of God's gift, three wounds" (125)]. Julian admits that her first desire to witness the Crucifixion in person as well as her second petition for a physical illness are extraordinary, and she makes them both conditional on God's will. The third request itself consists of a wish for three metaphorical wounds: "the wonnd(e) of contricyoun, the wonnde of compassyoun and the wonnde of wylfulle langgynge to god" (1:206); ["the wound of contrition, the wound of compassion and the wound of longing with my will for God" (127)]. Julian must have regarded this third petition as more conventional: confident that it was pleasing to God, she attached no condition to it. Even though these three requests are the only information that Julian conveys about her personal life aside from the immediate circumstances of her visionary experience, they provide a valuable clue to her intellectual and emotional formation by indicating the preparation and expectations she had for such an experience. As I will show, these three requests reveal the extent of Julian's familiarity with the tenets and practices of late medieval affective spirituality and situate the genesis of the short text of *A Book of Showings* within a specific cultural matrix.

Although Julian prays for five gifts, the first two, the vision and the illness, are outward manifestations of the three spiritual graces requested in the third petition: contrition, compassion, and longing for God.[20] Like the typical holy person in the late Middle Ages, Julian wants to achieve an identification with Christ by sharing in his suffering. She prays for both a physical *imitatio Christi* through the pain of bodily sickness and a psychological participation in his suffering through either a supernatural vision or the natural emotion of compassion. Richard Kieckhefer's observation about the affinity among these concepts in the thought of the fourteenth-century saints aptly describes Julian's attitude: "Compassion and imitation were responses that closed the distance between oneself and the suffering Christ: identifying oneself with him, one suffered along with him and strove to partake of his suffering."[21] In the book of instruction for anchorites, the twelfth-century *De institutione inclusarum* (*Rule of Life for a Recluse*), which he wrote for his sister, Aelred of Rievaulx regards compassion and imitation as the complementary foundations of the love of God.

> To þyse loue of God parteyneþ two þyngges: clene affeccioun of herte, and effecte of good deede. Þe affeccioun moot be in taste of gostly swetnesse, ant þe effecte of good deede moot be in excercise of vertus—þe which excercise of vertus is in a certayn god maner of lyuyngge, in fastyngge, in wakyngge, in trauayl, in redyngge, in preyeris, in pouerte, and swych oþere.[22]

> [To this love of God two things pertain: pure affection of heart and the carrying out of good deeds. The affection must be in the taste of spiritual sweetness, and the carrying out of good deeds must be in the exercise of

21

virtues—the exercise of which is in a certain good manner of living, in fasting, in keeping vigils, in hard work, in reading, in prayers, in poverty, and such other.]

In late medieval spirituality, compassion and imitation were directly related as motivation and manifestation, as *affectus* and *effectus*.

Julian recognizes that her initial request for a vision is simply a potent and unusual means of achieving the second wound of the third request, compassion; she wishes "that I myght have sene bodylye the passionn of oure lorde that he sufferede for me, that I myght have sufferede with hym as othere dyd that lovyd hym" (1:201–2) ["that I might have seen with my own eyes our Lord's Passion which he suffered for me, so that I might have suffered with him as others did who loved him" (125)]. A sensory perception of Christ's passion, Julian believes, will increase her compassion. However, the more typical way of attaining such a psychological identification with the Savior's anguish was through meditation. Aelred of Rievaulx, who provides one of the earliest examples of systematic meditation on the Passion in *De institutione inclusarum*, regards this devotional exercise as the initiation into loving God. "And as to speken of affeccioun, gostly and bodyly, þu most nursche hit wit holy and hoolsum meditacioun";[23] [And to speak of affection, spiritual and bodily, you must nourish it with holy and beneficial meditation]. That Julian engaged in such meditation seems clear from her association of a devotional practice with her desire for a visionary experience.

> For the fyrste [petition] come to my mynde with devocion; me thought I hadde grete felynge in the passyonn of Cryste, botte ʒitte I desyrede to haue mare be the grace of god. . . . I desyrede a bodylye syght, whare yn y myght have more knawynge of bodelye paynes of oure lorde oure savyoure, and of the compassyonn of oure ladye and of alle his trewe loveres that were be levande his paynes that tyme and sythene; for I wolde have beene one of thame and suffrede with thame. (1:201–2)

> [As to the first, it came into my mind with devotion; it seemed to me that I had great feeling for the Passion of Christ, but still I desired to have more by the grace of God. . . . I desired a bodily sight, through which I might have more knowledge of our Lord and saviour's bodily pains, and of the compassion of our Lady and of all his true lovers who were living at that time [and afterwards], for I would have been one of them and have suffered with them. (125–26)]

22

Julian thus articulates a central tenet of late medieval spirituality: compassion, the affective suffering with Christ, can be achieved through either devotional meditation or visionary experience.

Furthermore, the "bodelye syeknes" of Julian's second petition externalizes this inner compassion. *The Prickynge of Love*, a late fourteenth-century translation of the popular *Stimulus amoris*, probably written by James of Milan but attributed to Bonaventure, identifies such a literal reenactment of Jesus' physical pain as an appropriate initial response to meditation on the Passion.

> First þow shalt considere cristes passioun for to folwe hit þou shalt sette crist in syȝhte of [þi] sowle. . . . And make þat þi rewle & þi saunplarie for to lyue by & conforme þe to be like hym & his passioun. Þourȝe wilful sufferynge of al maner disese. And in þat be þi counfort & þi solace þat þou myȝt ouȝte suffre for his loue.[24]

> [First you should consider Christ's passion, for by concentrating on it you shall set Christ in the sight of your soul. . . . And make that your rule and your exemplar to live by and conform yourself to be like him and his passion through voluntary suffering of all kinds of discomfort. And in that be your comfort and your solace that you might in any way suffer for his love.]

In late medieval hagiography, intense compassion often manifests itself somatically. The thirteenth-century chronicles of Dominican convents in the Rhineland frequently recount the physical pains suffered by sisters engaged in ardent meditation on Christ's passion.[25] Likewise, in his *vita* of Elisabeth of Spalbeek, Philip of Clairvaux describes how she reenacted the episodes of the Passion at the appropriate canonical hours each Friday and concurrently received the stigmata.[26] The compassion she invoked through meditation resulted in a literal *imitatio Christi*. The stigmata of St. Francis of Assisi remain, of course, the most famous physical evidence of a visionary experience initiated by intense compassion. The bodily sight and bodily sickness for which Julian prays are thus extraordinary expressions of compassion, the second of the three "wounds" she asks for in her third petition.

Julian's two extraordinary requests are also related to the first and third of the "wounds" she desires in her third petition, contrition and longing for God. According to the premises of affective spirituality, compassion for Christ's suffering, achieved either through a vision or through meditation, evokes contrition, for the realization that his pain was caused by human sinfulness increases the individual's compunction. And the recognition of the love for humankind motivating Christ's sacrifice elicits the penitent's love in return. This chain of causality connecting compassion, penitence, and love-longing for God is clearly expressed in *The Prickynge of Love.*

> Prente þer-fore ihesu sadli in þi þouȝte for ofte mynd of his holy flesh & of his passioun. [*sic*] shal waste in þe al fleshli & vicios loue. and hit [schal] reise vp þi disire to loue of his godhede. hit shal shewe hou þou shalt worche. & hou þou shalt fele and hit shal enflaume þe herte to suffren hardnesse of penaunce.[27]

> [Therefore impress Jesus soberly in your thought, for thinking often of his holy flesh and of his passion shall destroy in you all fleshly and vicious love. And it [shall] incite your desire to love of his godhead. It shall show how you should work and how you should feel and it shall enflame your heart to suffer the hardship of penance.]

Likewise, the bodily pain that is an imitation of Christ's suffering is also a penance for the sins that made such suffering necessary and a reciprocation of divine love. Thus contrition and longing for God, the first and last of the three metaphoric wounds for which Julian prays, result from a compassionate participation in the Savior's pain and further motivate its imitation in penitential suffering.

The particular kind of "bodelye syeknes" that Julian desires, an illness that simulates the experience of dying, also corresponds with the third wound, longing for God, because literal or mystical death is the necessary condition for union with the divine. She writes, "In this sekenes I desyrede to hafe alle manere of paynes, bodelye and gastelye, that I schulde have ȝyf I schulde dye, alle the dredes and tempestes of feyndys, and alle manere of (oþere) paynes, safe of the owȝte passynge of the sawlle, for I hoped that it myȝt be to me a spede whenn I schulde dye, for I desyrede sone to be with my god" (1:203–4); ["In this sickness I wanted to have every kind of pain, bodily and spiritual, which I should have if I were dying, every fear and assault from devils, and every other kind of pain except the departure of the spirit, for I hoped that this would be profitable to me when I should die, because I desired soon to be with my God" (126)]. The experience of impending death, Julian believes, will be a penance for the sins of her past life and a preparation for the union with God she hopes to achieve in the future. Furthermore, illness and apparent death in late medieval hagiography, particularly of women, often presage a visionary experience. Citing the examples of Christina Mirabilis, Catherine of Siena, and Julian herself, Elizabeth Petroff observes, "A surprising number of biographies and autobiographies tell of an apparent dying, often when a teenager, of being taken for dead and perhaps even put in a coffin, but then miraculously coming back to life, often with an explicit visionary message for the world."[28] Julian's choice of the phrase "longing for God" indicates her familiarity with the rhetoric of desire used by mystics like Bernard of Clairvaux and the women in the German tradition of *Brautmystik*.[29] The physical illness of her second petition is thus an extraordinary means of expressing her longing for union with God, through either a mystical experience or actual death.

These correlations among the graces Julian requests reveal that they are not random wishes but steps in the program of affective spirituality. More particularly, Julian's prayer for the three "wounds"—contrition, compassion, and longing for God—discloses her familiarity with the typical sequence of spiritual progress articulated in popular treatises and handbooks about meditation. In his meditation on the death of Jesus in *Lignum vitae* (*The Tree of Life*), for example, Bonaventure sums up this spiritual progression in the same terms as Julian voices in her third request: "O Human heart, if you are not stricken with terror, moved with pity, riven with sorrow, softened with love, at the sight of such atonement, you are harder than the hardest rock."[30] That Julian assimilates these three traditional effects of meditation on Jesus' suffering into her third request indicates her awareness of the theory informing this devotional practice. Her desire to envision and imitate Christ's passion in order to enhance her compassion, contrition, and longing for God reveals her comprehension of the literature of affective spirituality prior to her visionary experience in May 1373.

II

Under Cistercian influence in the twelfth century and Franciscan in the thirteenth, affective spirituality fostered a three-stage program for spiritual growth progressing from compassion to contrition to contemplation. Bernard of Clairvaux, an early proponent of this program, regarded meditation on the life of Christ as the initiation into this process.[31] By imaginatively witnessing the events of Christ's life, Bernard argued, individuals could respond with the compassion and contrition appropriate to the Trinity's great act of love and could move toward a more spiritual love.

> The soul at prayer should have before it a sacred image of the God-man, in his birth or infancy or as he was teaching, or dying, or rising, or ascending. Whatever form it takes this image must bind the soul with the love of virtue and expel carnal vices, eliminate temptations and quiet desires. I think this is the principal reason why the invisible God willed to be seen in the flesh and to converse with men as a man. He wanted to recapture the affections of carnal men who were unable to love in any other way, by first drawing them to the salutary love of his own humanity, and then gradually to raise them to a spiritual love.[32]

Just as carnal love comes before spiritual love, meditation precedes contemplation, for devotion to the humanity of Christ is "carnal with comparison to that other love which does not know the Word as flesh so much as the Word as wisdom, as justice, truth, holiness, loyalty, strength, and whatever else could be said in this manner."[33] According to Bernard, then, the spiritual progression from compassion to contrition culminates in contemplation. Affective meditation on the humanity of Christ thus initiates a process of moral reform that prepares the meditator for the more spiritual contemplation of Christ's divinity.

Adopting the language of erotic desire from the Song of Songs, Bernard contends that meditation both sustains the Bride's love for Christ and attracts the Bridegroom to greater intimacy with the soul. Alluding to Song 2:6, "His left hand is beneath my head and his right hand embraces me," Bernard explains how meditation transcends the gap between past and future and transports the soul to the eternal present of union with God. "His left hand stands for the recollection of his love, than which nothing is greater, for he laid down his life for his friends (Jn 15:13). His right hand signifies the blessed vision which he promised to his friends, and the joys of the presence of his majesty."[34] As Etienne Gilson astutely observes, Bernard assumes that "*memoria*—and by that let us understand the memory, the sensible recollection of the passion of Christ—is in us the condition and herald of the *praesentia*, that is to say, in the full sense of the term, of the beatific vision in the future life, but also of these visitations of the soul by the Word in this life."[35] According to Bernard, the temporary union with Christ achieved through meditation prefigures the eternal participation in the deity attained by the blessed: "God's chosen ones will not be without the consolation of memory until they can enjoy the feast of God's presence. . . . And so memory is for the generations of this world; presence belongs to the kingdom of heaven."[36] Through recollection of the past the meditator anticipates the future.

Bernard's collapse of past and future into the present of the meditative moment, along with his identification of meditation on Christ's humanity as a preparation for mystical union and a presentiment of the beatific vision, may well be the ultimate source of Julian's request for the third "wound," longing for God. Her phrase recalls the psychology and language of desire informing Bernard's observation that "memory is sweet for those who long for God's presence. It does not satisy their longing but intensifies it."[37] In any case, the three metaphoric wounds for which Julian prays conform to the stages of spiritual development first enunciated by Bernard of Clairvaux: through meditation on the humanity of Christ, the soul moves from compassion to contrition to longing for union, both mystical and beatific, with God. According to the affective spirituality of the twelfth century, the practice of meditation begins the ascent to God.

In the thirteenth century the Franciscans give further impetus to this three-stage program of affective spirituality. Francis of Assisi provides a living example of its tenets; his compassion for Christ manifests itself somatically in his stigmata and spiritually in his mystical visions. And Francis's successor, Bonaventure, elected minister general of the Friars Minor in 1257, articulates the premises of this Franciscan spirituality and formulates a system of meditation based upon them. Like Bernard, Bonaventure believes that recollection of the events of Christ's passion is the best way to incite compassion for the God-man. In his *De perfectione vitae* (*On the Perfection of Life*), he writes: "Your heart is the altar of God. It is here that the fire of intense love must burn always. You are to feed it every day with the wood of the cross of Christ and the commemoration of His passion."[38] Bonaventure's *Lignum vitae* provides a sequence of systematic meditations on the Passion designed to elicit the meditator's compassion. He explains in the prologue that such meditation enables one to enact Gal. 2:19, "With Christ I am nailed to the cross":

No one will have the intimate and lively experience of such a feeling unless, far from forgetting the Lord's passion, or being ungrateful for it, he rather contemplates—with vivid representation, penetrating intelligence, and loving will—the labors, the suffering, and the love of Jesus crucified, so that he can truthfully repeat with the bride: *A bundle of myrrh is my Beloved to me: He shall abide between my breasts.*[39]

As Elizabeth Salter observes, "If we interpret St. Bonaventura's use of the word 'memoria' in the sense in which St. Bernard understood it—sensible recollection of the passion,—then the opening passages of the *Lignum vitae* describe his deliberate choice of materials according to their affective value."[40] Indeed, Bonaventure's allusion to the "bunch of myrrh" of Song 1:12 signals his recognition of his debt to Bernard.

In his forty-third sermon on the Song of Songs, Bernard interprets myrrh as a symbol of the "harshness of afflictions" recollected in meditation on the passion of Christ. "Preserve without fail the memory of all those bitter things he endured for you, persevere in meditating on him and you in turn will be able to say: 'My beloved is to me a little bunch of myrrh that lies between my breasts.'"[41] Moreover, like Bernard, Bonaventure regards such meditation as an initiation into the spiritual life. In the prologue to his treatise on mysticism, *Itinerarium mentis in Deum* (*The Journey of the Mind to God*, 1259), Bonaventure agrees with Bernard that compassion for the suffering Christ is the first step in the ascent to God. "Now, there is no path but through that most burning love for the Crucified which so transformed Paul the apostle when he was carried up to the third heaven that he could say: *With Christ I am nailed to the cross. It is no longer I that live, but Christ lives in me.*"[42] With Bernard, then, Bonaventure believes that the only means to achieve a contemplative union with God is through meditation on the Passion.

Such meditation on Christ's passion as recommended by Bernard and Bonaventure was initially practiced by those in religious rather than lay life, because the withdrawal from the world required for the third stage of contemplative union seemed most appropriate to them. Judging by the earliest references, this spiritual exercise seems to have been especially associated with anchorites. In 1080, almost two decades before Anselm of Canterbury wrote *Cur Deus homo*, Goscelin advises the English recluse Eve in his *Liber confortarius* to meditate on episodes from the Passion at the appropriate canonical hours in order to incite her love for the suffering Christ.[43] And less than a century later, another author writing to his English anchorite sister, the Cistercian Aelred of Rievaulx, presents one of the earliest systematic meditations on the life of Christ, in his *De institutione inclusarum*.[44] In the example he provides, Aelred leads the anchorite through the important events in the life of Christ from the Annunciation to the Resurrection, concentrating particularly on the episodes of the Passion. In the thirteenth century, Edmund Rich's *Speculum ecclesiae*, a work addressed to novice monks in his charge, puts into practice Goscelin's recommendation to Eve by providing a series of meditations on the Passion organized according to the canonical hours. As these representatives of the extant treatises show, the practice of meditation on Christ's passion, as a preparation for contemplation, was reserved in the twelfth and thirteenth centuries for those in religious life.

In the fourteenth century, however, meditation was increasingly divorced from contemplation, with the former recommended as a devotional practice appropriate for those in the active life and the latter still primarily reserved for professed contemplatives. The work most influential in introducing meditation to the laity is the *Meditationes vitae Christi* (*Meditations on the Life of Christ*). Often citing the authority of Bernard and wrongly attributed to Bonaventure, the *Meditationes*, dating from the mid-fourteenth century, popularized ideas about the value of compassion and provided an example of systematic meditation on the life of Christ.[45] Ostensibly addressed to a contemplative Poor Clare, this work expresses ambivalence about the preeminence of the contemplative life. "A major purpose of the *Meditationes* is to relieve the tension between action and contemplation by adapting the monastic ideal of solitude, fasting, prayer, and corporal suffering to the lay condition. 'Thus, you must withdraw in the mind,' [the author] teaches, 'not in the body, but in intent, devotion, and spirit.'"[46] Pseudo-Bonaventure even goes so far as to revise the three stages of perfection, placing the contemplative life as an intermediate step between the two phases of the active life:

> And between these two parts of the active life is the contemplative life, so that this be the order maintained: first, everyone exercises himself and wearies himself in prayer and in the study of the holy writings and in the other good deeds and services in common conversation, rectifying vices and acquiring virtue; in the second step, he reposes in contemplation, searching for solitude of mind and attending only to God with all his might; in the third, by means of the above two exercises of virtue, he becomes fervent, full of and illuminated by true wisdom—he is concerned with the salvation of others.[47]

29

Although the Pseudo-Bonaventure acknowledges the importance of the contemplative life, he begins the practice of divorcing the third stage, mystical union with God, from the program of affective spirituality.

By the early fifteenth century, when Nicholas Love translates the *Meditationes* into English as the *Myrrour of the Blessed Lyf of Jesu Christ*, he entirely disregards contemplation, traditionally the last stage of perfection, because his audience is lay rather than religious. As Salter observes, "throughout the *Myrrour* we find Love stating that the purpose of the set meditative passages is to induce love and compassion for Christ, and to teach moral thought and action. These are the first two 'fruits'; the third, union with God, is within the province of the mystic, and in the main, irrelevant to Love's purpose."[48] In his prologue, for example, Love explains that he translates the Latin text into English for the edification of "hem þat bene [of] symple vndirstondyng to þe which symple soules as seynt *Bernerde* seye contemplacion of þe monhede of cryste is more likyng more spedefull & more sykere þan is hyʒe contemplacion of þe godhed"[49] [those who are of simple understanding, to which simple souls, as Saint Bernard said, contemplation of the manhood of Christ is more pleasant, more advantageous, and more secure than is high contemplation of the godhead]. As it was gradually popularized for the laity in the late Middle Ages, the practice of meditating on the suffering of Christ's humanity, recommended only to those in religious life in the twelfth century, was divorced from its original role as the initial step toward contemplative union.

This separation of meditation from contemplation is evident in the work of the author who provides the most important context for understanding Julian of Norwich's intellectual and spiritual formation prior to her visionary experience, her contemporary Walter Hilton. Given his association with Cambridge, Ely, and Thurgarton in the last quarter of the fourteenth century and the influence of his writings, Hilton's work attests to the kind of guidance available to lay men and women as well as solitaries and religious in the vicinity of Norwich during Julian's lifetime. Although the short text of *A Book of Showings* probably antedates Book 1 of *The Scale of Perfection* (ca. 1386) by a decade or more, thus precluding Hilton's direct influence on Julian's first version, his discussion of contemplation indicates the familiarity of Bernard of Clairvaux's affective program in England during the last part of the fourteenth century.

In Book 1 of *The Scale of Perfection*, Hilton introduces Bernard's schema as he discusses the second of the three stages of contemplation. In contrast to the rational knowledge of God acquired by the learned, "the second part of contemplation lies principally in affection, without the understanding of spiritual things; this is commonly for simple and unlearned people who give themselves entirely to devotion."[50] As Hilton's examples suggest, despite his use of the term *contemplation*, this second part is modeled after the affective program articulated by Bernard; meditation on the humanity of Christ brings about contrition and prepares the meditator for a more spiritual love. Hilton divides this second part of contemplation into a lower and a higher degree, depending on the frequency and duration of the affective meditation. Although Hilton includes within the category of "simple and unlearned people" both lay and religious, women and men, he claims that those in the active life usually attain only the lower degree of affection because the higher degree "can be had and held only by people who are in great quietness of body and soul"—in other words, primarily those vowed to the contemplative life.[51]

The higher degree of the second part of contemplation leads to the third part of contemplation. Combining both cognition and affection or, as Hilton puts it, "the knowing and perfect loving of God," this third part corresponds to the spiritual union usually identified by the term *contemplation*. After a person is cleansed of sin and reformed to the image of Jesus, Hilton explains,

> he is visited and taken up from all earthly and fleshly affections, from vain thoughts and imaginations of all bodily things, and is as if forcibly ravished out of the bodily senses; and then is illumined by the grace of the Holy Spirit . . . so perfectly that by the rapture of this love the soul is for the time united and conformed to the image of the Trinity.[52]

Although Hilton presents the categories as somewhat fluid and overlapping, he distinguishes the second part of contemplation from the third in terms similar to Bernard's distinctions between carnal and spiritual love and between meditation on the humanity of Christ and contemplation of his divinity.

> That [second] part may be called burning love in devotion, but this [third part] is burning love in contemplation; that is the lower, but this is the higher; that is the sweeter to the bodily feeling, but this is the sweeter to the spiritual feeling, since it is more inward, more spiritual, more worthy and more wonderful; for this truly [is] a tasting and as it

were a sight of heavenly joy—not clearly but half in darkness—which shall be fulfilled and clearly revealed in the bliss of heaven, as St. Paul says: *Videmus nunc per speculum in aenigmate, tunc autem facie ad faciem.*[53]

Hilton claims that this third part of contemplation, though occasionally achieved by those active in the world, can be fully realized only by those dedicated to it as a way of life. By the last quarter of the fourteenth century, then, affective meditation was becoming a common devotional practice of the laity, although contemplation was still the prerogative of religious and solitaries.

In his discussion of the various kinds of meditation associated with the second part of contemplation, Hilton details the three-stage progression familiar from Bernard, but in the order of Julian's own third request for "the wonnd(e) of contricyoun, the wonnde of compassyoun and the wonnde of wylfulle langgynge to god" (1:206). According to Hilton, the first step in the spiritual life is contrition.

> At the start of someone's conversion, when he has been much soiled with worldly or fleshly sin, he commonly thinks most about those sins, with great compunction and sorrow of heart, great fits of weeping, and many tears from his eyes as he humbly and diligently asks mercy and forgiveness for them from God.

Contrition is followed by affective meditation on the life of Christ. "Then after this travail, and sometimes together with it, our Lord gives to such a person—or else to another who has been kept in innocence by the grace of God—a meditation of his humanity, his birth or his passion, or of the compassion of our Lady, St. Mary."[54] Hilton recounts such a meditation, briefly identifying the main episodes in the Passion and describing the compassion it incites. Invoking the authority of Bernard of Clairvaux, Hilton concludes that such meditation is the prelude to the third stage of contemplation.

> For it is an opening of the eye of the spirit into Christ's humanity, and it may be called the carnal love of God, as St. Bernard calls it, inasmuch as it is set in the human nature of Christ. It is very good, and a great help in destroying great sins, and a way to come to virtues, and so afterward into contemplation of the divine nature. For a person shall not commonly come to spiritual delight in the contemplation of Christ's divinity unless he first comes in imagination by anguish and compassion for his humanity.[55]

Although he reverses Bernard's order, Hilton nonetheless follows the abbot of Clairvaux in regarding contrition and compassion as necessary preparations for contemplation. However, he expands the audience for this spiritual program to include the laity, who are invited to engage in the first two stages even though the highest stage remains, except in rare cases, within the purview only of those vowed to a life of contemplation.

III

This difference between late medieval religious and lay people in their ultimate purpose in meditating on the life of Christ gives us some clue to Julian of Norwich's intellectual and spiritual development prior to her visionary experience. Her request for three "wounds" similar to the three traditional stages of spiritual development outlined by Bernard and Bonaventure—compassion, contrition, and contemplation—suggests that by 1373 she was already familiar with the devotional practices most common for those in religious or solitary life. Although no documentary evidence survives to indicate whether she was educated at a nunnery, had actually entered one, or was already an anchorite,[56] she twice indicates in the short text that her intended audience for *A Book of Showings* includes those vowed to the contemplative life.[57] Referring to the "nought" of the created world in chapter 4, Julian writes, "Of this nedes ilke man and woman to hafe knawynge that desyres to lyeve contemplatyfelye, that hym lyke to nouȝt alle thynge that es made for to hafe the love of god that es vn made" (1:215); ["Every man and woman who wishes to live contemplatively needs to know of this, so that it may be pleasing to them to despise as nothing everything created, so as to have the love of uncreated God" (131–32)]. And describing the showing in chapter 13, she concludes: "And eftyr this oure lorde schewyd hym to me mare gloryfyed as to my syght than I sawe hym before, and in this was I lerede that ilke saule contemplatyfe to whilke es gyffenn to luke and seke god schalle se hire and passe vnto god by contemplacionn" (1:243); ["And after this our Lord showed himself to me, and he appeared to me more glorified than I had seen him before, and in this I was taught that every contemplative soul to whom it is given to look and to seek will see Mary and pass on to God through contemplation" (147)]. Julian clearly regards contemplation of the godhead as the ultimate goal of her spiritual efforts. The fact that she is familiar with all three of the stages of ascent traditionally associated with meditation on the life of Christ indicates that she was well schooled in the theory and practice of affective spirituality as it was presented in medieval treatises for those in religious life. It seems probable, therefore, that she was a nun or anchorite at the time of her visionary experience in 1373.

Although we can only speculate about how Julian came to formulate her request for the three gifts and what her state of life was at the time she received the revelations, it is indisputable that she saw a causal connection between her desire and her visionary experience. Julian begins the short text of *A Book of Showings* by reporting her petition for these gifts; she obviously regards the events of 13 May 1373 as the answer to her earlier prayer. Although she claims to have forgotten her request for a "bodylye syght" and a "bodelye syeknes," she acknowledges that she concentrated her attention on the gifts of compassion, contrition, and longing for God (1:206). During the course of her severe illness, she asks again for the wound of compassion and immediately the visual showings of the suffering Christ commence. Undoubtedly, Julian's intense desire for the extraordinary graces of a vision and an illness, as well as her more conventional request for the three metaphorical wounds of affective spirituality, reveal her beliefs and expectations prior to her visionary experience. As such they provide the frame of reference for what she witnessed and how she chose to report it. Whatever the causes of the revelations, Julian understands them as she does because of these preconceptions. The desire for compassion, contrition, and longing for God thus constitutes the incorporated interpretation of the showings and accounts for the sequence of themes that she explores.

Although *A Book of Showings* has no plot in the usual sense, Julian's report of her visionary experience manifests a general progression from compassion to contrition to longing for God. Because she interlaces these themes with each other, the organization of *A Book of Showings* defies precise schematization; however, the outline of Julian's initial experience is clearest in the short text. In general, the theme of compassion, manifest primarily in visual showings of various moments in Christ's passion, dominates the first half of the *Showings*, chapters 1 through 13. The theme of sin and contrition, expressed most often in locutions either heard or brought to mind, prevails in the second half, chapters 14 through 25. And the various modes of union with God that constitute the subject of contemplative thought are considered in ghostly showings interspersed in chapters 4, 9, 13, 19, and 22. In the course of the revelations, Julian herself achieves both compassion and contrition, so *A Book of Showings* develops a counterpoint between what she witnesses and how she responds.

Julian takes up the theme of longing for God intermittently throughout the short text; it is, however, the least fully developed of the three topics in her first version of *A Book of Showings*, an indication that she was still a neophyte in the contemplative tradition at the time she received the revelations. In the first and final ghostly showings she introduces a topic that will be greatly expanded in the long text: the ontological union between the soul and the persons of the Trinity. In the revelation of God's "hamly lovynge" ["familiar love"] that she describes in chapter 4, Julian uses the metaphor of clothing to convey a sense of the Creator's all-encompassing love for humankind and the analogy of the hazelnut to express the meagerness of all creation sustained by this love. Since God is her maker, lover, and keeper, Julian concludes, "For to I am substancyallye aned to hym, I may nevere have love, reste ne varray blysse; that is to saye that I be so festenede to hym that thare be ryght nought that is made betwyxe my god and me" (1:213); ["For until I am substantially united to him, I can never have love or rest or true happiness; until, that is, I am so attached to him that there can be no created thing between my God and me" (131)]. This first ghostly showing of humankind dwelling in God is complemented by the final one of Jesus dwelling in the human heart, described in chapter 22 of the short text. The concept of an ontological union between Creator and creature implicit in both these showings provides the seed for the most extensive and distinctive additions that Julian makes in the long text, chapters 53 through 63 of Revelation Fourteen. In the short text Julian provides examples of three other modes of union, in reverse order of their chronological occurrence: in chapter 9 she explains the three degrees of bliss achieved in heaven by those who are saved; in chapter 13 she alludes to the beatific vision of Christ in glory attained by contemplatives; and in chapter 19 she examines prayer as a means to union with God. Undoubtedly, the subject of union with God dominated her reflections during the twenty years it took her to achieve an understanding of the revelations and complete the long text. I will examine Julian's mystical theology in the final version of *A Book of Showings* in chapter 5 below.

While revelations about union with God are interspersed throughout the short text, Julian alternately concentrates on the other two themes, counterpointing her descriptions of the visionary experience with her reactions to it. In the first half of the short text, for example, Julian's bodily sights of episodes from the Passion in chapters 3, 7, and 8 culminate in her own achievement of compassion as she stares into the face of the dying Christ in chapter 10. Realizing that this vision fulfills her earlier desire, she responds with intense compassion: "H(ere) felyd I sothfastlye that y lovede Criste so mekille abouen my selfe that me thought it hadde beene a grete eese to me to hafe dyede bodylye" (1:235); ["Here I felt truly that I loved Christ so much more than myself that I thought it would have been a great comfort to me if my body had died" (142)]. Following the example of Mary on Calvary, whom she witnesses in a ghostly showing, Julian enacts the affective power of her compassion in her refusal to take her eyes from the crucifix. Defying her impulse to look toward heaven, she affirms her faith in Jesus as her Savior. "I answerde and sayde: Naye, I may nought [look away from the cross], for thowe erte myne heuen. This I sayde for I walde nouȝt; for I hadde levyr hafe bene in that payne to domysdaye than hafe commenn to hevene othere wyse than be hym. For I wyste wele he that bought me so sare schulde vnbynde me when he walde" (1:236); ["I answered, and said: No, I cannot [look away from the cross], for you are my heaven. I said this because I did not want to look up, for I would rather have remained in that pain until Judgment Day than have come to heaven any other way than by him. For I knew well that he who had bought me so dearly would unbind me when it was his will" (143)]. Julian's allegiance to Jesus as her Redeemer is confirmed by the subsequent visions of the God-man's love for humankind. In chapter 12 she has a ghostly showing of the Trinity celebrating Christ's act of atonement in heaven, and in chapter 13 a bodily sight of his sacred heart, the symbol of his sacrificial love. At this point her visions cease, and the second part of the short text is dominated by aural revelations concerned with the question of sin and Julian's own experience of contrition.

Despite the evidence she receives in the first ghostly showing of the Trinity's "hamly lovynge" and the goodness of all creation, Julian remains troubled by the problem of evil. In response to the revelation that God is in all things and does all that is done, she asks, "Whate es synne?" (1:226); ["What is sin?" (137)]. The answer to this question is presented in the locutions that dominate chapters 14 through 18.

Throughout this second part of the short text Julian concentrates on the apparent contradiction between God's omnipotent beneficence, revealed in her ghostly showings, and his failure to forestall her own sinfulness. These revelations explain why sin is necessary and how all shall be well. As I will demonstrate in chapter 3, these aural showings provide the basis for the distinctive theodicy that Julian presents in the long text.

It is important to recognize, however, that Julian's theological resolution to the problem of evil is balanced by her own experience of temptation, sin, and contrition bracketing the final revelation. After Julian receives assurance that she will be saved, in the locution of chapter 20, the revelations cease and her pain returns. She falls into a state of doubt: "And I was als barane and drye as 3if I hadde neuer had comfort before bot litille, for fallynge to my paynes and faylynge of gastelye felynge" (1:266); ["And I was as barren and dry as if the consolation which I had received before were trifling, because my pains had returned and my spiritual perceptions failed" (162)]. Asked by a visitor how she is doing, Julian dismisses her visionary experience as ravings. She immediately repents her lack of faith and longs to confess, but hesitates: "Bot I couth telle it na preste, for I thoght, howe schulde a preste leue me? I leued nought oure lorde god" (1:266); ["But I could not tell it to any priest, for I thought: How could a priest believe me? I did not believe our Lord God" (162)]. Julian's dream that night of the Devil strangling her prefigures the second temptation following the final revelation, the ghostly showing of Jesus sitting in the city of her heart and the locution: "Witte it welle, it was na rauynge that thowe sawe to day, botte take it and leue it and kepe þe ther to, and þou schalle nought be ouercomenn" (1:269); ["Know it well, it was no hallucination which you saw today, but accept and believe it and hold firmly to it, and you will not be overcome" (164)]. When Julian perceives the stench, heat, and noise of the fiend immediately after this showing, she is able to resist the temptation to despair by fixing her eyes on the crucifix as she did in chapter 11 when she chose Jesus as her means to heaven.[58]

In her sin, contrition, and resistance to subsequent temptation, Julian enacts the lesson she has learned about the nature of evil in the showings. As she recognizes, the final locution complements the first one: "This laste wordes ware sayde to me for lernynge of fulle trewe sikernes that it is our lorde Jhesu that schewed me alle; for ryght as in

37

the fyrste worde that oure lorde schewed me, menande his blissyd passionn: Here with is the fende ouercomenn, ryght so he sayde in the laste worde with fulle trewe sikernesse: Thow schalle nought be ouercommen" (1:269); ["These last words were said to me to teach me perfect certainty that it is our Lord Jesus who revealed everything to me; for just as in the first words which our Lord revealed to me, alluding to his blessed Passion: With this the fiend is overcome, just so he said with perfect certainty in these last words: You will not be overcome" (164)]. By alluding to the revelation of chapter 8, Julian points to the causal connection between Christ's historical act of atonement and her own act of resistance. Just as she had seen Christ laugh at the fiend's attempt to lure people to damnation, so Julian, confident of the power of her Savior, can scorn the demons: "And I scorned thame, and thus was I delyuered of thamm be the vertu of Cristes passionn. For therewith is the fende ouercommenn, as Criste sayde before to me" (1:270); ["And I despised them, and so I was delivered from them by the strength of Christ's Passion. For it is so that the fiend is overcome, as Christ said before to me" (166)]. Her resistance to the second temptation to despair thus knots together the themes of compassion and contrition.

Julian interweaves the themes of contrition and union with God in the apostrophe to sin that concludes chapter 22. Alluding to the first and final ghostly showings of substantial union, all of humankind in God and Jesus in the human heart, she reiterates her Augustinian definition of sin as nonbeing.

> A wriched synne, whate ert þou? Thowe er nought. For I sawe that god is alle thynge; I sawe nought the. And when I sawe that god hase made alle thynge, I sawe the nought. And when I sawe that god is in alle thynge, I sawe the nought. And whenn I sawe that god does alle thynge þat is done, lesse and mare, I sawe the nought. And when I sawe oure lorde Jhesu sitt in oure saule so wyrschipfully, and luff and lyke and rewle and ȝeme all that he has made, I sawe nouȝt the. (1:271)

> [O, wretched sin, what are you: You are nothing. For I saw that God is in everything; I did not see you. And when I saw that God has made everything, I did not see you. And when I saw that God is in everything, I did not see you. And when I saw that God does everything that is done, the less and the greater, I did not see you. And when I saw our Lord Jesus Christ seated in our soul so honourably, and love and delight and rule and guard all that he has made, I did not see you. (166)]

The revelations of the soul's union with God thus confirm those about the nature of sin. At the conclusion of the short text of her *Showings*, then, Julian regards herself as a contrite individual who hopes to progress in the contemplative life through her realization that it is only sin that separates her from God.

Although this summary oversimplifies the complex interlace of themes in the short text, it does reveal Julian's focus on issues associated with compassion, contrition, and contemplation. Her further pondering of these topics, particularly the last two, over a quarter of a century, culminates in the long text of *A Book of Showings*. Even though she makes changes throughout, her most substantial revisions occur in the section that corresponds to the second half of the short text and comprises more than two-thirds of the long text, Revelations Thirteen through Sixteen. In chapters 3, 4, and 5, I will analyze these revelations in order to explain the distinctive features of Julian of Norwich's theology. In the next chapter I investigate further her development of the theme of compassion in the cultural context of the meditative tradition. I will demonstrate that her evocative descriptions of episodes from Christ's passion indicate that she was proficient in the kind of visualization encouraged by this devotional practice and that Julian's visionary experience was engendered by her habit of meditation on Christ crucified.

From Visualization to Vision:
Meditation and the
Bodily Showings

ALTHOUGH the Passion was a frequent subject of medieval religious literature, few works achieve the evocative power of *A Book of Showings* in depicting the physical distress of the dying Jesus. The intensely visual character of Julian's bodily showings has led scholars to compare her prose account to late medieval paintings and sculptures of the Crucifixion. Richard Kieckhefer, for example, observes that Julian achieves verbally the same violence of emotion that the German plague crosses do visually.

> German crucifixes of the fourteenth century frequently portray Christ's body in grotesquely distorted fashion, with blood gushing profusely from his wounds. Something of the same effect comes from Julian of Norwich's vision of the crucifixion, in which Christ's body undergoes almost kaleidoscopic transformation through various shades of blue, brown, and black, as a piercing cold wind dries his flesh.[1]

Catherine Jones attributes Julian's descriptive powers to the influence of the school of East Anglian art, at its height during the fourteenth century. The vivid pictorial quality of the bodily showings, Jones contends, "might well be compared to the skilled modeling techniques and fine colors used so sensitively by the East Anglian artists, who characteristically excelled at endowing passion scenes with exquisite pathos."[2] Sixten Ringbom even suggests that an artistic rendering of the Crucifixion was the catalyst for Julian of Norwich's visionary experience.[3] Certainly these scholars correctly recognize the similarities between Julian's visions and the prevailing style of representing the Passion in late medieval art. The extant art from East Anglia produced during this period provides numerous examples of the *Christus patiens*; undoubtedly Julian was familiar with the conventions of depicting the crucified Christ in affective spirituality. Later in this chapter I will consider some very specific instances of the influence of iconography on her visions, but for now two generic examples will suffice.

40

1. Crucifixion, Horsham St. Faith's Priory, Norfolk.
From E. W. Tristram, *English Medieval Wall Painting:
The Thirteenth Century*, plate 205.

The first is a wall painting in the building that was once the refectory of St. Faith's Priory, a Benedictine foundation in Horsham, near Norwich.[4] Probably executed around 1250, this fresco, despite its damaged condition, presents an image of the suffering Savior that continues to evoke empathy. The crucified Christ, his eyes closed and head bowed, is interposed between Mary and John, both expressing grief through their posture and gestures; Mary holds one hand under her cheek, as if to support her head, and John is clasping his hands in front of his chest. Blood flows from the nail wounds in Christ's hands and feet as well as from the upwardly curved lance wound in his side; blood also trickles from a green band circling his head, though it is not discernibly a crown of thorns. The bones of the torso press against the

41

flesh suggesting the emaciation of the body. Though conventional in its representation of the Crucifixion, this painting is remarkable for its size. Beginning at about ten feet above the original floor level, the sixteen-foot cross extends into the gable. The figures are double life size. The imposing proportions of this scene of pathos serve to enhance its evocative power. If, as E. W. Tristram concludes, this wall painting is the work of an artist associated with a Benedictine center, probably at Norwich, Julian might have seen a similar portrayal of the Passion in her own city.

The second example, also of Norwich provenance, is the Gorleston Psalter, executed around 1325 for a parish church in the town of that name in Suffolk.[5] A full-page Crucifixion, added a few years after the psalter's original composition, follows the calendar. The influence of Sienese painting, similar to the style of Duccio, renders this a moving image. The setting is a jagged bluff littered with skulls. Again the dying body of Christ hanging from an elongated cross dominates the picture space. The figures of Mary and John, proportional to Christ, stand on either side with their hands clasped together and their faces expressing grief: Mary looks up toward her son; John looks down and away. A smaller Mary Magdalen kneels with her arms around the base of the cross, dwarfed by its imposing height. Again a green band, rather than a distinctive crown of thorns, surrounds Christ's head, and blood streams toward his brow. Blood from the nail wounds runs down the arms and lower portion of the cross. Blood from the wound just under the right breast flows down the length of the chest to the loincloth. The thick torso exerts a great strain on the thin arms. Christ's head is bowed, eyes apparently closed; he is either dead or dying. The quiet intensity of this painting suggests that it is a devotional rather than a didactic image.[6] Judging by some additions made later in the fourteenth century, the manuscript might have been in the Norwich cathedral priory during Julian's lifetime. Since Norwich, like London, was a center for the production of illuminated manuscripts during the fourteenth century, the presence of artists and artisans in and around the city insures that Julian would have seen representations of the Passion similar in evocative power to the Gorleston Crucifixion.[7]

The detailed descriptions of the Passion in *A Book of Showings* express the power of Julian of Norwich's visual imagination and suggest the influence of such contemporary devotional art on her visionary experience.[8] She reveals her familiarity with affective images of Christ's suffering similar to the St. Faith's wall painting and the Gorleston Crucifixion when she claims, near the beginning of the short text, "I

2. Crucifixion, Gorleston Psalter. From Sydney Cockerell,
The Gorleston Psalter.

leevyd sadlye alle the peynes of Cryste as halye kyrke schewys and
techys, and also the payntyngys of crucyfexes that er made be the grace
of god aftere the techynge of haly kyrke to the lyknes of Crystes
passyonn, als farfurthe as man ys witte maye reche" (1:202); ["I believed
firmly in all Christ's pains, as Holy Church shows and teaches, and as

paintings of the Crucifixion represent, which are made by God's grace according to Holy Church's teachings, to resemble Christ's Passion, so far as human understanding can attain" (125–26)]. However, while devotional art undoubtedly influenced the showings Julian experienced, as I will demonstrate at the end of this chapter, her final phrase indicates that she found both the verbal and visual teachings about the Passion inadequate to her own spiritual needs. Indeed, she refers to the limitations of artists' renderings of Christ's suffering to account for her own desire for an unmediated vision of the Passion, the "bodylye syght" she requests as the first gift. In this chapter I will show that Julian's desire for such an immediacy was most likely incited by her meditation on the suffering and death of Christ.[9] Although the corporeal showings are probably an amalgam of devotional works of art that she had seen in her Norwich environment and her own imaginative reenactment of the Passion narrative, her practice of meditation focused her eye and trained her powers of visualization. While contemporary devotional art certainly shaped what Julian saw, such images were not the primary catalyst for her visionary experience.

I

The preliminary devotional practice of affective spirituality, meditation involved an imaginative participation in the events of Jesus' life. The meditator is encouraged to close the gap between the present time and the past time of the historical Christ by being engaged "either as an eyewitness or as an actor in the drama of the event. He is present to the event and the event is present to him."[10] Writers of manuals for meditation used a variety of techniques to evoke such a sense of presence. Primary among these techniques are frequent injunctions to the meditator to "see" the scene being described with concrete imagery and intensely evocative language. Pseudo-Bonaventure often appeals to the meditator to envision the events of Christ's life in "the mind's eye."[11] For example, the fourteenth-century Middle English translation of the Passion section of the *Meditationes vitae Christi*, "The Privity of the Passion," begins with a promise of "newe gostely comforthe" to the person who raises up

all þe scharpenes of his mynde & opyne whyde the Inere eghe of his soule In to be-holdynge of þis b[l]esside passione, and forgett & caste be-hynd hyme for þe tyme all oþer Ocupacyouns & besynes; and that he make hym-selfe present in his thoghte as if he sawe fully with his bodyly eghe all the thyngys þat be-fell abowte þe crosse and þe glorious passione of oure lorde Ihesu; and þat noghte schortly & passandly, bot lufandly, besely, habundandly, & lastandly; noghte sturdandly, ne with dullnes & hevines of sperit.[12]

[all the acuity of his mind and opens wide the inner eye of his soul to behold this blessed Passion, and forgets and casts behind him for the time all other occupations and business; and he who makes himself present in his thought as if he saw completely with his bodily eye all the things that befell concerning the cross and the glorious passion of our lord Jesus, not briefly and fleetingly, but lovingly, busily, abundantly, and lastingly; not harshly, nor with dullness and heaviness of spirit.]

Introducing the meditation on Christ's Last Supper with his disciples, Pseudo-Bonaventure continues this appeal to the visual imagination: "Be-holde nowe besylye to euery poynte as if þou were there bodyly.... Goo thow amange theme, & be-holde how lufandly, how felandly he gose with theme and spekes, & steres theme to praye";[13] [Pay attention now carefully to every point as if you were there bodily.... Go you among them, and behold how lovingly, how feelingly he goes with them and speaks and stirs them to pray]. To aid the meditator in this process of visualization, writers of meditative treatises use vivid and evocative language. The Middle English translator follows Pseudo-Bonaventure in describing Christ's scourging with precise details and concrete imagery.

And as some doctours says, one euery knott was a scharpe hok of Iryne, þat with euery stroke þey rofe his tendyr flesche.... He es betyne and betyne agayne, blester appone blester, and wonde appone wonde, to bothe þe beters & þe [be]-holders were wery, & þene þei vn-bonde hyme. Be-holde hym here mekly & habondandly, and if þou can haue here no compassione of þi lorde Ihesu, wete þou wele þi herte es hardere þane þe stone.[14]

[And as some doctors say, on every knot was a sharp hook of iron, so that with every stroke they tore his tender flesh.... He is beaten and beaten again, blister upon blister, and wound upon wound, until both the beaters and the spectators were weary, and then they unbound him. Behold him here meekly and diligently, and if you can have here no compassion for your lord Jesus, know you well that your heart is harder than stone.]

45

Such efforts to witness imaginatively the events of Christ's passion and death certainly sharpened the meditator's eye for details.

The direct address to the meditator in the final sentence of Pseudo-Bonaventure's description provides an example of another technique writers employed to encourage imaginative participation in the events of Christ's life. Aelred of Rievaulx in *De institutione inclusarum* similarly places the anchorite at the historical scene through imperatives and injunctions. Describing Christ before Pilate, he writes:

> Avyse þe inwardly and tak tent how bonerly he stant by-fore þe jugge, wit is heed enclined, wit his eȝen icast adoun, wit good chiere and fiewe wurdes, al redy for þi sake to dispysyngge, al redy to harde betyngge. I am siker, suster, þu miȝt not longe suffre þis, þu miȝt not suffre his comely ryg be so to-torn wit schurges, his gracious face to be bouyd wit bofattes, his wurschipful heed to be corouned wit scharpe thornes to þe brayn, his riȝt hand, þat made heuen and irþe, be dishonest[ed] wit a ryed; I wot wel þu miȝt not longe dure to see þis wit þyn eȝen.[15]

> [Consider inwardly and pay attention to how courteously he stands before the judge, with his head inclined, with his eyes cast down, with a good expression and few words, all ready for hard beating. I am sure, sister, that you might not long suffer this; you might not suffer his comely back to be so torn with scourges, his gracious face to be bowed by buffets, his honorable head to be crowned with sharp thorns pressed into the brain, his right hand, that made heaven and earth, to be dishonored with a reed; I well know that you might not long endure to see this with your eyes.]

In addition to addressing the meditator, the writers speak to the historical persons who are the subject of meditation. After asking a series of questions about the cruelty and audacity of the tormentors, for example, the translator of "The Privity of the Passion" follows Pseudo-Bonaventure in addressing Christ as though he were present: "A, lorde Ihesu, what made the to suffire all þis hard penance, tourmenteȝ and payneȝ? Sothely thynne vnmesurabyll luffe þat þou hade to vs, and owre grette wikkednes þat myghte not be weschenðe awaye bot with þe precyouse licoure of þi precyouse blode";[16] [Ah, lord Jesus, what made you suffer all this hard penance, torments and pains? Truly the immeasurable love that you had for us, and our great wickedness that might not be washed away except with the precious liquid of your precious blood]. Aelred also enhances the meditator's impression of being present at the scene by including prayers spoken in the first person by the hypothetical anchorite to the subjects of meditation. As these examples demonstrate, writers in the meditative tradition used a variety of techniques to create a sense of immediacy in order to induce the meditator to suffer with Christ. Through these meditative techniques, "the imagination transforms the nonpresent and the immaterial into the concrete and visible."[17]

It seems reasonable to speculate that Julian of Norwich's bodily sights of Christ's passion owe much to this tradition of meditation.[18] The graphic language she uses and the sense of presence she creates closely resemble the immediacy invoked by what Ewert Cousins terms this "mysticism of the historical event."[19] Julian feels herself transported into the past, as she had asked to be in her first request, to be present "that tyme with Mary Mawdeleyne and with othere that were Crystes loverse, that I myght have sene bodylye the passionn of oure lorde that he sufferede for me, that I myght have sufferede with hym as othere dyd that lovyd hym" (1:201–2) ["at that time with Mary Magdalen and with the others who were Christ's lovers, so that I might have seen with my own eyes our Lord's Passion which he suffered for me, so that I might have suffered with him as others did who loved him" (125)]. Introducing each bodily showing with a reference to seeing or beholding, Julian seems to be obeying the frequent injunctions of the meditative manuals to visualize the events in Christ's life. She recounts the various episodes of the Passion with the concrete visual details of an eyewitness. For example, the graphic and evocative language Julian uses to describe her vision of the bleeding body of the scourged Christ seems to be a response to the vivid descriptions of the scourging in the passages cited above from Pseudo-Bonaventure and Aelred.

> And aftyr this I sawe be haldande the bodye plentevouslye bledande, hate and freschlye and lyfelye, ryȝt as I sawe before in the heede. And this was schewyd me in the semes of scowrgynge, and this ranne so plenteuouslye to my syght that me thought, ȝyf itt hadde bene so in kynde, for þat tyme itt schulde hafe made the bedde alle on blode and hafe passede onn abowte. (1:227)

> [And after this as I watched I saw the body bleeding copiously, the blood hot, flowing freely, a living stream, just as I had before seen the head bleed. And I saw this in the furrows made by the scourging, and I

saw this blood run so plentifully that it seemed to me that if it had in fact been happening there, the bed and everything around it would have been soaked in blood. (137)]

The eidetic expressiveness of Julian's account of the bodily showings most likely results from a sensitivity to concrete detail gained by frequent concentration on devotional art, particularly paintings, and through repeated practice of the imaginative visualization required for meditation.

The content of Julian's bodily showings also bears the imprint of meditation on the Passion. She describes seven corporeal visions: the head of Christ crowned with thorns, the face of the mocked Christ, the bleeding body of the scourged Christ, the discolored face of the crucified and dying Christ, the blissful countenance of the Savior, the wound in his side, and Christ in glory.[20] Julian regards the first five of these showings as a sequence, for she says in the long text that "oure curteyse lorde shewyd his passyon to me in fyue manneres" (9.23.389) ["our courteous Lord showed his Passion to me in five ways" (218)], and she lists the first four bodily sights as examples of the pains of the Passion and the fifth as a revelation of the resulting joy and bliss. The sixth and seventh visions simply affirm the love that Christ expressed for humankind in the Passion. Julian's concentration on the torments that preceded the Crucifixion accords with the emphasis on these same events in the serial Passion narratives used for meditation from the thirteenth through fifteenth centuries.[21] These narratives, which displaced the earlier, unsystematic meditation on the Crucifixion alone, usually begin with the Last Supper and end with the Resurrection. Although Julian's last three bodily showings perhaps owe more to iconography than to meditation, her attention to expressive details in these visions also reflects her training in meditation.

In contrast to the meditative treatises on the Passion, however, Julian does not narrate the entire story of Christ's suffering and death but rather focuses on particular moments. She concentrates on the pains that he endured and makes no mention of his tormentors. Unlike the account in "The Privity of the Passion," for example, Julian describes the results of the scourging instead of the act itself. She sees the blood flowing from the stripes rather than the men inflicting them. Her visions include none of the personages who play such a large role either as torturers or as compassionate witnesses in the serial Passion narratives and much of the devotional art of the late medieval period. Only Jesus appears in bodily likeness; even her visions of Mary at the time of the Incarnation and at the Crucifixion are not corporeal. She evokes compassion for the suffering Christ by allowing her eyes to linger over the evidence of his pain. Julian reads her vision like a picture rather than a story. In contrast to the crowded and bustling scenes described in the *Meditationes* or depicted in many contemporary paintings of the Crucifixion, both of which are similar to the dramatic and spectacular effects of a motion picture, Julian's style achieves the intimacy of a photographic close-up.

One example suffices to demonstrate this difference. As in the *Meditationes vitae Christi*, Julian interprets Jesus' fifth word on the cross, "Sicio," as both a bodily and a ghostly thirst. But while the meditative treatise concentrates on the circumstances surrounding Christ's utterance, Julian focuses on the effects of bodily thirst on his dying body. The Middle English translator, following Pseudo-Bonaventure, simply amplifies the Gospels, particularly John 19:28–30.

> The fyfte worde was: "I thryste". This was a bitter worde full of compassione bothe to his modir & to seynt Iohn & to all his frendis þat louede hym tendirly, and to vnpeteuose Iewes it was comforthe & grete gladnes. For þof it were so þat hym thrystede for þe hele of manes soule, neuerþe-les in sothefastnes hym thrystede bodily; & þat was no wondyr, for thurghe scheddynge of hys precyouse blode so habundandly, & for grete angwyse þat he sufferde withowttyne cessynge fro þe thursedaye at euene to þe ffrydaye at hey-none, he was all Inwardly drye and thristy. And whene þise vnpetouse mene vmbethoghte theme in what thynge þey myghte moste dere hyme, they tuke aysell & gall & mengede to-gedir, and gafe hym drynke.[22]

> [The fifth word was: "I thirst." This was a bitter word full of compassion both for his mother and for Saint John and all his friends who loved him tenderly; and to the unpitying Jews it was a comfort and great gladness. For although he undoubtedly thirsted for the health of man's soul, nevertheless he also thirsted bodily; and that was no wonder, for through shedding of his precious blood so profusely, and for great anguish that he suffered without ceasing from Thursday evening until high noon on Friday, he was all inwardly dry and thirsty. And when these unpitying men considered how they might most injure him, they mixed together vinegar and gall and gave it to him to drink.]

This passage exemplifies the Pseudo-Bonaventure's interest in the circumstances of Christ's suffering: he analyzes the attitudes of those on Calvary, both friends and foes; he explains the reasons for Jesus' thirst; and he follows the Gospels in reporting the act of Christ's tormentors that both increased his pain and fulfilled the messianic prophecy of Ps. 68:22.

Like the Middle English translator of the *Meditationes vitae Christi*, Julian refers to Christ's double thirst, but she defers discussion of the "gastelye thyrste" until chapter 15. Instead she develops the brief mention of Christ's inward dryness in the *Meditationes* into a graphic description of his desiccated body, abandoning Pseudo-Bonaventure's account of the public events for a much more intimate portrait of the suffering Savior.[23] In chapter 10 of the short text Julian concentrates on the pitiful and painful death of Jesus. Her eyes linger over the physical effects on Christ's face of the process of drying and dying. She describes this face turning pale and then blue, with the lips changing from ruddy red to bluish black and the nostrils shriveling.

> The blyssyd bodye dryede alle ane lange tyme, with wryngynge of the nayles and paysynge of the hede and weyght of the bodye, with blawynge of wynde fra withoutynn that dryed mare and pyned hym with calde, mare thann mynn herte can thynke, and alle othere paynes. Swilke paynes I sawe that alle es to litelle þat y can telle or saye, for itt maye nouȝt be tolde, botte ylke saule aftere the sayinge of saynte Pawle schulde feele in hym þat in Criste Jhesu. (1:234)

> [The blessed body was left to dry for a long time, with the wrenching of the nails and the sagging of the head and the weight of the body, with the blowing of the wind around him, which dried up his body and pained him with cold, more than my heart can think of, and with all his other pains I saw such pain that all that I can describe or say is inadequate, for it cannot be described. But each soul should do as St. Paul says, and feel in himself what is in Christ Jesus. (141–42)]

The graphic details Julian provides render her account closer than Pseudo-Bonaventure's to that of an eyewitness and evoke greater compassion for the suffering Savior.

I have argued that *A Book of Showings* owes its genesis, to some extent, to the religious culture of affective spirituality, especially the practice of meditating on the Passion. However, the difference in style between the meditative manuals and Julian's descriptions of her bodily showings is also significant, for her more intimate and focused accounts suggest that she did in some sense actually "see" the moments in the Passion that she describes. I do not wish to deny the validity of Julian's visionary experience or to speculate about its metaphysical or psychological causes. Rather, I propose to demonstrate that, like any other human experience, it occurs within a specific frame of reference. Given this fact, it seems reasonable to conclude that the particular showings of the Passion that Julian of Norwich receives are influenced by her contemporary religious culture of affective spirituality. The visualization induced by meditation on the passion of Christ is the catalyst for her visions.

II

By providing insight into Julian's preparations and expectations for a visionary experience, a study of the influence of the meditative tradition on *A Book of Showings* presents a frame of reference for appreciating what her incorporated interpretation derives from her cultural circumstances. However, the final version of Julian's *Showings* owes a double debt to the process of meditation, for just as visualization of Christ's passion precipitated Julian's visions, so retrospection of the visions precipitated her illumination as she struggled for nearly a quarter of a century to understand the showings she had witnessed. Thus, the revelations themselves become a "text" for meditation and, in turn, spur re-visions in both the spiritual and literary senses of the word. An examination of the changes Julian makes in her accounts of the bodily showings from the short to the long text reveals that she hones her descriptive powers in order to present her own visions in a manner designed to elicit her reader's compassion for the suffering Christ.[24]

In revising the short text Julian often includes more graphic details of Christ's suffering in her descriptions of the corporeal visions. Some of her most memorable passages in the long text are additions of this kind. For example, her description of the scourged Christ is even more gruesome in the long text than in the short-text passage cited above.

> And after this I saw beholdyng the body plentuous bledyng in semyng of the scoregyng, as thus. The feyer skynne was broken full depe in to the tendyr flessch, with sharpe smytynges all a bout the sweete body. The hote blode ranne out so plentuously that ther was neyther seen skynne ne

wounde, but as it were all blode. And when it cam wher it shuld haue falle downe, ther it vanysschyd. Not with standyng the bledyng continued a whyle, tyll it myght be seen with avysement. And this was so plentuous to my syght that me thought if it had ben so in kynde and in substance, for that tyme it shulde haue made the bedde all on bloude, and haue passyde over all about. (4.12.342–43)

[And after this as I watched, I saw the body bleeding copiously in representation of the scourging, and it was thus. The fair skin was deeply broken into the tender flesh through the vicious blows delivered all over the lovely body. The hot blood ran out so plentifully that neither skin nor wounds could be seen, but everything seemed to be blood. And as it flowed down to where it should have fallen, it disappeared. Nonetheless, the bleeding continued for a time, until it could be plainly seen. And I saw it so plentiful that it seemed to me that if it had in fact and in substance been happening there, the bed and everything all around it would have been soaked in blood. (199–200)]

The short text only includes sentences resembling the first and the last; instead of identifying this moment as the scourging and describing the torn flesh and profuse bleeding, Julian writes more abstractly of "the bodye plentevouslye bledande, hate and freschlye and lyfelye, ryȝt as I sawe before in the heede" (1:227) ["the body bleeding copiously, the blood hot, flowing freely, a living stream, just as I had before seen the head bleed" (137)].

Another example of Julian's enhanced descriptions occurs near the end of Revelation One in the long text. The corresponding passage in the short text is very brief: "And in that tyme that oure lorde schewyd this that I haue nowe saydene in gastelye syght, I saye the bodylye syght lastande of the plentyuouse bledynge of the hede" (1:217); ["And during the time that our Lord showed me this spiritual vision which I have now described, I saw the bodily vision of the copious bleeding of the head persist" (132)]. In chapter 7 of the long text Julian expands this brief statement into three paragraphs as she endeavors to provide a precise account of the shape, color, and amount of the blood streaming from the crown of thorns.

The grett droppes of blode felle downe fro vnder the garlonde lyke pelottes, semyng as it had comynn ouȝte of the veynes. And in the comyng ouȝte they were bro(wn)e rede, for the blode was full thycke; and in the spredyng abrode they were bryght rede. And whan it camme at the

browes, ther they vanysschyd; and not wythstonding the bledyng con-
tynued tylle many thynges were sene and vnderstondyd. (1.7.311–12)

[The great drops of blood fell from beneath the crown like pellets, looking as if they came from the veins, and as they issued they were a
brownish red, for the blood was very thick, and as they spread they
turned bright red. And as they reached the brows they vanished; and
even so the bleeding continued until I had seen and understood many
things. (187–88)]

In order to enhance the visual image, Julian uses three similes. "Thes
thre thynges cam to my mynde in the tyme: pelettes for the roundhede
in the comyng ouȝte of the blode, the scale of herying for the roundhede in the spredyng, the droppes of the evesyng of a howse for the
plentuoushede vnnumerable" (1.7.312–13); ["At the time three things
occurred to me: The drops were round like pellets as the blood issued,
they were round like a herring's scales as they spread, they were like
raindrops off a house's eaves, so many that they could not be counted"
(188)]. This analysis of her own descriptive technique attests Julian's
self-consciousness about her efforts to increase the eidetic expressiveness of the bodily showings in the long text. Her choice of images from
daily life, like raindrops or the scales of a herring, provide evidence of
her keen powers of observation and her synthetic visual imagination.

In Revelation Eight Julian describes her final bodily sight of Christ's
passion and her own attainment of compassion. The two phenomena
presented in chapter 10 of the short text—the visual showing of the
drying and dying face of Jesus and the aural showing of his words "I
thryste"—are divided between chapters 16 and 17 of the long text. In
each case Julian elaborates on the phenomenon with the addition of
graphic details of the suffering. She doubles the short text's description
of the drying face by transposing the discussion of its external causes,
the cold and the wind, from later in chapter 10, and expounds on its
internal causes, loss of blood and pain. Julian's expanded account of the
drying of Christ's body enhances her insistence in both texts on the
gradual and painful process of his dying. At the end of chapter 16 she
emphasizes the slow progress of his death by adding a penultimate
sentence that recapitulates all he suffered. "And ther I say it semyd as
he had bene sennyght deed, it specyfyeth that the swet body was so
dyscolouryd, so drye, so clongyn, so dedly and so pytuous as he had
bene sennyght deed, contynually dyeng" (8.16.359); ["And when I say
that it seemed as if he had been dead for a week, that means, as I have

explained, that the sweet body was so discoloured, so dry, so shrivelled, so deathly and so pitiful that he might have been dead for a week, though he went on dying" (207)]. The greater detail of the long text enables the reader to follow the steps in this process more affectively than the short text does and imaginatively to witness the agony of the Crucifixion with increased compassion.

In chapter 17 Julian continues to enhance her reader's ability to visualize Christ's final pain by increasing fourfold her commentary on his dying words, "I thirst." In the short text Julian had been at a loss for words to describe Christ's death: "Swilke paynes I sawe that alle es to litelle þat y can telle or saye, for itt maye nouȝt be tolde, botte ylke saule aftere the sayinge of saynte Pawle schulde feele in hym þat in Criste Jhesu" (1:234); ["I saw such pain that all that I can describe or say is inadequate, for it cannot be described. But each soul should do as St. Paul says, and feel in himself what is in Christ Jesus" (141–42)]. In fact this showing of the drying body of Christ had marked a turning point in her own condition, for in the short text she tells us that her mother, believing Julian dead, closed her daughter's eyes. This personal detail, like most others in the short text, Julian omits from her final version of *A Book of Showings*, probably in order to universalize her experience.[25] Compensating for her previous silence, Julian concentrates in the long text on an evocative description of the loose skin clinging to the coagulated blood where the crown of thorns had pierced Christ's forehead. Again using an image from daily life, she develops a simile comparing the shredded flesh to a torn and ragged cloth. "Wher thorow it was broken on pecys as a cloth, and saggyng downwarde, semyng as it wolde hastely haue fallen for heuynes and for lowsenes" (8.17.362); ["Through this it was torn in pieces like a cloth, and sagged down, seeming as if it would soon have fallen because it was so heavy and so loose" (208)]. Then she describes a crown of clotted blood circling the crown of thorns. Julian concludes her description of this dried body with a second simile: "The skynne and the flesshe that semyd of the face and of the body was smalle rympylde with a tawny coloure, lyke a drye bord when it is agyd, and the face more browne than the body" (8.17.363); ["The skin and the flesh of the face and the body which showed were covered with fine wrinkles, and of a tawny colour, like a dry board which has aged, and the face was more brown than the body" (208)]. Summarizing chapters 16 and 17, Julian ends the description of this final episode of the Passion by reiterating the four ways in which Christ's body lost moisture, thus drawing the affective material together with analytic precision. Despite the details she has added in the long text, she still feels that her words fall short of her visionary experience: "for which paynes I saw that alle is to lytylle that I can sey, for it may nott be tolde" (8.17.364); ["and with all his other pains, I saw that all that I can say is inadequate, for it cannot be described" (209)]. Nonetheless, as B. A. Windeatt remarks, "[Julian's] description has power to evoke a fresh response of feeling to this most familiar of icons, through the unusualness of its attention to the details of the extraordinary violation of Christ's body in the Passion."[26]

Julian's amplifications of these descriptions indicate the manner in which her memory and imagination contributed to her initial impression. In the course of recollecting and recording what she had seen, she improves her memory of the details and enhances her descriptive powers. As Windeatt puts it, "Julian quite literally alters her way of looking at the original shewings. . . . The details of colour, quality, and extent reflect an emotional response in Julian and summon a corresponding response from the reader."[27] Her own visionary experience incites her to foster her reader's powers of visualization. By increasing the evidence of Christ's physical distress through concrete details, Julian hopes to evoke her audience's compassion in the manner of writers of meditative treatises on the Passion. The meditative tradition thus influences not only what Julian sees, but also how she chooses to report it.

III

Although Julian's first four bodily sights appear to have been engendered by her familiarity with handbooks on meditation, her last three do not correspond to episodes from narratives of the Passion like the *Meditationes vitae Christi*. Rather, her visions of the crucified Christ's blissful face, of the wound in his side, and of his glorified body indicate the direct influence of late medieval iconography, for all three express the theme of Christ's love for humankind by presenting an *imago* that transcends historical events. Perhaps these last three bodily showings provide early evidence of what became the common fifteenth-century practice of referring the meditator to a visual representation, either an illustration in the text or a statue or painting in the church.[28] Since iconography was usually derived from written texts and not vice versa, it is impossible to ascertain whether Julian knew a motif from a meditative treatise or its artistic manifestations. And the ubiquity of this iconography militates against identifying any specific works of art that Julian might have seen. However, as I will show, the fifth and sixth visions derive from the same iconographic tradition, for the ghostly revelation of the three heavens discussed in the fifth showing resembles the visual image of the Throne of Grace, a motif often associated with the icon of the Man of Sorrows informing the sixth bodily showing.[29]

Julian's fifth bodily showing is very brief. Watching Christ die, she witnesses a surprising change in his face. "And sodaynlye, me behaldande in the same crosse, he channchede in to blysfulle chere. The chawngynge of his chere channgyd mynne, and I was alle gladde and mery as yt was possybille. Than brought oure lorde merelye to my mynde: Whate es any poynte of thy payne or of þy grefe? And I was fulle merye" (1:239); ["And suddenly, as I looked at the same cross, he changed to an appearance of joy. The change in his appearance changed mine, and I was as glad and joyful as I could possibly be. And then cheerfully our Lord suggested to my mind: Where is there any instant of your pain or of your grief? And I was very joyful" (144)]. Although the corporeal vision is too general to attribute to any particular source, it is accompanied by a locution and a ghostly revelation, both of which resemble traditional devotional motifs. First, Julian engages in a brief dialogue with the Savior:

> Than sayde oure lorde, askande: Arte thou wele payde that I suffyrde for the? 3a, goode lorde, quod I; gramercy, goode lorde, blissyd mut thowe be. 3yf thowe be payede, quod oure lorde, I am payede. It is a ioye and a blysse and ane endlesse lykynge to me that euer y suffyrde passyonn for the, for 3yf I myght suffyr mare, I walde suffyr. (1:239)

> [Then our Lord put a question to me: Are you well satisfied that I suffered for you? Yes, good Lord, I said; all my thanks to you, good Lord, blessed may you be! If you are satisfied, our Lord said, I am satisfied. It is a joy and a bliss and an endless delight to me that ever I suffered my Passion for you, for if I could suffer more, I would. (144)]

The last sentence of this locution initiates a ghostly revelation of three heavens and further reflection on the meaning of her preceding bodily sight.

Although Julian's vision of the three heavens is a ghostly rather than a bodily showing, it may well bear an affinity with the iconography of the Throne of Grace. As she gazed at the blissful face of the crucified

Christ, Julian's "vndyrstandynge was lyftyd vppe in to heuenn, and thare I sawe thre hevens; ... I sawe thre hevenns, and alle of the blessyd manhede of Cryste" (1:239) ["understanding was lifted up into heaven, and there I saw three heavens; ... I have seen three heavens, and all are of the blessed humanity of Christ" (144–45)]. She explains these heavens in terms of the locution brought to her mind: "And in this thre wordes: It is a ioye, a blysse and ane endeles likynge to me, ware schewed to me thre hevens, as thus. For the ioye I vndyrstode the plesannce of the fadere, for the blysse the wirschippe of the sonne, and for the endeles lykynge the haly gaste" (1:240); ["And in these three sayings: It is a joy, a bliss and an endless delight to me, there were shown to me three heavens, and in this way. By 'joy' I understood that the Father was pleased, by 'bliss' that the Son was honoured, and by 'endless delight' the Holy Spirit" (146–47)]. Even though Julian's account includes few concrete details, she seems to be describing a scene analogous to the iconography of the Throne of Grace. This depiction of the Trinity shows Christ on the cross being supported by the Father in human form, often sitting on a throne, and with the wings of a dove representing the Holy Spirit usually connecting the two. As Gertrud Schiller observes, this pictorial type confirms the efficacy of the atonement by indicating that Christ is both God and man and by dramatizing the acceptance of his sacrifice by the other persons of the Trinity. "When God exhibits or offers his crucified Son as a propitiation in the image of the Throne of Grace, the spectator's gaze is directed towards the Death of the Redeemer, yet it is also clear that this figure who was crucified on earth is part of the divine Trinity and has been exalted to join the Father."[30] The Trinity rejoices because humankind's salvation has been won through the passion of the God-man. This is precisely the conclusion that Julian draws from this ghostly sight: "Jhesu wille that we take heede to this blysse that is in the blyssedfulle trinite of oure saluacionn, and that we lyke als mekylle with his grace whyles we er here" (1:241); ["Jesus wants us to pay heed to this bliss for our salvation which is in the blessed Trinity, and to take equal delight, through his grace, whilst we are here" (146)].

Julian interprets the words formed in her understanding during this fifth bodily showing as evidence of Christ's immense love for humankind. The final clause of the locution, "for ȝyf I myght suffyr mare, I walde suffyr" ["for if I could suffer more, I would" (144)], alludes to Isa. 5:4: "What is there that I ought to do more to my vineyard, that I have not done to it?" Understood as a prophecy of Christ's sacrifice, this

3. Throne of Grace, Luttrell Psalter.
From *The Luttrell Psalter*.

verse is cited in the *Improperia* for Good Friday and became the basis
for numerous medieval lyrics of reproach.[31] However, Julian transforms
this locution from a complaint into an expression of love.

> And in this wordes: ȝyf I myght suffyr mare, I walde suffyr mare, I sawe
> sothly that ȝif he myght dye als ofte als fore euer ilke man anes that
> schalle be safe, as he dyd anes for alle, love schulde neuer late hym hafe
> reste to he hadde done it. And whenn he hadde done it, he walde sette
> it atte nought for luff, for alle thyn(k)e hym botte litylle in regarde of his
> love. (1:240)

> [And in these words: If I could suffer more, I would suffer more, I saw
> truly that if he could die as often as once for every man who is to be
> saved, as he did once for all men, love would never let him rest till he had
> done it. And when he had done it, he would count it all as nothing for
> love, for everything seems only little to him in comparison with his love.
> (145)]

In her reflections on this locution Julian appreciates the astonishing strength of Christ's love; she is convinced of his willingness to endure the torments of the Passion over and over for each individual who is to be saved. Her concentration on this love enacts one of the tenets of affective spirituality, for, as Bernard of Clairvaux remarks, "the more surely you know yourself loved, the easier you will find it to love in return."[32] Julian's transformation of a scriptural verse usually regarded as a reproach into an expression of Christ's love epitomizes her emphasis throughout *A Book of Showings* on the affection of God for sinful humankind. Her use of the *quid ultra debui facere* thus resembles the less common association of these words in Middle English lyrics with the motif of Christ as lover-knight or with the iconography of the Sacred Heart,[33] for not only does she interpret this locution as evidence of Christ's love, but the next bodily showing is of the wound in his side.

The sixth bodily showing provides further evidence of divine affection as Julian sees Christ look to his side and say, "My childe, ȝif thow kan nought loke in my godhede, see heere how I lette opyn my syde and my herte be clovene in twa and lette oute blude and watere, alle þat was thare yn; and this lykes me and so wille I that it do the" (1:242); ["My child, if you cannot look on my divinity, see here how I suffered my side to be opened and my heart to be split in two and to send out blood and water, all that was in it; and this is a delight to me, and I wish it to be so for you" (146)]. This bodily showing reflects the popular iconography of the Man of Sorrows. The crucified Christ, with eyes either closed or opened, bends his head to his right to draw attention to the lance wound in his side whence flow blood and water. As Schiller observes, "the Man of Sorrows in its many artistic forms is the most precise visual expression of the piety of the Late Middle Ages, which took its character from mystical contemplation rather than from theological speculation. The Latin *Imago pietatis* might be translated 'image of self-sacrificing love.'"[34] Although not based on an episode from the historical narrative of Christ's suffering and death, the Man of Sorrows is the visual epitome of the Passion's purpose. The heart broken in two by the lance appropriately symbolizes the love that incited Jesus' sacrificial death. In her short text Julian concentrates on the salvific significance of the wound: the blood and water flowing from the side of the God-man redeem humankind. As a synopsis of the doctrine of the Passion, the Man of Sorrows with his bleeding heart provides a fitting image for Julian's penultimate bodily showing.

After receiving a ghostly showing of Mary in glory, Julian sees the Man of Sorrows transfigured into the glorified Christ. Although she provides no visual description, she introduces this revelation as a bodily showing. "And eftyr this oure lorde schewyd hym to me mare glory-fyed as to my syght than I sawe hym before, and in this was I lerede that ilke saule contemplatyfe to whilke es gyffenn to luke and seke god schalle se hire and passe vnto god by contemplacionn" (1:243); ["And after this our Lord showed himself to me, and he appeared to me more glorified than I had seen him before, and in this I was taught that every contemplative soul to whom it is given to look and to seek will see Mary and pass on to God through contemplation" (147)]. Julian's final corporeal vision is, paradoxically, ineffable, for the glorified body of Christ is beyond the powers of any human to describe. She can only report the words formed in her understanding on this occasion when she attained the contemplative union.

> And eftyr this techynge, hamelye, curtayse and blysfulle, and verray lyfe, ofte tymes oure lorde Jhesu sayde to me: I it am that is hiaste. I it am that þou luffes. I it am that thowe lykes. I it am that þowe serves. I it am þat þou langes. I it am that þowe desyres. I it am that thowe menes. I it am þat is alle. I it am that haly kyrke preches the and teches the. I it am that schewed me are to the. (1:243)

> [And after this teaching, familiar, courteous, full of bliss and true life, our lord Jesus often said to me: I it am who is highest. I it am whom you love. I it am in whom you delight. I it am whom you serve. I it am for whom you long. I it am whom you desire. I it am whom you intend. I it am who is all. I it am whom Holy Church preaches and teaches to you. I it am who showed myself before to you. (My translation)]

This locution echoes the vocabulary and syntax used to identify mystical experience in the contemplative tradition. Julian's repetition of the phrase *I it am* alludes to God's identification of himself when he appeared to Moses in the burning bush: "I am who am" (Exod. 3:14). Augustine interprets these words on several occasions as an articulation of the divine essence and proof of God's eternal existence.[35] Richard of St. Victor alludes to Augustine's interpretation of Exod. 3:14 in his discussion of the ecstasy of the contemplative state in *The Mystical Ark* (ca. 1155). "And then [the mind] falls asleep 'in the same' when by means of contemplation and wonder it rests in Him to whom it is one and the same thing to be everything that is, and who alone can truly say, 'I am who I am.'"[36] Julian amplifies the original phrase from Exodus in an effort to articulate the allness of God that she experiences through this vision of the glorified body of Christ. Her inclusion of personal, emotive terms relates this showing to the third wound she requests, love longing for God. Her effort to achieve compassion through means of a bodily showing of the Passion thus culminates in a glimpse of the godhead revealed in the mystical and beatific visions.

Julian's descriptions of these last three bodily showings are much briefer and less graphic than her preceding accounts of the episodes from the Passion. Perhaps the evocative power of her language declines because these images were not part of her meditative program or because they are less dramatic than the first four. More significantly, Julian has reached the point where meditation gives way to contemplation and visionary experience progresses to mysticism. It seems appropriate that as she moves from the elementary to the higher stages of spirituality, her experience becomes less sensory and concrete. After chapter 13, the corporeal visions cease until she sees the Devil that night in a dream; in the second stage of her visionary experience she receives instruction "be worde formede in myne vndyrstandynge, and be gastelye syght" (1:224) ["by words formed in my understanding and by spiritual vision" (135)]. Language itself begins to fail Julian as the revelations become more theoretical.

> Botte the gastelye syght I maye nought ne can nought schewe it vnto ʒowe oponlye and als fullye as I wolde; botte I truste in oure lorde god alle myghtty that he schalle of his goodnes and for ʒoure love make ʒowe to take it mare gastelye and mare swetly than I can or maye telle it ʒowe, and so motte it be, for we are alle one in loove. (1:224)

> [But I may not and cannot show the spiritual visions to you as plainly and fully as I should wish; but I trust in our Lord God Almighty that he will, out of his goodness and for love of you, make you accept it more spiritually and more sweetly than I can or may tell it to you, and so may it be, for we are all one in love. (135–36)]

Julian's sense that she cannot adequately express her experience impels her to years of further reflection. Just three months short of twenty years later, she achieves the understanding that enables her to complete the long text of *A Book of Showings*.

Six times the length of the original version, the long text of the *Showings* develops the theological implications of Julian's visionary

experience. Although, as I have already shown in this chapter, she revises her account of the visual showings of Christ's passion in order to
evoke her reader's compassion, the more significant additions that Julian makes in Revelations Thirteen and Fourteen of the long text bear
witness to her maturation over the course of two decades as a moral
and mystical theologian. Chapters 3 and 4 will investigate the resolution she provides in Revelations Thirteen and Fourteen to the problem
of evil. And chapter 5 will explain the anthropology underlying her
analysis of the motherhood of Jesus in the second part of Revelation
Fourteen. Julian ascribes her understanding of these complex issues to
two decades of reflection on her visionary experience; any identification of the specific sources for these additions must remain speculative.
Nonetheless, as I shall demonstrate in the next three chapters, Julian
explores the implications of these showings with a thoroughness and
precision that transform the primarily devotional short text into the
theologically sophisticated long text.

"Alle Shalle Be Wele":
The Theodicy of
Julian of Norwich

SYNNE IS behouely, but alle shalle be wele, and alle shalle be wele, and alle maner of thynge shalle be wele." These words from the thirteenth revelation of Julian of Norwich's *Book of Showings* have been inscribed on modern consciousness by T. S. Eliot's quotation of them in the *Four Quartets*. Although Eliot's incorporation of Julian's voice into his dialogue with the past has brought her recognition within the literary establishment, it has also reduced the message of her *Showings* to a conservative, secular mysticism. Echoing as they do through "Little Gidding," Julian's words have the resonance of an incantation, a desire transformed by the ritual of repetition into an assertion. But the charm of Julian's language belies the complexity of her thought, for these words from Revelation Thirteen epitomize her critique of the medieval ideology of sin. Without violating orthodoxy, Julian of Norwich formulates her own original response to a theological dilemma at the center of Christian belief: the problem of evil. Her analysis of the contradiction between the reality of sin and suffering in creation and the Christian conception of the Creator places her in the tradition of Western theodicy, the endeavor, as Milton puts it, "to justify the ways of God to man."[1]

A Book of Showings presents the problem of evil in terms that identify unmistakably the conundrum it presents for Christians. The observable fact of evil, either as sin or as suffering, controverts the belief that the universe was created by a good God who is omnipotent and omniscient. Julian's own apprehension of sin, both in her and around her, violates her vision of God as a benevolent Creator enclosing all in love. In Revelation Three, incited by "a softe drede," she confronts the dilemma of evil: "What is synne? For I saw truly that god doth alle thyng, be it nevyr so lytyle. And I saw veryly that nothyn is done by happe ne by aventure, but alle by the for(eseing) wysdom of god" (3.11.336–37); ["What is sin? For I saw truly that God does everything, however small it may be, and that nothing is done by chance, but all by God's prescient wisdom" (197)]. If the Creator does all and knows the consequences of all that he does, how does evil come to exist in creation? The human experience of sin and suffering appears to contradict the qualities of power, knowledge, and goodness attributed to the deity. In her formulation of the question, Julian inquires not only about the nature of evil but also about the nature of God and the relationship between the Creator and humankind.

The enigma of sin haunted Julian for the twenty years that passed between her initial vision and the final revision of the *Showings*; it acted as the irritant around which the interpretive accretions of the long text formed. Revelations Thirteen and Fourteen in the final version, the locus of Julian's solution to the problem of evil, contain the most significant expansions of the short text. Of the thirteen chapters that constitute the thirteenth showing, eight (28, 32, 33, 35, 36, 38, 39, 40) include substantial additions. And only the chapters on prayer (41 through 43) in Revelation Fourteen appear in the earlier text; the parable of the lord and servant and the analogy of Jesus as Mother, both central to Julian's theodicy, are new to the final version. As she admits in her interpretation of the parable in chapter 51, its meaning was not apparent to her at the time of the initial vision although she did realize that "it was gevyn me for answere to my desyer" (14.51.519) ["it had been given as an answer to my petition" (269)] to understand God's attitude toward sinners. Undoubtedly, Julian's anxiety about sin impelled her revision of the *Showings* as her solution to the problem of evil became clear to her over nearly a quarter-century of contemplation.

Julian's preoccupation with sin bespeaks the challenge that it posed to her personally and to medieval Christians. As her exploration of the issue in *A Book of Showings* reveals, she was not satisfied by either the heretical or the orthodox solution to the problem of evil. Both theodicies tried to defend God by imputing the origin of evil to another source. The heterodox solution, offered by the Manichaeans of the early Christian era and the Cathars of the high Middle Ages, posed a force of evil in the universe, equal in power to God but separate from him, that was responsible for sin and suffering. The orthodox solution, definitively articulated by Augustine of Hippo, attributed evil to the free will of creatures, either angelic or human, who deliberately chose to disobey God. Although Julian of Norwich refutes dualism with a definition of evil similar to Augustine's, she also challenges the juridical premises of orthodox theodicy.

Julian rejects heretical dualism by denying the substantial reality of evil. In response to her question about the nature of sin, Revelation Three affirms the omnipotence and immanence of the Creator and the goodness of creation: "for [God] is in the myd poynt of all thynges, and all he doth. And I was sewer that he doth no synne; and here I saw verely that synne is no dede, for in alle thys, synne was nott shewde" (3.11.338); ["for [God] is at the centre of everything, and he does everything. And I was certain that he does no sin; and here I was certain that sin is no deed, for in all this sin was not shown to me" (197–98)]. In Revelation Thirteen, as she begins to address the haunting question of "why, by the grete forsey(ng) wysdom of god, the begynnyng of synne was nott lettyd" (13.27.404) ["why, through the great prescient wisdom of God, the beginning of sin was not prevented" (224)], Julian asserts again that sin has no autonomous essence. "But I saw nott synne, for I beleue it had no maner of substannce, ne no part of beyng, ne it myght not be knowen but by the payne that is caused therof" (13.27.406); ["But I did not see sin, for I believe that it has no kind of substance, no share in being, nor can it be recognized except by the pain caused by it" (225)]. By defining sin as nonbeing Julian rejects the central premise of dualistic theodicy, the concept of evil as an independent force.

Julian's repudiation of dualism rests on the conventional Christian definition of evil articulated by Augustine (A.D. 354–430) and Pseudo-Dionysius (late fifth century) and repeated by numerous medieval theologians. In the *Confessions* Augustine relates his break with Manichaean dualism to his reading of Plotinus. Influenced by the Neoplatonic view of evil as nonbeing, he comes to regard it as a privation of the good: "Therefore, whatsoever is, is good. Evil, then, the origin of which I had been seeking, has no substance at all; for if it were a substance, it would be good."[2] Pseudo-Dionysius likewise presents a Plotinian conception of evil in *The Divine Names*. "So, then, evil has no being nor does it inhere in the things that have being. There is no place for evil as such and its origin is due to a defect rather than to a capacity."[3] That the Fourth Lateran Council invokes this same argument in 1215 to condemn the Cathars' conception of evil as an autonomous entity demonstrates the pervasiveness of this definition throughout the Middle Ages.[4]

In response to the challenge of dualism, both Augustine and Pseudo-Dionysius adapt Plotinus's conception of the universe as a plenitude in which evil, as a privation of the good, is a metaphysical trompe l'oeil, a misperception due to the inadequate perspective of creatures who cannot understand the divine plan. Addressing the omniscient Creator in the *Confessions*, for example, Augustine proclaims, "To thee there is no such thing as evil, and even in thy whole creation taken as a whole, there is not. . . . But in the parts of creation, some things, because they do not harmonize with others, are considered evil. Yet those same things harmonize with others and are good, and in themselves are good."[5] In *The Divine Names* Pseudo-Dionysius also argues that evil, although a privation of the good, serves a purpose in the divine plan. "Good comes from the one universal Cause, and evil originates in numerous partial deficiencies. God knows evil under the form of good, and with him the causes of evil things are capacities which can produce good."[6] This conception of evil recurs again and again in the writings of medieval theologians and echoes as late as the eighteenth century in Pope's aphorism "All partial evil is universal good."

Julian proposes a similar response to the problem of evil in Revelation Three as she contrasts the flawed judgment of humankind with the perfect judgment of God.

> For man beholdyth some dedys wele done and some dedys evylle, and our lorde beholdyth them not so, for as alle that hath beyng in kynde is of gods makyng, so is alle thyng that is done in properte of gods doyng. For it is esy to vnderstand that the beste dede is wele done; and so wele as the best dede that is done and the hyghest, so wele is the least dede done, and all in the properte and in the order that our lord hath it ordeynyd tofor withouȝte begynnyng, for ther is no doer but he. (3.11.339–40)

> [For a man regards some deeds as well done and some as evil, and our Lord does not regard them so, for everything which exists in nature is of God's creation, so that everything which is done has the property of being of God's doing. For it is easy to understand that the best of deeds is well done; and the smallest of deeds which is done is as well done as the best and the greatest, and they all have the property and the order ordained for them as our Lord had ordained, without beginning, for no one does but he. (198)]

Julian's faith in providence and her experience of God's immanence in creation lead her to affirm the goodness of the divine plan despite the limitations of human comprehension. From God's point of view, she asserts, evil does not exist because it is not an entity and because it works toward the ultimate good.

Although she accepts the definition of evil as a privation of the good, Julian of Norwich does not claim that sin and suffering are merely illusions. Instead, she identifies pain as the experiential manifestation of the ontological privation. The defect has an effect: "synne is cause of alle thys payne" (13.27.407); ["sin is the cause of all this pain" (225)]. In order to confront the reality of sin and suffering, this time from the point of view of human experience, she again poses the problem of evil by asking in Revelation Thirteen about God's purpose in allowing sin. In her response throughout this showing and the next, Julian calls into question the orthodox medieval solution, first proposed by Augustine, to the problem of evil.

Based on a juridical paradigm, orthodox medieval theodicy ascribes both moral and natural evil to the deliberate violation of divine injunctions. As Augustine asserts: "whatever is called evil is either sin or the punishment of sin. Sin is nothing but the evil assent of free will, when we incline to those things which justice forbids and from which we are free to abstain."[7] In accord with this legalistic definition of sin, explanations of the problem of evil based on Augustine's argument concentrate on its etiology or origins: What is the cause of evil in the individual, and how was evil introduced into a cosmos created by a God who is all-good, all-powerful, and all-knowing?

Like heretical dualism, orthodox theodicy attempts to defend God from responsibility for evil. Rather than proposing an independent power, though, it attributes both the origin and the persistence of evil in the universe to the decision of free creatures, either angelic or human, who rejected good by the exercise of their unrestrained wills. As a result of the original sin of their first parents, Augustinian theodicy argues, all humans are born with a will already inclined toward evil. Despite their inherited weakness, however, God is just in punishing sinners because both the initial and subsequent offenses are committed voluntarily. In his account of his break with Manichaean dualism in the *Confessions*, Augustine summarizes these two premises informing his theodicy: "that free will is the cause of our doing evil, and that [God's] just judgment is the cause of our having to suffer from its consequences."[8] Because of his insistence that evil is due either to human transgressions or to divine punishment of them, Augustine's argument is referred to as the "free-will defense" or "retributive theodicy."[9] As these terms indicate, this solution to the problem of evil is juridical; it is concerned with origins because it is an effort to place blame.

The premises of Augustine's solution to the problem of evil inform the medieval ideology of sin. These assertions—that evil results from the free choice of individuals who inherit a propensity to sin and that sinners must suffer the consequences of God's wrath—are theological axioms of the Middle Ages. Although Julian of Norwich may not have been familiar with the texts in which Augustine develops his theodicy, she undoubtedly knew the general outline of his argument from pastoral teaching. In Revelations Thirteen and Fourteen of *A Book of Showings*, Julian develops a theodicy that implicitly challenges the Augustinian solution to the problem of evil by calling into question its fundamental premises.

While Augustinian theodicy fears that humankind will deny their culpability and impugn the just anger of the Creator, Julian fears that her fellow Christians will be overwhelmed by their guilt for sin and their dread of a wrathful God. She writes to comfort those who are, like herself, vexed by a sense of personal sinfulness that conflicts with their belief in God's all-encompassing love. Julian responds to the problem of evil with the consolation that "synne is behouely, but alle shalle be wele, and alle shalle be wele, and alle maner of thynge shalle be wele" (13.27.405); ["sin is necessary, but all will be well, and all will be well, and every kind of thing will be well" (225)]. Instead of the Augustinian emphasis on causes and consequences, her writing reflects a concentration on purpose and ends. Given the fact of sin, she explores its function in the divine plan and God's disposition toward sinners, both now and at the end of time. In contrast to the etiological preoccupation of Augustinian theodicy, Julian's solution to the problem of evil is teleological.

As I shall demonstrate in this chapter and the two that follow, Julian's theodicy counteracts the Augustinian paradigm at each crucial point. Rather than assert that individuals suffer as punishment for sin, she argues in Revelation Thirteen that the pain caused by sin serves a pedagogical purpose. Julian provides the theological justification for her teleological theodicy in the additions she makes in Revelation Fourteen of the long text. In chapters 44 through 52 she rejects the related claims, central to the Augustinian reading of Genesis 3, that original sin was deliberate and that God is vindictive. In chapters 53 through 62 she amplifies her notion of the godly will, first mentioned in chapter 37 of Revelation Thirteen, into an anthropology that challenges the notion of the depraved will crucial to the doctrine of original sin. Despite their diversity, Revelations Thirteen and Fourteen both develop Julian's unique solution to the problem of evil. Her originality, as I will show, results from her ability to incorporate concepts from other areas of theological discourse into her theodicy and, without violating orthodoxy, to present an alternative to the juridical ideology of sin.

I

The teleological focus of Julian's theodicy becomes apparent in her explication of the aural showing of Revelation Thirteen. In response to her inquiry about why God has allowed sin, she is told that "synne is behouely, but alle shalle be wele, and alle shalle be wele, and alle maner of thynge shalle be wele" (13.27.405). Instead of looking back to the causes of evil, as Augustinian theodicy does, Julian looks forward to its ultimate consequences. Regarding sin from an eschatological perspective, she consoles rather than condemns her fellow creatures by distinguishing between an evident and a secret meaning of the phrase "alle shalle be wele." The evident meaning, revealed by the Holy Spirit and holy church, is the possibility of redemption by Christ. As Julian puts it, "That one party is oure saviour and oure saluacyon. Thys blessyd parte is opyn, clere, feyer and lyght and plentuouse, for alle mankynde that is of good wylle and that shalle be is comprehendyd in this part" (13.30.414); ["One portion is our saviour and our salvation. This blessed portion is open, clear, fair and bright and plentiful, for all men who are of good will are comprehended in this portion" (228)]. In expounding her solution to the problem of evil, Julian concentrates on this manifest promise of salvation and provides a theodicy for all who will be saved. However, she complements her theodicy for the predestined with her discreet speculation about the second meaning of "alle shalle be wele" in the middle chapters of Revelation Thirteen. Although this solution to the problem of evil will remain secret until the end of time, Julian suggests that it might entail universal salvation. As I will discuss at the end of this chapter, she thus provides the basis for a theodicy addressed even to those who are not predestined.

Julian begins her explication of the aural showing by re-envisioning

Christ's passion. "In þis nakyd worde: Synne, oure lorde brouȝte to my mynde generally alle that is nott good, and the shamfull despyte and the vttermost trybulation that [Jesus] bare for vs in thys lyfe, and hys dyeng and alle hys paynes, and passion of alle hys creatures gostly and bodely" (13.27.405); ["In this naked word 'sin', our Lord brought generally to my mind all which is not good, and the shameful contempt and the direst tribulation which [Jesus] endured for us in this life, and his death and all his pains, and the passions, spiritual and bodily, of all his creatures" (225)]. Julian's initial allusion to the passion of Christ not only links Revelation Thirteen to her preceding visions of the suffering Savior but also indicates the theological justification for her theodicy. As she implies throughout Revelation Thirteen and explains in chapter 51 of Revelation Fourteen, Christ's act of atonement provides the means by which "alle shalle be wele" for those who will be saved. In chapters 27 and 28 Julian assures her audience that the suffering of Christ in the historical past remains a present comfort and a promise of future recompense to the elect. And in chapter 29 she grounds her solution to the problem of evil in the theology of redemption. Just as Christ atoned for Adam's sin, so the Lord "shalle make wele alle that is lesse" (14.29.413) ["shall set right everything which is less" (228)].[10] Departing from Augustinian theodicy, Julian does not concentrate on Adam's transgression as the cause of evil, but rather on Christ's reparation as the consequence. In chapter 51 of Revelation Fourteen, she develops a typological interpretation of Genesis 3 based on the topos of original sin as a *felix culpa*. However, in Revelation Thirteen, she applies the notion of the fortunate fall to the life of the individual Christian.

Julian's assertion that "synne is behouely" ["sin is necessary"] demonstrates her radical understanding of the Christian commonplace of the *felix culpa* and transforms this topos into a logically and psychologically satisfying theodicy for the elect. The *Middle English Dictionary* defines *behouely* not only as "requisite, necessary," but also as "useful, profitable, beneficial, good."[11] Julian evokes both of these definitions in Revelation Thirteen. She argues that sin is necessary because it serves a beneficial function: sin is a means of achieving self-knowledge and knowledge of God. Though Julian does not deny that sin causes suffering, she regards the pain as pedagogical. Through the experience of sin and suffering, the *viator* comes to know herself in relationship to God. "And thys payne is somthyng, as to my syȝte, for a tyme, for it purgyth and makyth vs to know oure selfe and aske mercy" (13.27.406–

7); ["And it seems to me that this pain is something for a time, for it purges and makes us know ourselves and ask for mercy" (225)]. In those who are to be saved, the suffering caused by sin incites the process of justification. "Synne is the sharpest scorge þat ony chosyn soule may be smyttyn with, whych scorge alle to betyth man or woman, and alle to brekyth hym, and purgyth hym in hys owne syght" (13.39.449); ["Sin is the sharpest scourge with which any chosen soul can be struck, which scourge belabours man or woman, and breaks a man, and purges him in his own sight" (244)]. Julian's choice of the word *scourge* points to a paradox undergirding her theodicy: for the predestined, sin initiates the purgation, the first stage of the progression to perfection.[12] Through the suffering caused by sin, those who will be saved attain consciousness of their own unworthiness and of God's generosity. Julian summarizes this premise of her theodicy near the end of Revelation Fourteen: "for it nedyth vs to falle, and it nedyth vs to see it; for yf we felle nott, we shulde nott knowe how febyll and how wrechyd we be of oure selfe, nor also we shulde not so fulsomly know þe mervelous loue of oure maker" (14.61.603); ["for we need to fall, and we need to see it; for if we did not fall, we should not know how feeble and how wretched we are in ourselves, nor, too, should we know so completely the wonderful love of our Creator" (300)]. Julian's theodicy involves a moral or tropological interpretation of the *felix culpa*; she considers personal sin in those who will be saved as a fortunate fault with beneficial consequences far exceeding the initial culpability.

Julian's theory that "synne is behouely" depends, of course, on her conviction that "alle shalle be wele." Referring to the assurance about the Trinity's providential plan for creation that she gained in the first and particularly the third revelations, Julian explains the interaction between divine righteousness and mercy that insures spiritual well-being despite the fact of sin.

> Ryghtfulhed is that thyng þat is so good þat may nott be better than it is, for god hym selfe is very ryghtfulhed, and all hys werkes be done ryghtfully, as they be ordeyned fro withouȝt begynnyng by hys hygh myght, hys hygh wysdom, hys hygh goodnesse. And ryght as he hath ordeyne(d) it to the best, ryght so he werkyth contynually, and ledyth it to the same ende. . . .
>
> And marcy is a werkyng þat comyth of the goodnes of god, and it shalle last wurkynge as long as synne is sufferyd to pursew ryghtfulle soules. . . . By hys sufferannce we falle, and in hys blessyd loue with his

myght and hys wysdom we are kept, and by mercy and grace we be reysyd to manyfolde more joy. And thus in ryghtfulnes and in mercy he wyll be know and lovyd, now and withouȝt ende. (13.35.434–35)

[Righteousness is that which is so good that it cannot be better than it is, for God himself is true righteousness, and all his works are righteously performed, as they are ordained from eternity by his exalted power, his exalted wisdom, his exalted goodness. And what he has ordained for the best he constantly brings to pass in the same way, and directs to the same end. . . .

And mercy is an operation which comes from the goodness of God, and it will go on operating so long as sin is permitted to harass righteous souls. . . . By his toleration we fall, and in his blessed love, with his power and his wisdom, we are protected, and by mercy and grace we are raised to much more joy. And so in righteousness and in mercy he wishes to be known and loved, now and forever. (237–38)]

Julian's pairing of righteousness and mercy here repeats the joining of the two terms in Revelation Three but reverses the context. In the third showing she focuses on the divine foresight that renders evil part of a plan for good. In the thirteenth showing she concentrates on the pedagogical process by which God accomplishes this plan. She epitomizes the stages in this process with the terms *falling*, *keeping*, and *raising*, repeated throughout the second part of this showing.

As she develops her teleological theodicy in chapters 36 through 40, Julian reiterates these terms to articulate orthodox teachings about how Christians participate in Christ's act of atonement through the sacrament of penance. Using the example of sinners who were saved, such as David, Paul, Mary Magdalen, and particularly the Yorkshire saint John of Beverley,[13] Julian insists in chapter 38 that the grace received by penitents surpasses the gifts they would have obtained if they had not sinned. Referring to an event in John's life thus far unidentified by scholars, she writes:

And nevyrthelesse god sufferyd hym to *falle*, hym mercifully *kepyng* that he perysschyd nott ne lost no tyme; and afterward god *reysed* hym to manyfolde more grace, and by the contrycion and the mekenesse that he had in hys lyuyng, god hath gevyn hym in hevyn manyfolde joyes, over passyng that he shuld haue had yf he had nott synnyd or fallen. (13.38.448; italics mine)

[And nevertheless God allowed him to *fall*, mercifully *protecting* him so that he did not perish or lose any time; and afterwards God *raised* him to many times more grace, and for the contrition and the meekness that he had as he lived, God has given him in heaven manifold joys, exceeding what he would have had if he had not sinned or fallen. (243; italics mine)]

In chapter 39 Julian describes the sacramental procedures of contrition, confession, and satisfaction by which penitents can recapitulate John of Beverley's conversion. Repeating the litany of *keeping* and *raising* from the previous chapter, Julian also identifies this penitential process with her own request for three wounds prior to her visionary experience. "By contryscion we be made clene, by compassion we be made redy, and by tru longyng to god we be made wurthy. Theyse be thre menys, as I vnderstode, wher by that alle soules com to hevyn, that is to sey that haue ben synners in erth and shalle be savyd" (13.39.451–52); ["By contrition we are made clean, by compassion we are made ready, and by true longing for God we are made worthy. These are three means, as I understand, through which all souls come to heaven, those, that is to say, who have been sinners on earth and will be saved" (245)]. Because sin teaches humans to understand their impotence and God's mercy, it is, according to Julian, "behouely," both necessary and beneficial to the divine plan for salvation.

Since they are consoled by their Savior and assured of salvation, sin is indeed a fortunate fault for the elect. As Julian concludes in chapter 59 of Revelation Fourteen:

And all this blysse we haue by mercy and grace, whych manner blysse we myght nevyr haue had and knowen, but yf that properte of goodnesse whych is in god had ben contraryed, wher by we haue this blysse. For wyckydnesse hath ben sufferyd to ryse contrary to þat goodnesse; and the goodnesse of mercy and grace contraryed agaynst that wyckydnesse, and turnyd all to goodnesse and wurshyppe to all that shall be savyd. (14.59.589)

[And we have all this bliss by mercy and grace, and this kind of bliss we never could have had and known, unless that property of goodness which is in God had been opposed, through which we have this bliss. For wickedness has been suffered to rise in opposition to that goodness; and the goodness of mercy and grace opposed that wickedness, and turned everything to goodness and honour for all who will be saved. (295)]

Just as Christ's atonement far exceeds Adam's loss, so too, in the lives of the elect, the beneficial effects of sin and suffering outweigh their adverse consequences.

II

Despite the fact that Julian's interpretation of the aural showing of Revelation Thirteen implicitly challenges orthodox Augustinian theodicy, she subscribes to a thoroughly Augustinian understanding of human peccability and predestination. She regards justification of sinners as a gratuitous gift of God. "Owre lorde god shewde that a deed shalle be done and hym selfe shalle do it, and it shall be wurschypfulle and mervelous and plenteuous, and by (me)[14] it shall be done, and hym selfe shalle do it. . . . and I shalle do ryght nought but synne; and my synne shall nott lett his goodnes workyng" (13.36.436); ["Our Lord God revealed that a deed will be done, and he himself will do it, and it will be honourable and wonderful and plentiful, and it will be done with respect to me, and he himself will do it. . . . and I shall do nothing at all but sin; and my sin will not impede the operation of his goodness" (238)]. Despite their sinfulness, the elect are insured salvation. "For as it was afore shewde to me that I shuld synne, ryght so was the comfort shewyde: suernesse of kepyng for alle myn evyn cristen" (13.37.442–43); ["For just as it was first revealed to me that I should sin, so was consolation revealed—assurance of protection for all my fellow Christians" (241)]. Julian thus repudiates the Pelagian belief that salvation is a reward for good works and the more prevalent semi-Pelagian notion that her own effort to do her best initiates God's gift of justifying grace.

Although it is very unlikely that Julian was directly familiar with contemporary scholastic theology, her views on human peccability and predestination in some respects resemble the teachings of theologians such as Thomas Bradwardine and Gregory of Rimini. While most medieval theology is Augustinian in the sense that it "can be seen as a series of 'Augustinian syntheses,' in each of which one or another aspect of the world view associated with the name of Augustine had been dominant,"[15] these fourteenth-century theologians revived Augustine's late, anti-Pelagian texts. They emphasized human sinfulness and the gratuity of election in their debate with the so-called Pelagians about the powers of the divine and human will. Arguing against thinkers like Ockham and Holcot, who endorsed human freedom by espousing the semi-Pelagian idea that efforts to do well elicit God's grace, Bradwardine and Rimini insisted that salvation is a gift of God, not a reward for human merits.

This reaffirmation of God's role in salvation, with its emphasis on grace (*sola gratia*), predestination before foreseen merits (*praedestinatio ante praevisa merita*) based on God's decree rather than God's foreknowledge, double predestination (that the final condition of the damned represents a conscious decision on God's part just as much as the beatitude of the elect), and the perseverance of the saints, went hand in hand with a stronger view of divine omnipotence that sometimes bordered on divine omnivolence.[16]

Julian of Norwich agrees with all but the third of these premises; as I will demonstrate at the end of this chapter in my discussion of the second secret of Revelation Thirteen, she does not accept the idea of double predestination, a concept never endorsed by the medieval church.

Remarkably, though, Julian's affirmation of Augustinian predestination counteracts the harshness of Augustinian theodicy. Throughout the Middle Ages, Augustine's anti-Pelagian arguments were usually invoked to depreciate human worth. As William Courtenay observes, "the fourteenth-century crisis over Pelagianism was only one episode in a recurring struggle between an optimistic assessment of human nature ... and the traditional Augustinian emphasis on human limitations and, correspondingly, divine activity through grace."[17] Julian, however, articulates the usually dismaying tenets of human culpability and gratuitous election in a theodicy designed to console rather than condemn her "evyn cristen" ["fellow Christians"]. She transforms the typical tenor of these doctrines by integrating the conviction of human sinfulness fundamental to theories of predestination into an optimistic anthropology derived from mystical theology.

Although Julian defers its development until the last ten chapters of Revelation Fourteen, she presents the first clue to this anthropology in her reference to the "godly wylle" of the elect in Revelation Thirteen. "For in every soule that shalle be savyd is a godly wylle that nevyr assentyth to synne, nor nevyr shalle" (13.37.443); ["For in every soul which will be saved there is a godly will which never assents to sin and never will" (241–42)]. This godly will, the nexus between Julian's theodicy and her anthropology, contrasts with the depraved will central to Augustinian theodicy. As Augustine moves from the definition of evil to a discussion of its causes, he displaces the vocabulary of *deprivatio* with that of *depravatio*. "And I asked what wickedness was, and I found that it was no substance, but a perversion of the will bent aside from thee,

O God, the supreme substance, toward these lower things, casting away its inmost treasure and becoming bloated with external good."[18] This conception of human depravity is the cornerstone of Augustine's juridical theodicy and the medieval theology of sin: "An evil will, therefore, is the cause of all evils."[19]

With her conception of the godly will, Julian attempts to reconcile the fact of sin with her faith in predestination. Her insistence on the pervasiveness of human guilt does indeed seem to contradict her confidence in the ultimate salvation of the elect. She resolves this apparent discrepancy by distinguishing between two aspects of the soul, the substance or higher part and the sensuality or lower part. "Ryght as there is a bestely wylle in the lower party that may wylle no good, ryght so there is a godly wyll in the hygher party, whych wylle is so good that it may nevyr wylle evylle, but evyr good" (13.37.443); ["Just as there is an animal will in the lower part which cannot will any good, so there is a godly will in the higher part, which will is so good that it cannot ever will any evil, but always good" (242)]. Even though those predestined to glory may not refrain from sin, the godly will keeps them from the state of unrepented mortal sin that would exclude them from heaven. Interpreting her parable of the lord and servant in chapter 51, Julian concludes: "We may nott in this lyfe kepe vs fro synne alle holy, in full clenesse as we shall be in hevyn. But we may wele by grace kepe vs fro the synnes whych wolde lede vs to endlesse payne, as holy chyrch techyth vs, and eschewe venyall resonably vppe oure myght" (14.52.551); ["We cannot in this life keep ourselves completely from sin, in the perfect purity that we shall have in heaven. But we can well by grace keep ourselves from the sins which would lead us to endless torment, as Holy Church teaches us, and eschew venial sin, reasonably, to the extent of our power" (281)]. Julian's arguments about the pedagogical benefits of sin throughout Revelation Thirteen thus depend on her conviction that those chosen for salvation are incapable of ultimate defection and damnation.

Several scholars have claimed that Julian of Norwich derives her notion of the godly will from the twelfth-century Cistercian William of St. Thierry. John P. H. Clark identifies *De natura et dignitate amoris* (Concerning the nature and dignity of love, 1121–1124), as the source, while Colledge and Walsh cite his *Epistola ad fratres de Monte Dei* (Letter to the brethren of Mont Dieu or *Golden Epistle*, 1144–1145).[20] Given the popularity of these works during the late Middle Ages and their mistaken attribution to Bernard of Clairvaux, these claims are certainly plausible. Walter Hilton was familiar with *The Golden Epistle*, and Richard Rolle may have known it either directly or indirectly.[21] A brief examination of the passages cited as Julian's sources, however, reveals that there are important differences between her ideas and William's.

Clark attributes the concept of the godly will to William's discussion of those "born of God" in *De natura et dignitate amoris*. Interpreting 1 John 3:9, William writes: "Note the force of the words, *He does not commit sin*, it says, because he who is born of God endures more than acts: and *he is not able to sin*, namely persevere in sin, who serves with his mind the law of God, even though as he hastens to subject his flesh, through which he incurs temptation and sin, he seems to serve the law of sin."[22] William's statement resembles Julian's concept of the godly will to the extent that both claim, paradoxically, that individuals can sin and not sin simultaneously. Both acknowledge that humans remain susceptible to temptation owing to their corporeal natures, the "flesh" for William and the "sensuality" for Julian. William asserts that such sin, because involuntary, does not destroy charity. His statement does not, however, foreshadow Julian's idea, developed in Revelation Fourteen, of an ontological connection between the will of the elect and the divine will.

Colledge and Walsh cite the following passage from William of St. Thierry's *Golden Epistle*:

> For love (*amor*) is a great will towards God, another love (*dilectio*) is a clinging to him or uniting to him, and a third love (*charitas*) is delight in him. Yet the unity of the spirit with God in a man who lifts up his heart towards God is the perfection of his will, when he not only wills God's will, he is not only drawn to God, but in that drawing he is so made perfect that he can will nothing but what God wills. For to will what God wills, this is to be like God; not to be able to will except what God wills, this is to be what God is, for whom willing and being are one and the same.[23]

This source seems more plausible than the one suggested by Clark because William, like Julian, identifies the will as the site of union with God. However, he is describing perfection; she, election. According to William's model of spiritual progress, this unity of spirit marks the final stage achieved only by the contemplative. Julian also speaks of such a contemplative union in her discussion of prayer in chapters 42 through 44, but she distinguishes this condition from the natural union enacted in the godly will. "Ful glad and mery is oure lord of oure prayer; and he lokyth ther after, and he wyll haue it, for with his grace it makyth vs lyke to hym selfe in condescion as we be in kynde, and so is his blessyd wylle" (14.41.463–64); ["Our Lord is most glad and joyful because of our prayer; and he expects it, and he wants to have it, for with his grace it makes us like to himself in condition as we are in nature, and such is his blessed will" (249)]. As Julian will explain in Revelation Fourteen, it is this resemblance "in kynde" ["in nature"] that makes possible the resemblance "in condescion" ["in condition"]; she focuses on this initial ontological union, while William traces the steps to the contemplative reunion.

Insofar as Julian derives her anthropology from the same model as does William, their ideas are analogous.[24] Too many differences in details and emphases exist between their discussions, however, to permit us to infer that the anchorite was strongly influenced by the monk. Unlike William, who addresses his letter to those who would be perfect, the Carthusians of Mont-Dieu, Julian is writing to an audience of those who hope to be saved, her fellow Christians. She proposes the godly will as the mechanism by which they persevere in grace, for it originates in God's eternal predestination of the elect to glory. As my analysis of Julian's anthropology in chapter 5 will demonstrate, a better analogue for the godly will can be found in the work of William of St. Thierry's mentor and friend, Bernard of Clairvaux, who moves the image of God from the *mens* or mind, where Augustine locates it, to the will. In discussing her concept of Jesus as Mother, I will propose that Julian's idea of the godly will is her original elaboration of the Bernardine interpretation of the *imago Dei*.

The optimistic anthropology implied by Julian's notion of the godly will in Revelation Thirteen is reinforced by a rhetorical stance that is reassuring rather than recriminating. She expresses neither anxiety nor arrogance about herself or her readers as she presents her theodicy for the predestined. Rather, she writes with humble confidence about those who will be saved to an audience whom she addresses as "myn evyn cristen" ["my fellow Christians"]. These two groups often appear to be one and the same. Julian certainly implies such an alignment when she writes, "What may make me more to loue myn evyn cristen than to see in god that he louyth alle that shalle be savyd, as it were alle one soule?" (13.37.443); ["What can make me love my fellow Christians more than to see in God that he loves all who will be saved, all of them as it were one soul?" (241)]. And she closely identifies herself with her audience through her use of the first-person plural pronoun and her insistence that she represents humankind. "And thys is the vnderstondyng of this worde, that it shalle be done by me, that is, the generalle man, that is to sey alle that shalle be safe" (13.36.438); ["And this is the meaning of this saying, that it will be done with respect to me, that is, men in general, that is to say all who will be saved" (239)]. Despite the uniqueness of her visionary experience, Julian regards herself simply as an intermediary between her fellow Christians and God. "For yf I looke syngulery to my selfe I am ryʒt nought; but in generall I am, I hope, in onehede of cheryte with alle my evyn cristen. For in thys oned stondyth the lyfe of alle mankynd that shalle be savyd" (1.9.322); ["If I pay special attention to myself, I am nothing at all; but in general I am, I hope, in the unity of love with all my fellow Christians. For it is in this unity that the life of all men consists who will be saved" (191)]. Although she expresses confidence about her own election, she does not do so in order to set herself apart from others. Rather, Julian regards herself as only one among the many who shall be saved.

III

While the theodicy that Julian presents for the elect in Revelation Thirteen rests on her uniquely optimistic attitude toward predestination, she shows even greater originality in her speculation about the fate of those who are not predestined. In explaining the secret meaning of the thirteenth showing, Julian cautiously refers to a deed that the Trinity will perform at the end of time to make all things well. The context makes it clear that she is alluding to the promise of universal salvation. Julian is understandably hesitant to discuss this second interpretation of the phrase "alle shalle be wele," for it contradicts the church's teaching about the eternal damnation of sinners. As she acknowledges:

> And one poynt of oure feyth is that many creatures shall be dampnyd, as angelis that felle ouʒt of hevyn for pride, whych be now fendys, and meny in erth that dyeth out of the feyth of holy chyrch, that is to sey tho

79

that be hethyn, and also many that hath receyvyd cristondom and lyvyth vncristen lyfe and so dyeth ouȝte of cheryte. All theyse shalle be dampnyd to helle withouȝt (e)nde, as holy chyrch techyth me to beleue. (13.32.425)

[And one article of our faith is that many creatures will be damned, such as the angels who fell out of heaven because of pride, who now are devils, and many men upon earth who die out of the faith of Holy Church, that is to say those who are pagans and many who have received baptism and who live unchristian lives and so die out of God's love. All these will be eternally condemned to hell, as Holy Church teaches me to believe. (233)]

However, as Julian boldly points out, such orthodoxy denies the visionary authority of Revelation Thirteen, for if many are eternally damned, she continues, "me thought it was vnpossible that alle maner of thyng shuld be wele" (13.32.425); ["it seemed to me that it was impossible that every kind of thing should be well" (233)]. She implies the universality of salvation on the authority of the divine response: "That þat is vnpossible to the is nott vnpossible to me. I shalle saue my worde in alle thyng, and I shalle make althyng wele" (13.32.426); ["What is impossible to you is not impossible to me. I shall preserve my word in everything, and I shall make everything well" (233)].

Julian is chary about specifying the nature of God's act to save humankind: "There is a deed the whych the blessydfulle trynyte shalle do in the last day, as to my syght, and what the deed shall be and how it shall be done, it is vnknowen of alle creaturys whych are beneth Crist, and shall be tylle whan it shalle be done" (13.32.423–24); ["There is a deed which the blessed Trinity will perform on the last day, as I see it, and what the deed will be and how it will be performed is unknown to every creature who is inferior to Christ, and it will be until the deed is done" (232)]. When her request for a vision of hell and purgatory is not granted, Julian carefully avoids any repudiation of the church's teachings on these matters, conceding that the damned have been blotted out from the Book of Life. Nonetheless, the fact that she entertains the possibility of universal salvation contradicts the position of contemporary theologians on this issue.

Julian's guarded proposal of universal salvation has scriptural warrant in 1 Tim. 2:4 with the assertion that God "will have all men to be saved and to come to the knowledge of the truth." This text had proved a "perpetual crux of interpretation" for medieval analyses of predestination.[25] In fourteenth-century England, as I have already indicated, the uneasy compromise in Augustine's theology between individual culpability and predestination comes under scrutiny in the debate between the Ockhamists and the Augustinians. Despite their differences of opinion, however, both sides constrain the claim for universal salvation implicit in 1 Tim. 2:4.

The Ockhamists, wanting to preserve human freedom, interpret 1 Tim. 2:4 in terms of John of Damascene's distinction between God's antecedent and consequent wills. Ockham, for example, argues that God predestines some for glory because he foresees that they will cooperate with grace. He contends that God gives all people the means to salvation but leaves it to them to take advantage of these means. If an individual freely pursues salvation, God cooperates to insure its achievement. Those who neglect the opportunity by failing to act meritoriously bring about their own eternal damnation. For Ockham, then, God's decision to elect certain persons rather than others depends on human freedom of choice; damnation results not from God's reprobation of sinners, but from their own refusal to use their abilities to gain salvation.[26]

The fourteenth-century Augustinians, in contrast, repeat Augustine's own interpretation of 1 Tim. 2:4, limiting the referent of *all men* to the predestined.[27] Claiming conformity to the bishop of Hippo's authentic teachings, they insist that election is due to grace, not human merit. Gregory of Rimini, for example, asserts that meritorious or sinful acts are not the causes of predestination or reprobation but the results. God wills the salvation of some and the damnation of others without regard to their foreseen response to grace; both decisions are inscrutable. Furthermore, in arguing for double predestination, either to election or reprobation, Gregory makes explicit a tacit premise of Augustine's thought; in contending that grace is given to the elect and withheld from the damned without regard to their merits, the bishop of Hippo implies God's ultimate responsibility for human destinies.[28] Although the medieval church never endorsed the idea of double predestination, arguing that God allowed but did not actively will the damnation of sinners, Gregory disassociated himself from the traditional modification of Augustine's late anti-Pelagianism by "placing the onus of reprobation squarely upon God's free refusal to bestow His mercy."[29]

Despite the radical differences between their doctrines of predestination and their interpretations of 1 Tim. 2:4, neither the Ockhamists nor the Augustinians considered the possibility of universal salvation. Like Augustine himself, each group believed that the number of the elect was already established and that it was far less than the number of the damned.[30] Julian's speculations about the second meaning of "alle shalle be wele" are thus in bold contrast to the scholastic theology of her day. By alluding to God's prerogative to save all people, she interrogates the *aporia* that undermines orthodox medieval theodicy. Whether election is attributed to foreseen human merit, as the Ockhamists claimed, or solely to the grace of God, as the Augustinians asserted, the doctrine of predestination implied that for those who are not saved all shall not be well. Although Augustine's solution to the problem of evil argues that Adam's sin was fortunate for the predestined, John Hick contends that "so far as the rest of fallen humanity are concerned, no justification has been offered, but on the contrary, the problem has been exacerbated by the appalling doctrine that God creates persons who he knows will merit damnation and who He is content should be damned."[31] Julian's conjecture about the great deed at the end of time by which God will fulfill his promise is thus the necessary corollary to her theodicy for the elect.

By focusing in Revelation Thirteen on the teleology or ends of evil instead of its etiology or origins, Julian of Norwich introduces a solution to the problem of evil that challenges the juridical paradigm of Augustinian theodicy. Rather than expounding the causes of sin, she examines its consequences. And instead of trying to place blame and justify God's punishment of sinners, she explores the manner in which "alle shalle be wele" at the end of time for all people. Stressing the gratuitousness of salvation over the justice of damnation, Julian presents predestination as a comforting rather than a terrifying prospect. Her optimism about the large number of the elect and the possibility of salvation even for those not predestined contrasts with the far more distressing opinion of contemporary theologians that the great majority of humankind are damned.

The Parable of the Lord and
Servant and the Doctrine
of Original Sin

ONE OF THE most striking features of Julian of Norwich's solution to the problem of evil is her refusal to attribute wrath to God. She insists in Revelation Thirteen that God ascribes "no maner of blame to me ne to none that shalle be safe" (13.27.407) ["no kind of blame to me or to anyone who will be saved" (225)]. And she commences Revelation Fourteen by acknowledging that her showings seem to contradict the teachings of the church in regard to God's attitude toward sinners. In rejecting the depiction of God as wrathful, Julian calls into question a central premise of orthodox medieval theodicy. Claiming that "whatever is called evil is either sin or the punishment of sin,"[1] Augustine's solution to the problem of evil concentrates on justifying God's retribution against those who transgress divine injunctions. Invoking a juridical paradigm, Augustine argues: "Sinners are ordained to punishment. This order is contrary to their nature, and is therefore penalty. But it suits their fault and is therefore just."[2] Drawing on the rhetoric of the Old Testament and the Pauline Epistles, medieval teachings about sin follow Augustine in portraying God as wrathful in his reprisals against the wicked.

The fear of such a wrathful judge pervades the medieval preoccupation with penance. Following the Fourth Lateran Council's decree in 1215 that all the faithful confess their sins at least once a year, the themes of guilt and punishment came to dominate verbal and visual pastoral instruction. A complex ecclesiastical apparatus developed based on "the conviction that God the Creditor kept an exact account of every sin and every debt."[3] Summae for confessors and manuals for penitents, designed to aid in the examination of conscience and the assessment of culpability, proliferated. To the sculptural programs of the virtues and vices developed in the high Middle Ages were added the more macabre images of the dead and dying in the late medieval period.[4] And the relief of the Last Judgment usually found on the tympanum over the west portal of the Gothic cathedral warned the faithful of the horrifying torments that those who die in sin will suffer eternally.[5] Based on a survey of similar evidence, Jean Delumeau concludes, "To thus re-create the image of God as it was proposed by theologians leads to the very heart of a history of mentalities, which reveals a link between the devaluation of a horribly sinful humanity and the rigor of the Supreme Judge."[6]

Although medieval theologians, in contrast to the uneducated laity, recognized that their characterization of God as wrathful was metaphoric, they insisted on the legal paradigm informing the orthodox Augustinian solution to the problem of evil. Augustine himself, explaining that Scripture often uses "words which even the most simple customarily use among themselves," concedes that God punishes without passion. "Because it is very difficult for a man to avenge something without experiencing anger, the authors of Scripture have decided to use the name *wrath* for God's vengeance, although God's vengeance is exercised with absolutely no such emotion."[7] Aquinas, likewise, acknowledges, "In attributing anger to God what is signified is not an emotion but a just judgment and the will to punish sin."[8] While both theologians deny that God feels anger, they nonetheless continue to regard the deity as punitive. The characterization of God as wrathful, despite its figurative status, thus betrays the juridical economy of human transgression and divine retribution informing Augustinian theodicy.

This theology of retribution troubled Julian of Norwich. She was not upset, as might be expected, by a fear of punishment, but rather by the depiction of God as wrathful. Without denying human sinfulness, Julian refuses to attribute to God the malevolence toward sinners that is characteristic of Augustinian theodicy. She admits that her showing seems to contradict the church's teachings and that this contradiction poses a dilemma for her. Referring to the two different perspectives from which humankind is judged, she writes:

> The furst dome, whych is of goddes ryghtfulnes, and that is of his owne hygh endlesse loue, and that is that feyer swete dome that was shewed in alle the feyer revelation in whych I saw hym assign(e) to vs no maner of blame. And though theyse were swete and delectable, ȝytt only in the beholdyng of this I culde nott be fulle esyd, and that was for the dome of holy chyrch, whych I had before vnderstondyn and was contynually in my syght. And therfore by this dome me thought that me

behovyth nedys to know my selfe a synner. And by the same dome I
vnderstode that synners be sometyme wurthy blame and wrath, and
theyse two culde I nott see in god. And therfore my desyer was more
than I can or may telle, for the hygher dome god shewed hym selfe in the
same tyme, and therfore (m)e behovyd nedys to take it. And the lower
dome was lernyd me before tyme in holy chyrche, and therfore I myght
nott by no weye leue the lower dome. (14.45.487–88)

[The first judgment, which is from God's justice, is from his own great
endless love, and that is that fair, sweet judgment which was shown in all
the fair revelation in which I saw him assign to us no kind of blame. And
though this was sweet and delectable, I could not be fully comforted only
by contemplating it, and that was because of the judgment of Holy
Church, which I had understood before, and which was continually in
my sight. And therefore it seemed to me that by this judgment I must
necessarily know myself a sinner. And by the same judgment I understood that sinners sometimes deserve blame and wrath, and I could
not see these two in God, and therefore my desire was more than I
can or may tell, because of the higher judgment which God himself revealed at the same time, and therefore I had of necessity to accept
it. And the lower judgment had previously been taught me in Holy
Church, and therefore I could not in any way ignore the lower judgment.
(257)]

The discrepancy between her vision and the teachings of the church
perplexed Julian. Although the resolution to her dilemma was revealed
in "a mervelous example of a lorde and of a seruannt, as I shall sey
after, and that full mystely shewed" (14.45.488) ["a wonderful example
of a lord and a servant, as I shall tell later, and that was very mysteri-
ously revealed" (257)], she confesses that it took her two decades of
reflection to achieve an understanding of its meaning.

The difficulty that Julian must have had in comprehending this example is corroborated by her silence about all but the first three chapters of Revelation Fourteen in the summary of the showings she gives
in chapter 1 of the long text; her failure to mention either the parable
of the lord and servant or the idea of Jesus as Mother suggests that
most of this revelation was composed during her second revision of the
short text.[9] Nonetheless, as I will demonstrate in this chapter and the
next, Revelation Fourteen completes the teleological theodicy that Julian commences in Revelation Thirteen. In the last ten chapters of

Revelation Fourteen, she offers an ontological confirmation of her theodicy by developing an anthropology derived from mystical theology. In chapters 45 through 52 she expresses her disagreement with Augustinian premises about the nature of sin and the character of God's response to it.

The parable of the lord and servant in chapter 51 of Revelation Fourteen is the linchpin of Julian's solution to the problem of evil. Through this parable she offers an alternative to the doctrine of original sin crucial to Augustine's juridical theodicy. Based on his reading of Genesis 3 and Romans 5, Augustine proposes a theory of original sin to account for the depravity of the will that, he believes, renders individuals inevitably wicked but nonetheless culpable. By attributing the eruption of evil in creation to the free acts of rational creatures, angelic and human, who chose to disobey divine injunctions, Augustine and his medieval successors exonerate the all-knowing, all-good, and all-powerful Creator. Because Adam and Eve deliberately transgressed, God justly punishes their descendants, who inherit both guilt and weakness as a result of the original sin.

Julian's parable of the lord and servant revises the prevailing Augustinian reading of Genesis 3 and epitomizes her opposition to retributive theodicy. Augustine's interpretation is primarily etiological; hers, teleological. He reads the narrative as a literal, historical account; she, disregarding many of the details, stresses the typological relationship of Adam to Christ. Augustine emphasizes Adam's freedom in offending God and God's subsequent condemnation of the human race to punishment; Julian emphasizes the atonement made by Christ and God's subsequent gifts of justification and perseverance to the elect. Although both allude to chapter 5 of Paul's Epistle to the Romans, they concentrate on different parts of that text. The bishop of Hippo verifies his teachings on original sin by invoking Rom. 5:12–14; the anchorite of Norwich derives her dual interpretation of the vision of the lord and servant from Rom. 5:15–21. While both regard Adam's sin as a *felix culpa*, Augustine focuses his attention on the last word of the phrase; Julian, on the first. The distinctive metaphors that Augustine and Julian choose to define sin reveal a significant difference in their thinking about evil and in the emphasis of their theodicies. Both consider sin a deviation from the original created order, but Augustine's dominant metaphors for this condition are those of political conflict, whereas Julian's are those of physical separation.

As Elaine Pagels has shown, Augustine consistently discusses the etiology of evil, both historically and psychically, in terms of rebellion.[10] His impotence to resist sin despite his desire to do so he describes as an internal war. "I neither willed with my whole will nor was I wholly unwilling. And so I was at war with myself and torn apart by myself."[11] This *psychomachia*, this war within, is the penalty for an ancestral rebellion against God. "And this strife was against my will; yet it did not show the presence of another mind, but the punishment of my own. Thus it was no more I who did it, but the sin that dwelt in me—the punishment of a sin freely committed by Adam, and I was a son of Adam."[12] Augustine thus attributes his self-estrangement, the disobedience of his own will to his conscious desires, to the original disobedience of Adam to God. Writing of the Fall in *The City of God*, he concludes, "In the punishment of [Adam's] sin the retribution for disobedience is simply disobedience itself. For man's wretchedness is nothing but his own disobedience to himself, so that because he would not do what he could, he now wills to do what he cannot."[13] The *depravatio* that causes personal, actual sin is also the inherited punishment for a primordial, ancestral sin.

Augustine asserts the justice of such an inherited punishment on the grounds that God is just in punishing the rebellion of free agents. "The important point is that through the justice of God, who is our Lord and master and whom we refused to serve as his subjects, our flesh, which had been subject to us, now gives us trouble through its noncompliance, whereas we by our defiance of God have only succeeded in becoming a nuisance to ourselves, and not to God."[14] Although Augustine derives the idea of the inherited weakness or *vitium* from Paul, he presents it in a juridical context alien to the Apostle.[15] His theory of original sin holds not only that human beings commit actual, personal sins because of this inherited propensity, but also that all individuals are equally guilty of the first sin through their seminal identity in Adam. He thus speaks of the legacy of original sin as a defect in human nature and as a moral offense, as *vitium* and as *reatus*, both of which merit punishment.

Although Augustine attempts to legitimize his concept of original guilt by the use of political metaphors of freedom, authority, and rebellion, such legalisms are suspect when applied to the descendants of the act's perpetrator.[16] Nonetheless, ignoring the illogic of these political metaphors in his theodicy, Augustine exempts God from responsibility for evil by arguing that it is just for the all-good, all-knowing, and all-powerful deity to punish the uncompelled transgression of the parents by inflicting on their progeny both moral culpability for the primordial sin and the compulsion to further sin, each eternally damnable.

Augustine's concept of original sin provides the context and contrast for Julian's parable of the lord and servant. In her retelling of Genesis 3, she refuses to attribute disobedience to Adam or wrath to God. She presents the original transgression as an inadvertent separation from God rather than a deliberate act of rebellion. And she shows God's response to be compassionate mercy instead of justified anger. In so transforming the conventional reading of Genesis 3, Julian reveals her familiarity with the notion of the *regio dissimilitudinis*, or land of un-likeness, particularly as presented by the twelfth-century Cistercians, and with the theory of salvation developed by Anselm of Canterbury in *Cur Deus homo*. Representing original sin as a fall into the self, she mitigates the malice assigned to Adam in the Augustinian interpreta-tion. And stressing the typological relationship between Adam and Christ, she nullifies any emphasis on the just wrath of God in response to such a transgression. In contrast to the traditional Augustinian ex-plication of Genesis 3, Julian's does not concentrate on the justness of God's punishment of the initial transgression but on the promise of a restoration. As in her discussion of the pedagogical effects of actual sin in Revelation Thirteen, she focuses on the teleology or purpose rather than the etiology or cause of original sin.

I

Julian admits that the example of the lord and servant was very difficult for her to comprehend. Presenting it in chapter 51, she attempts to recapitulate the process by which she came to understand its mean-ing. As she explains, this revelation was manifest in two ways: "That one perty was shewed gostly in bodely lycknesse. That other perty was shewed more gostly withoute bodely lyckness" (14.51.514); ["One part was shown spiritually, in a bodily likeness. The other part was shown more spiritually, without bodily likeness" (267)]. In addition to the two different kinds of showings combined in the example of the lord and servant, Julian identifies three levels of understanding.

> The furst is the begynnyng of techyng that I vnderstode ther in in the same tyme. The secunde is the inwarde lernyng that I haue vnderstonde there in sythen. The thyrd is alle the hole revelation fro the begynnyng

to the ende whych oure lorde god of his goodnes bryngyth oftymes frely
to the syght of my vnderstondyng. And theyse thre be so onyd, as to my
vnderstondyng, that I can nott nor may deperte them. (14.52.519–20)

[The first is the beginning of the teaching which I understood from it
at the time. The second is the inward instruction which I have understood from it since. The third is all the whole revelation from the beginning to the end, which our Lord God of his goodness freely and often
brings before the eyes of my understanding. And these three are so unified, as I understand it, that I cannot and may not separate them. (269)]

Although Julian had an immediate comprehension of one level, her
full interpretation develops over a period of time. She tries to recapitulate this growth of awareness by presenting the example recursively,
moving from the description of the bodily likeness to her immediate
response and then to the subsequent interpretation.

Julian begins with a description of the scene she envisioned. Her
focus moves from the pair to the servant and then back to the lord. She
presents the initial relationship between lord and servant as mutually
benevolent: "The servannt stondyth before his lorde, reverently redy to
do his lordes wylle. The lorde lokyth vppon his seruannt full louely and
swetly and mekely" (14.51.514); ["The servant stands before his lord, re-
spectfully, ready to do his lord's will. The lord looks on his servant very
lovingly and sweetly and mildly" (267)]. Then Julian observes the servant in the act of falling. She emphasizes the good will with which he
sets out to perform the lord's command and depicts his fall as a consequence of his eagerness to obey.

[The lord] sendyth hym in to a certeyne place to do his wyll. The servannt nott onely he goyth, but sodenly he stertyth and rynnyth in grett
hast for loue to do his lordes wylle. And anon he fallyth in a slade, and
takyth ful grett sorow; and than he gronyth and monyth and wallowyth
and wryeth, but he may nott ryse nor helpe hym selfe by no manner of
weye. (14.51.514–515)

[[The lord] sends him to a certain place to do his will. Not only does the
servant go, but he dashes off and runs at great speed, loving to do his
lord's will. And soon he falls into a dell and is greatly injured; and then
he groans and moans and tosses about and writhes, but he cannot rise or
help himself in any way. (267)]

Surprised by the cause of the fall, Julian scrutinizes the servant closely
to ensure that she perceives his motivation correctly.

I merveyled how this seruannt myght thus mekely suffer all this woo; and I behelde with avysement to wytt yf I culde perceyve in hym ony defauȝte, or yf the lorde shuld assigne in hym ony maner of blame; and verely there was none seen, for oonly hys good wyll and his grett desyer was cause of his fallyng. And he was as vnlothfull and as good inwardly as he was when he stode before his lorde, redy to do his wylle. (14.51.516)

[I was amazed that this servant could so meekly suffer all this woe; and I looked carefully to know if I could detect any fault in him, or if the lord would impute to him any kind of blame; and truly none was seen, for the only cause of his falling was his good will and his great desire. And in spirit he was as prompt and as good as he was when he stood before his lord, ready to do his will. (268)]

As a result of this fall, the servant is no longer able to see the lord nor to recognize his love. Julian identifies seven pains the servant suffers: bruising, bodily heaviness, a consequent feebleness, diminution or blinding of his reason, inability to rise, loneliness, and isolation in a desolate place.

Next Julian turns her attention to the lord. His outward expression shows his ruth and pity for the fallen servant, but his inward expression, as her subsequent understanding has revealed, is one of enjoyment. Recognizing that the servant suffers as a consequence of his good will, the lord promises to reward him "aboue that he shulde haue be yf he had nott fallen, yea, and so ferforth that his fallyng and alle his wo that he hath takyn there by shalle be turnyd in to the hye ovyr-passyng wurschyppe and endlesse blesse" (14.51.518) ["above what he would have been if he had not fallen, yes, and so much that his falling and all the woe that he received from it will be turned into high, sur-passing honour and endless bliss" (269)]. After interrupting this initial presentation of what "was shewed gostly in bodely lycknesse" ["was shown spiritually, in a bodily likeness"], Julian returns to focus on other significant details later in chapter 51. She offers more information about the lord's position and appearance (14.51.523–24) and about the servant's position, appearance, and task (14.51.527–32).

Julian indicates that she immediately interprets the scene as an enactment of the original sin, the representative of all human transgressions.

The lorde that satt solemply in rest and in peas, I vnderstonde that he is god. The seruannt that stode before hym, I vnderstode that he was shewed for Adam, that is to sey oone man was shewed that tyme and his fallyng to make there by to be vnderstonde how god beholdyth alle manne and his fallyng. For in the syghte of god alle man is oone man, and oone man is alle man. (14.51.521–22)

[I understood that the lord who sat in state in rest and peace is God. I understood that the servant who stood before him was shown for Adam, that is to say, one man was shown at that time and his fall, so as to make it understood how God regards all men and their falling. For in the sight of God all men are one man, and one man is all men. (270)]

Julian subsequently realizes, however, that the servant is also the typological second Adam, Christ. "In the servant is comprehendyd the seconde person of þe trynyte, and in the seruannt is comprehendyd Adam, that is to sey all men" (14.51.532); ["In the servant is comprehended the second person of the Trinity, and in the servant is comprehended Adam, that is to say all men" (274)]. Any analysis of Julian's example of the lord and servant must account for all the details of the scene from this double perspective, as appropriate both to Adam and to Christ. Four issues are particularly significant: the servant's good will in responding to the lord's command, the suffering that results from the servant's fall, the lord's refusal to blame the servant for the fall, and the greater reward the servant receives as a result of his suffering.

As Julian explains, she immediately identifies the lord as God and the servant as Adam, the representative of sinful humanity. Although she acknowledges that Adam and humankind suffer as a consequence of his fall, she insists that his fall was not the result of rebellion or disobedience.

This man was hurte in his myghte and made fulle febyll, and he was stonyd in his vnderstandyng, for he was turnyd fro the beholdyng of his lorde, but his wylle was kepte in gods syght. For his wylle I saw oure lorde commende and aproue, but hym selfe was lettyd and blyndyd of the knowyng of this wyll. And this is to hym grett sorow and grevous dysses, for neyther he seeth clerly his lovyng lorde whych is to hym full meke and mylde, nor he seeth truly what hym selfe is in the syght of his louyng lord. (14.51.522)

[This man was injured in his powers and made most feeble, and in his understanding he was amazed, because he was diverted from looking on his lord, but his will was preserved in God's sight. I saw the lord commend and approve him for his will, but he himself was blinded and hindered from knowing this will. And this is a great sorrow and a cruel suffering to him, for he neither sees clearly his loving lord, who is so meek and mild to him, nor does he truly see what he himself is in the sight of his loving lord. (270–71)]

The originality of Julian's insistence on Adam's good will becomes apparent when her account of the Fall is compared to one that closely resembles it.

In *Cur Deus homo* Anselm of Canterbury also refers to original sin as a metaphoric fall into a pit. Although, as I will demonstrate later in this chapter, Julian invokes Anselm's soteriology in her interpretation of the servant as Christ, her conception of Adam's fall differs from his Augustinian view of original sin. Anselm attributes this fall to the servant's malicious disobedience and insists that he deserves to be punished. The dialogue between Anselm and the interlocutor Boso articulates the major premises of the doctrine of original sin at the heart of retributive theodicy.

> A[nselm]. . . . Suppose that a man enjoins some task on his servant, and charges him not to throw himself into a pit which he [the master] points out to him, out of which he [the servant] cannot possibly escape. But that servant despises the command and the warning of his master and, of his own free will, throws himself into the pit that has been shown him, so that he is unable to carry out his assigned task. Do you think that this inability is worth anything as an excuse for not performing the assigned task?
>
> B[oso]. Not at all. On the contrary, it increases his guilt, since he brought this inability on himself. For he sinned doubly, because he did not do what he was ordered to do, while what he was commanded not to do he did.[17]

Both speakers in the dialogue insist that the servant's fall is the result of his deliberate disobedience of a divine injunction. As a result, the servant is incapable of performing the tasks assigned him, but he is nonetheless morally culpable for his incapacity because his initial offense was voluntary. Anselm thus endorses the Augustinian position that the legacy of original sin is both weakness and guilt. The former does not excuse the latter since Adam freely chose to transgress and all of Adam's descendants are seminally present in him.

The differences between Anselm's example and Julian's strikingly demonstrate her disagreement with the conventional interpretation of Genesis 3. Julian, remarkably, denies that Adam's fall into the pit is deliberate or voluntary. In fact, it results from his efforts to perform the lord's command, not disobey it. Julian provides a clue about what this command entails for Adam when she resumes the description of the bodily likeness later in chapter 51. She sees the servant standing to the left of the lord, dressed as a laborer in a ragged, white garment stained with perspiration. The lord commands the servant to go to earth to seek a treasure.

> And then I vnderstode that he shuld do the grettest labour and the hardest traveyle that is. He shuld be a gardener, deluyng and dykyng and swetyng and turnyng the erth vp and down, and seke the depnesse and water the plantes in tyme. And in this he shulde contynue his traveyle, and make swete flodys to rynne and nobylle plentuousnesse fruyte to spryng, whych he shulde bryng before the lorde, and serve hym therwith to his lykynk. And he shulde nevyr turne ageyne, tyll he had dyȝte this mett alle redy, as he knew that it lykyd to þe lorde; and than he shulde take thys mett with the dryngke, and bere it full wurschypply before the lorde. (14.51.530–31)

> [And then I understood that he was to do the greatest labour and the hardest work there is. He was to be a gardener, digging and ditching and sweating and turning the soil over and over, and to dig deep down, and to water the plants at the proper time. And he was to persevere in his work, and make sweet streams to run, and fine and plenteous fruit to grow, which he was to bring before the lord and serve him with to his liking. And he was never to come back again until he had made all this food ready as he knew was pleasing to the lord; and then he was to take this food, and drink, and carry it most reverently before the lord. (273–74)]

Julian's imagery of productive labor alludes to two events in Genesis: God's bestowal on the newly created Adam of dominion over the earth (Gen. 2:19–20) and his curse on the ground to punish the disobedient Adam (Gen. 3:17–19). Medieval iconography of Adam delving typically represents the second event.[18] Although Julian admits that the cultivation of the land requires hard manual labor, she transforms its punitive implications with her description of the earth's bounty and the lord's pleasure. Julian's celebration of Adam's labor presages the positive attitude toward the human body that she expresses in her analogy of Jesus as Mother later in Revelation Fourteen. It also indicates that she regards the Adamic narrative as a story about creation rather than transgression.

In her interpretation of Genesis 3, Julian invokes the theological commonplace of the fall into a region of unlikeness and thus evokes the anthropology of the *imago Dei* that she develops more thoroughly in chapters 53 through 63 of Revelation Fourteen. "Adam fell fro lyfe to deth, in to the slade of this wrechyd worlde, and aftyr that in to hell" (14.51.533–34); ["Adam fell from life to death, into the valley of this wretched world, and after that into hell" (274)]. The ontological separation indicated by the phrase "fro lyfe to deth" suggests the Neoplatonic implications of this concept as it was developed by Augustine and adapted by the Cistercians and other medieval theologians. Based on the assertion in Gen. 1:27 that humankind is created in the image and likeness of the Trinity, this anthropology regards separation from God as an exile into a land of unlikeness.[19] Most often medieval theologians ascribe this distance from God to either a natural or a moral breach. The natural separation from God results from the difference between Creator and creature. This ontological distance between God and humankind is further increased by a moral separation that occurs as a result of sin. Medieval theologians thus refer to both creation and transgression as a fall into a region of unlikeness.

Although his use of the metaphor is frequent and varied, Bernard of Clairvaux on several occasions refers to Adam's fall as a descent into the region of unlikeness.[20] In his *Sermons on the Song of Songs* (*Sermones super cantica canticorum*, 1135–1153), for example, Bernard associates the region of unlikeness with the exile of Adam and Eve, identifying their sin specifically as a descent from the spiritual to the material realm due to ignorance of their true natures. In sermon 35 Bernard attributes Adam's expulsion to a lack of self-understanding that led him to pride and subsequent bestiality.

> Placed in a position of honor, [Adam] was so intrigued by the dignity of his rank that he did not understand that he was but clay. . . . From then on this fairest of creatures was reduced to the level of the herd; from then on the likeness of God was changed to the likeness of a beast; from then on association with the animals took the place of fellowship with the angels. You see how careful we must be to shun this ignorance that has brought evils by the thousands on the whole human race![21]

In sermon 82 Bernard likewise argues that Eve sinned because she forgot her true spiritual resemblance to God. "Consider Eve, and how her immortal soul of immortal glory was infected by the stain of mortality through her desire for mortal things. Why did she not spurn mortal and transitory things, when she was immortal, and satisfy herself with the immortal and eternal things which were proper to her?"[22] These two examples reveal the duality of the ontological relationship between Creator and creatures. On the one hand, as in the case of Adam, human beings are dissimilar to their Creator because of their material bodies; God remains trancendent. On the other hand, as in the case of Eve, human beings are similar to their Creator because of their spiritual souls through which the image of God is immanent within them.[23] Through creation and transgression, then, humankind is distanced from God and exiled into the world of matter, the *regio dissimilitudinis*.

The Neoplatonic assumptions informing this concept of an ontological fall into the region of unlikeness are even clearer in Bernard's source, Augustine's *Confessions*. Addressing God, Augustine writes:

> When I first knew thee, thou didst lift me up, that I might see that there was something to be seen, though I was not yet fit to see it. . . . I realized that I was far away from thee in the land of unlikeness, as if I heard thy voice from on high: "I am the food of strong men; grow and you shall feed on me; nor shall you change me, like the food of your flesh into yourself, but you shall be changed into my likeness."[24]

The digestive metaphor Augustine uses to refer to the substantial union between God and humankind reveals the Neoplatonic influence on his thought; this Neoplatonism becomes more explicit in his discussion of the first chapter of Genesis in the last three books of the *Confessions*.[25] Analyzing Augustine's meditation on Gen. 1:2 in book 11 of the *Confessions*, Gilson explains how Augustine's notion of the region of unlikeness fits into his exemplarist theory of creation, for matter, lacking form, is most dissimilar to God who is absolute form.[26] Although created in the image of God, human beings are dissimilar to their Creator insofar as they consist of body as well as soul. This ontological distance is further increased by their moral offense. Associating the region of unlikeness with matter, Augustine regards both creation and transgression as causes of humankind's exile into this land alien to the spirit.

Julian's discussion of Adam's fall also seems to be informed by Christian Neoplatonism. In claiming that Adam's fall was a descent from life into death, she implies an exemplarist theory of creation, similar to though not necessarily derived from Augustine's, for, as Cousins observes, "from the time of Augustine until the Reformation and even beyond, Christian Neoplatonism was the mainstream philo-

sophical-theological tradition in the spirituality of Western Christianity."[27] Julian interprets the lord's position "syttyng on the erth, bareyn
and desert" ["sitting on the ground, barren and waste"] as a sign of this
ontological separation between Creator and creature that occurs when
the soul is embodied.

> He made mannes soule to be his owne cytte and his dwellyng place,
> whych is most pleasyng to hym of all his workes. And what tyme man
> was fallyn in to sorow and payne, he was not all semely to serve of þat
> noble offyce; and therfore oure kynde fader wolde haue dyght hym noon
> other place but to sytt vppon the erth, abydyng man kynde, which is
> medlyd with erth, tyll what tyme by his grace hys deerwurthy sonne had
> brought agayne hys cytte in to the nobyll feyernesse with his harde
> traveyle. (14.51.525–26)

> [He made man's soul to be his own city and his dwelling place, which is
> the most pleasing to him of all his works. And when man had fallen into
> sorrow and pain, he was not wholly proper to serve in that noble office,
> and therefore our kind Father did not wish to prepare any other place,
> but sat upon the ground, awaiting human nature, which is mixed with
> earth, until the time when by his grace his beloved Son had brought back
> his city into its noble place of beauty by his hard labour. (272)]

As I shall show in my discussion of Julian's anthropology in the next
chapter, she also associates this process of embodiment with Jesus'
motherhood in creation.

The ontological union involves the Son as well as the Father, for
each individual who will be saved has been predestined in Christ from
all eternity. Julian alludes to this eternal union between the elect and
Christ when she explains Adam's fall.

> When Adam felle godes sonne fell; for the ryght onyng whych was made
> in hevyn, goddys sonne myght nott be seperath from Adam, for by
> Adam I vnderstond alle man. Adam fell fro lyfe to deth, in to the slade
> of this wrechyd worlde, and aftyr that in to hell. Goddys son fell with
> Adam in to the slade of the meydens wombe, whych was the feyerest
> doughter of Adam, and that for to excuse Adam from blame in hevyn
> and in erth; and myghtely he fechyd hym out of hell. (14.51.533–34)

> [When Adam fell, God's Son fell; because of the true union which was
> made in heaven, God's Son could not be separated from Adam, for by
> Adam I understand all mankind. Adam fell from life to death, into the
> valley of this wretched world, and after that into hell. God's Son fell with

Adam, into the valley of the womb of the maiden who was the fairest daughter of Adam, and that was to excuse Adam from blame in heaven and on earth; and powerfully he brought him out of hell. (274–75)]

The predestination of humanity in the second person of the Trinity from all eternity necessitates the incarnation of Christ when Adam falls from union with God into the region of unlikeness; Jesus' motherhood in creation incites his motherhood in restoration. Julian's anthropology is thus closely connected to her soteriology. However, before we examine the influence of Anselm of Canterbury's theory of atonement on Julian's interpretation of the Adamic myth, it is important to note how Julian modified the tradition of the region of unlikeness.

In sermon 36 of *On the Song of Songs*, Bernard of Clairvaux presents the consequences of sin, both original and actual, as a fall into a region of unlikeness. A comparison of Julian's list of the pains the servant suffers with this similar account from Bernard epitomizes the difference between her attitude toward the body and his, a difference that I will explore in greater detail in my discussion in the next chapter of Julian's concept of Jesus as Mother. Bernard focuses on the dangers posed by embodiment.

> When a man thus takes stock of himself in the clear light of truth, he will discover that he lives in a region where likeness to God has been forfeited. . . . How can he escape being genuinely humbled on acquiring this true self-knowledge, on seeing the burden of sin that he carries, the oppressive weight of his mortal body, the complexities of earthly cares, the corrupting influence of sensual desires; on seeing his blindness, his worldliness, his weakness, his embroilment in repeated errors; on seeing himself exposed to a thousand dangers, trembling amid a thousand fears, confused by a thousand difficulties, defenceless before a thousand suspicions, worried by a thousand needs; one to whom vice is welcome, virtue repugnant?[28]

The seven pains the servant suffers as a result of his fall in chapter 51 of *A Book of Showings* bear some resemblance to Bernard's catalog.

> And of all this the most myschefe that I saw hym in was feylyng of comfort, for he culde nott turne his face to loke vppe on his lovyng lorde, whych was to hym full nere, in whom is full comfort; but as a man that was full febyll and vnwyse for the tyme, he entendyd to his felyng and enduryng in woo, in whych woo he sufferyd vij grett paynes. The furst was the soore brosyng that he toke in his fallyng, whych was to hym moch payne. The seconde was þe hevynesse of his body. The thyrde was

97

fybylnesse that folowyth of theyse two. The iiij was that he was blyndyd in his reson and stonyd in his mynde so ferforth that allmost he had forgeten his owne loue. The v was þat he myght nott ryse. The vj was payne most mervelous to me, and that was that he leye aloone. I lokyd alle about and behelde, and ferre ne nere ne hye ne lowe I saw to hym no helpe. The vij^th was that the place whych he ley in was alang, harde and grevous. (14.51.515–16)

[And of all this, the greatest hurt which I saw him in was lack of consolation, for he could not turn his face to look on his loving lord, who was very close to him, in whom is all consolation; but like a man who was for the time extremely feeble and foolish, he paid heed to his feelings and his continuing distress, in which distress he suffered seven great pains. The first was the severe bruising which he took in his fall, which gave him great pain. The second was the clumsiness of his body. The third was the weakness which followed these two. The fourth was that he was blinded in his reason and perplexed in his mind, so much so that he had almost forgotten his own love. The fifth was that he could not rise. The sixth was the pain most astonishing to me, and that was that he lay alone. I looked all around and searched, and far and near, high and low, I saw no help for him. The seventh was that the place in which he lay was narrow and comfortless and distressful. (267–68)]

Of the seven pains Julian identifies, the middle three have a counterpart in Bernard's catalog in sermon 36: the weight of the mortal body, weakness or feebleness, and blindness. However, while Bernard emphasizes the burdens of sensuality and earthly cares, Julian stresses the servant's isolation and loneliness. She is not as worried as Bernard about the problems posed by the body and the world; instead, she is troubled by the separation from God. Julian articulates the servant's suffering in medical and psychological rather than forensic terms; she focuses on the ontological rather than the moral consequences of Adam's fall.

In contrast to the Augustinian doctrine of original sin, which attributes malevolence to both Adam and his descendants, Julian denies that either disobeys God deliberately. Her definition of personal sin, like her version of the Genesis narrative, emphasizes the consequences of separation from God, not the revolt of the will causing such separation.

Man is channgeabyll in this lyfe, and by sympylnesse and vncunnyng fallyth in to synne. He is vnmyghty and vnwyse of hym selfe, and also his wyll is ovyr leyde in thys tyme he is in tempest and in sorow and woe.

And the cause is blynnes, for he seeth not god; for yf he saw god contynually, he shulde haue no myschevous felyng ne no maner steryng, no sorowyng that servyth to synne. (14.47.496)

[Man is changeable in this life, and falls into sin through naivete and ignorance. He is weak and foolish in himself, and also his will is over-powered in the time when he is assailed and in sorrow and woe. And the cause is blindness, because he does not see God; for if he saw God con-tinually, he would have no harmful feelings nor any kind of prompting, no sorrowing which is conducive to sin. (260)]

Julian consistently stresses weakness rather than guilt as the legacy of the ancestral transgression. Accordingly, she portrays actual sin as the result of ignorance rather than depravity.

And therfore we fayle oftymes of the syght of hym, and anon we falle in to oure selfe, and than fynde we felyng of ryght nowght but the contraryous that is in oure selfe, and that of the olde rote of oure furst synne with all that folowyth of oure owne contynuance; and in this we be traveyled and temptyd with felyng of synne and of payne in many dyverse maner, gostely and bodely, as it is knowyn to vs in this lyfe. (14.46.498–99)

[And therefore often we fail to perceive him, and presently we fall back upon ourselves, and then we find that we feel nothing at all but the op-position that is in ourselves, and that comes from the old root of our first sin, with all that follows from our own persistence; and in this we are belaboured and tempted with the feeling of sin and of pain in many dif-ferent ways, spiritually and bodily, as is known to us in this life. (261)]

For Augustine, sin causes separation from God; for Julian, sin ensues from such separation. She considers the suffering that results from sin not as a penalty inflicted by a wrathful God, but as the natural conse-quence of the sinner's violation of his or her "feyer kynde" (14.63.615) ["fair nature" (304)], the breach of the ontological union between Cre-ator and creature. And whereas Augustine emphasizes the perverse will of Adam's descendants, Julian concentrates on the godly will of the elect, "that nevyr assentyd to synne ne nevyr shall" (14.53.555) ["which never assented to sin nor ever will" (283)].

Moreover, in Julian's parable the lord regards the servant as a com-passionate healer rather than a just judge.[29] In contrast to the wrathful God of retributive theodicy, Julian's lord beholds his servant with a "doubyll chere" ["double aspect"]: outwardly of pity and ruth for the

servant's suffering, inwardly of joy at the prospect of his eventual restoration (14.51.516–17). This showing confirms Julian's earlier insistence,
despite church teaching, that God feels no wrath toward sinners. "And
then I saw that oonly payne blamyth and ponyschyth, and oure curteyse lorde comfortyth and socurryth, and evyr he is to the soule in
glad chere, lovyng and longyng to bryng vs to his blysse" (14.51.523);
["And then I saw that only pain blames and punishes, and our courteous Lord comforts and succours, and always he is kindly disposed to
the soul, loving and longing to bring us to his bliss" (271)]. Julian thus
implies that sin is its own punishment and that the conception of God
as wrathful is itself a consequence of the blindness that is sin.

Furthermore, Julian provides the theological justification for her refusal to regard God as punitive in her subsequent interpretation of the
servant as Christ, the second Adam. As she explains, the lord's outward expression of pity and ruth is directed toward Adam, who falls
inadvertently rather than deliberately; his inward expression of joy is
directed toward Christ, who rescues Adam and restores him to an even
greater reward than that originally intended for him (14.51.524–25). In
presenting this second interpretation of the example of the lord and
servant, Julian invokes the soteriology or theory of salvation first developed by Anselm of Canterbury in *Cur Deus homo*.

II

As Gillian Evans observes, "Anselm was the first thinker since Augustine to take a comprehensive fresh look at the problem of evil."[30] In
Cur Deus homo (*Why God Became Man*, 1098) Anselm resolves the contradiction between the conception of divine retribution underlying Augustinian theodicy and the idea of divine mercy informing the theory
of redemption. Boso, the interlocutor in the dialogue with Anselm,
poses the problem by claiming that unbelievers regard the incarnation
and crucifixion of Christ as affronts to God's honor and dignity. Why,
they ask, did the Father demand that his Son endure such humiliation
and suffering? Repeating the hypothetical words of such a nonbeliever,
Boso states the apparent contradiction:

> If you say that God, who, according to you, created all things by his
> commandment, could not do all this by a simple command, you contra-
> dict yourselves by making him powerless. Or if you admit that he could

have done this, but preferred to act as he did, how can you prove that he is wise, when you assert that he was willing to suffer such unseemly things without any reason? For all the things that you allege depend on his will. For the wrath of God is nothing but his will to punish.[31]

The anthropomorphization of God as wrathful had in some sense, as this hypothetical objection claims, paralyzed divine omnipotence within the constraints of divine vengeance.

Anselm solves this problem by displacing the rhetoric of divine retribution with that of cosmic rectitude. As Jaroslav Pelikan explains:

> Instead of speaking of the "wrath" of God, . . . Anselm spoke of his justice; the justice of God had been violated by the failure of man to render to God what he owed him; the justice of God also made it impossible for God to forgive this sin by mere fiat, for this would have been a violation of the very order in the universe that God had to uphold to be consistent with himself and with his justice. Any scheme of human salvation, therefore, had to be one that would render "satisfaction" to divine justice and leave the "rightness" and moral order intact.[32]

Anselm's doctrine of atonement depends on an understanding of the satisfaction rendered by Christ as a restoration of the moral order rather than an appeasement of an angry God. The fall of Adam had disrupted the moral order and appropriate restitution was necessary for humankind's violation of rectitude. No human being could make this restitution, however, since no one was without sin; only the guiltless God was capable of making amends. Therefore, as Anselm concludes, "the person who is to make this satisfaction must be both perfect God and perfect man, because none but true God can make it, and none but true man owes it."[33] The dual nature of Christ as God and man achieved through the Incarnation resolved the seeming contradiction between divine justice and divine mercy. As God, Christ restored the moral order; as man, he offered expiation for the transgressions of humankind.

Anselm contends that the God-man's act of atonement renders Adam's fall a *felix culpa*, both because of its result and because of its means. First of all, the restoration of humankind exceeds its original creation, "since the former was done to a sinner against his desert, but the latter neither to a sinner nor against his desert." Moreover, Anselm continues, the means by which this restoration is accomplished is also remarkable. "Again, what a great thing it is for God and man to meet in one person, so that, while the integrity of both natures is preserved, the same person is man and God!"[34] Interpreting Rom. 5:19, Anselm develops the typological parallels between Adam and Christ:

> For when death had entered into the human race through man's disobedience, it was fitting that life should be restored through the obedience of man. When the sin which was the cause of our condemnation had its beginning from a woman, it was fitting for the author of our justice and salvation to be born of a woman. Since the devil, when he tempted man, conquered him by the tasting of a tree, it was fitting for him to be conquered by man's bearing of suffering on a tree.[35]

As the second Adam, the God-man satisfies the demands of divine justice at the same time that he demonstrates the immensity of divine mercy.

By the fourteenth century Anselm's argument had become the definitive soteriology of the medieval church.[36] Even though Julian of Norwich may not have known *Cur Deus homo* directly, she invokes concepts similiar to Anselm's in proposing her second interpretation of the showing of the lord and servant. Over the course of time she comes to understand the characteristics of the servant as appropriate for Jesus as well as for Adam. In presenting this subsequent reading, Julian shows that every detail about the servant in the "bodely lycknesse" is also true of Christ because ontologically and morally Christ and humankind are one. Connected with humankind for all eternity through the predestination of the elect in the second person of the Trinity, as will be discussed in the next chapter, Christ falls into the maiden's womb just as Adam falls into this wretched world. Like Adam, Jesus stumbles to earth as he eagerly sets out to do the will of God the Father by taking on a human body. "His stertyng was þe godhed, and the rennyng was þe manhed; for the godhed sterte fro þe fader in to þe maydyns wombe, fallyng in to the takyng of oure kynde, and in this fallyng he toke grete soore" (14.51.539–40); ["His rushing away was the divinity, and his running was the humanity; for the divinity rushed from the Father into the maiden's womb, falling to accept our nature, and in this falling he took great hurt" (277)]. Christ, like Adam, is injured by his fall, but Julian clearly identifies these pains as the physical torments of the Passion rather than those of separation from God (14.51.540–42). Using the metaphor of the body as a garment, Julian explains that Christ takes on Adam's flesh and becomes a God-man in order to atone for the sins of humankind. "And thus hath oure good lorde Jhesu taken vppon hym all oure blame; and therfore oure fader may nor wyll no more blame assigne to vs than to hys owne derwurthy son Jhesu Cryst" (14.51.535); ["And so has our good Lord Jesus taken upon him all our blame; and therefore our Father may not, does not wish to assign more blame to us than to his own beloved Son Jesus Christ" (275)]. Julian's interpretation of the servant as Christ thus conforms to Anselm's atonement theory of salvation.

Although this redemptive relationship between Christ and Adam is the most significant dimension of Julian's example, other details of chapter 51 are also doubly appropriate. Like Adam, for example, Jesus comes to earth to be a gardener; however, his task is metaphoric rather than literal, for the ground he cultivates is the human soul. Julian alludes to the same traditional image that Langland develops in *Piers Plowman* when he places the tree of charity "'in a gardyn . . . þat god made hymselue / Amyddes mannes body; . . . / Herte highte þe herber þat it Inne groweþ'",[37] ["in a garden . . . that God made himself / Amid man's body; . . . / The garden that it grows in is called heart"]. Although Julian does not invoke the Devil's rights theory as Langland does, she may have in mind the same metaphoric apples of fallen humanity that Piers/Christ rescues from Satan when she refers to the treasure hidden in the garden of the heart as "a mete whych is louesom and plesyng to the lorde" (14.51.530) ["a food which is delicious and pleasing to the lord" (273)]. As Wolfgang Riehle indicates, this familiar metaphor of the soul as a garden was developed from biblical passages such as "the New Testament parable of the treasure hidden in the field (Matt. 13:44), or a verse from the Book of Proverbs which states that whoever searches for wisdom as for hidden treasures will find the knowledge of God (Prov. 2:4), but above all the 'hortus conclusus' of the *Song of Songs* (S. of S. 4:12)."[38]

Julian completes her exposition of the showing of the lord and servant by explaining the lord's promise to restore his servant to glory. Again, she insists that this promise applies to both the first and second Adam. Chapter 51 ends with her description of the victorious Christ seated in peace and rest at the right hand of the Father. Alluding to Revelation Nine, she identifies the crown that he wears as those he has redeemed. And chapter 52 explains what this restoration means for Adam and the elect. Thanks to Christ's sacrifice, sin, both original and personal, becomes a *felix culpa*, for those predestined will receive an even greater reward in heaven than the bliss the first parents experienced in paradise (14.52.550).[39] For Julian and her fellow Christians, however, this restoration is yet to come. Nonetheless, through her final interpretation of the servant (chapter 52), she is able to reconcile the apparent contradiction posed earlier in Revelation Fourteen between the inevitability of human sinfulness and God's promise of salvation to the elect.

Julian reveals that she and her fellow Christians, like the servant, also have a dual identity; they are both Adam and Christ.

> For þe tyme of this lyfe we haue in vs a mervelous medelur both of wele and of woo. We haue in vs oure lorde Jhesu Cryst vp resyn, and we haue in vs the wrechydnesse and the myschef of Adams fallyng. Dyeng by Cryst we be lastynly kept, and by hys gracyous touchyng we be reysed in to very trust of saluacyon. And by Adams fallyng we be so broken in oure felyng on dyverse manner by synne and by sondry paynes, in whych we be made derke and so blynde that vnnethys we can take any comforte. (14.52.546–47)

> [During our lifetime here we have in us a marvellous mixture of both well-being and woe. We have in us our risen Lord Jesus Christ, and we have in us the wretchedness and the harm of Adam's falling. Dying, we are constantly protected by Christ, and by the touching of his grace we are raised to true trust in salvation. And we are so afflicted in our feelings by Adam's falling in various ways, by sin and by different pains, and in this we are made dark and so blind that we can scarcely accept any comfort. (279)]

Returning to the theme she developed at the end of Revelation Thirteen, Julian explains how this dual identity of those who will be saved insures that personal sin is indeed a *felix culpa*, for Christ atoned not only for Adam's offense but also for the past and future transgressions of all the elect. Reiterating the metaphor of falling and rising, she reconciles the apparent contradiction—between the propensity to sin inherited from Adam and the promise of salvation merited by Christ—by discriminating between venial and mortal sin and by emphasizing the efficacy of the sacrament of penance (14.52.551).

Julian also clarifies how the distinction between two parts of the soul resolves the apparent contradiction between her showings and the church's teachings about God's wrath. At the beginning of chapter 45, she had related this distinction between the higher and lower parts of the soul to the difference between God's excusing and the church's accusing of sinners. "God demyth vs vpon oure kyndely substance, whych is evyr kepte one in hym, hole and safe, without ende; and this dome is of his ryghtfulhede. And man demyth vppon oure channgeable sensualyte, whych semyth now oone and now a nother, after that it takyth of the partyes and shew(yth) outward" (14.45.486); ["God judges us in our natural substance, which is always kept one in him, whole and safe, without end; and this judgment is out of his justice. And man judges us in our changeable sensuality, which now seems one thing and now another, as it derives from parts and presents an external appearance" (256)]. In chapter 52 Julian associates these two judgments with the "doubyll chere" ["double aspect"] of the lord. His outward expression of ruth and pity she attributes to two causes: Adam's fall and the suffering Christ endured to atone for it. She also focuses this outward expression on the lower part of the soul, capable of sin and in need of mercy and grace.

> Thus wylle oure good lorde þat we accuse oure selfe wylfully, and truly se and know (our fallyng and all þe harmes þat cum therof, seand and witand þat we may never restoren it; and therwith, if we wilfully and truly sen and knowen,) his evyrlastyng loue that he hath to vs and his plentuous mercy. And thus gracyously to se and know both to geder is þe meke accusyng that oure good lorde askyth of vs. And hym selfe wurkyth there it is, and this is the lower party of mannys lyfe. (14.52.552–53)

> [So does our good Lord want us willingly to accuse ourselves, and to see truly and know our falling, and all the harms which come from it, seeing and knowing that we can never repair it; and also we willingly and truly see and know the everlasting love which he has for us, and his plentiful mercy. And so by grace to see and know both together is the meek self-accusation which our good Lord asks from us. And he himself works where it is, and this is the lower part of man's life. (281–82)]

The lord's inward expression of love and joy, however, indicates God's exoneration of the higher part of the soul, the substance that is eternally united to its maker. Because humans can see only the outward manifestation of the lower part, or sensuality, it is appropriate for them to blame themselves for sin. But God, who beholds the sensuality united to the substance of the soul, can excuse human frailty. Bringing her argument full circle from chapter 45, Julian thus resolves the dialectic contradiction between the Augustinian ideology of guilt and her own vision by distinguishing between the limited human perspective and the comprehensive divine one.

105

Recognizing that Augustine's juridical theodicy reduces the divine nature to deceptive human proportions, Julian rejects the anthropomorphic characterization of a punitive God. Her conclusion to the parable of the lord and servant clarifies her declaration earlier in Revelation Fourteen that wrath is impossible for God because it would violate the divine nature. "I saw verely that oure lorde was nevyr wroth nor nevyr shall. . . . God is that goodnesse that may nott be wroth, for god is nott but goodnes. Our soule is onyd to hym, vnchanngeable goodnesse. And betwen god and oure soule is neyther wrath nor forgevenesse in his syght" (14.46.493); ["I saw truly that our Lord was never angry, and never will be. . . . God is that goodness which cannot be angry, for God is nothing but goodness. Our soul is united to him who is unchangeable goodness. And between God and our soul there is neither wrath nor forgiveness in his sight" (259)]. Avoiding even a metaphorical attribution of anger to God, Julian locates wrath within humans. "For I saw no wrath but on mannes perty, and that forgevyth he in vs. . . . For we by synne and wrechydnesse haue in vs a wrath and a contynuant contraryousnes to pees and to loue" (14.48.500–501); ["For I saw no wrath except on man's side, and he forgives that in us. . . . For we through sin and wretchedness have in us a wrath and a constant opposition to peace and to love" (262)]. Without denying human sinfulness, Julian of Norwich refuses to attribute to God the malevolence toward sinners that is characteristic of Augustinian theodicy. While she affirms her submission to church teachings, she nonetheless presents a solution to the problem of evil that interrogates the retributive premises of orthodox theodicy.

Reconceiving the *Imago Dei*:
The Motherhood of Jesus and
the Ideology of the Self

In Revelation Fourteen of *A Book of Showings* Julian of Norwich states a critical tenet of her theology: "And thus I saw full suerly that it is redyer to vs and more esy to come to þe knowyng of god then to know oure owne soule" (14.56.570); ["And so I saw most surely that it is quicker for us and easier to come to the knowledge of God than it is to know our own soul" (288)]. This assertion that one knows the self by knowing God situates Julian within the Western project of self-consciousness initiated by the Delphic injunction, "Know thyself." The responses of various religious and philosophical systems to this injunction indicate not only their epistemological assumptions about how humans know but also their ontological and anthropological theories about what constitutes the self. Investigators are only beginning to write the history of ideologies of selfhood, but surely the tradition represented by Julian of Norwich will constitute an important chapter.[1]

Julian's claim that knowledge of God and of the self coincide reverses the original, pre-Socratic interpretation of the Delphic oracle as a warning to humans to know that they are not gods, and it locates her *Showings* within the Christian discourse of introspective mysticism. The enabling premise of this self-reflexive mysticism originates in the account of creation at Gen. 1:26–27: "And he said: 'Let us make man to our image and likeness; . . .' And God created man to his own image; to the image of God he created him. Male and female he created them." These verses, as interpreted by Augustine in *De trinitate* (*On the Trinity*, 400–416), authorize the occidental practice of contemplative mysticism.[2] Julian's assertion that "oure soule is a made trynyte lyke to the vnmade blessyd trynyte" (14.55.568) ["our soul is a created trinity, like the uncreated blessed Trinity" (287)] indicates her familiarity with the tradition of Augustinian spirituality, although the pervasiveness of this topos throughout the Middle Ages precludes identification of her specific source. As I will demonstrate in this chapter, her understanding of the theology informing this type of mysticism allows her to interrogate the medieval ideology of sin from within the Christian tradition. Substituting a concept of the self with the potential for deification for the self depraved by sin, she justifies her critique of Augustine's theodicy on the authority of his own anthropology. This maneuver indicates Julian's astute comprehension of medieval theology as well as her awareness of the tensions within the Augustinian system.

Julian of Norwich's learning and acuity as a theologian are apparent not only in her challenge to the polarities of medieval Christianity, but also in her creativity within its constraints. Complementing the belief that humankind, male and female, are created in the image of God, she envisions God as encompassing both sexes. She realizes that the deity can be referred to only metaphorically as a person and that any assignment of sex or attribution of gender to the Creator projects the conditions of creatureliness onto the ineffable. Regarding her own vision of the lord and servant in chapter 51, Julian explains that although God's manifestation assumes the male form, "we ought to know and beleue that the fader is nott man" (14.51.525) ["we ought to know and believe that the Father is not man" (272)]. She explores the all-encompassing nature of God by complementing the traditional male images of the Father and Son with the analogy of Jesus as Mother in Revelation Fourteen. Even though there are scriptural and patristic antecedents for this motif, Julian's representation of the second person of the Trinity as a Mother calls attention to medieval Christianity's ambivalence toward women.[3] Using Gen. 1:27, again as interpreted by Augustine in *De trinitate*, theologians, though asserting the equality of men and women before God, constructed a gendered model of the essential self which denied that the part characterized as female, the lower reason, contained the image of God. Julian's amplification of the motif of Jesus as Mother both reflects and refracts her socially constituted identity as woman. As a reaction against the contradictory attitudes toward women expressed by the church, Julian of Norwich's androgynous deity provides both an index to the stereotypes associated with each gender in Christianity and a paradigm for transcending the theology of sexual difference.

I

Despite differences between their attitudes toward the female, Julian of Norwich grounds her conception of the self in the conventions of contemplative mysticism developed from Augustine's writings. Regardless of the scholarly controversy about the nature of mysticism and the debate about whether Augustine himself was an authentic mystic, it is obvious that his introspective method influenced the medieval practice of contemplation.[4] Augustine's self-analysis in the *Confessions* as well as his practice of offering his own experiences as examples or evidence in his treatises stemmed from his belief that knowledge of the self constituted the foundation of all knowledge, particularly that of God.[5] This paradigm of the self is the inspiration, either directly or indirectly, for Julian's assertion that one must know God to know oneself.[6]

Augustine articulates the model of the self underlying this introspective epistemology in *De trinitate*. In his effort to understand the divine Trinity that he accepts on faith, Augustine assumes that humankind, created in the image and likeness of God, embodies a similar trinitarian unity. After analyzing and rejecting several interior triads, Augustine settles on memory, understanding, and will as the trinitarian *imago Dei* that best approximates its divine archetype.[7] Conceding that the human mind is not divine by nature, Augustine asserts that it nonetheless has the potential to participate in divinity. "For [the mind] is His image by the very fact that it is capable of Him, and can be a partaker of Him; and it cannot be so great a good except that it is His image."[8] Augustine's emphasis on capacity inscribes a circular trajectory for self-development, with the goal a fulfillment of the pattern imposed at the beginning. Having been created in the image of their Creator, individuals have the potential for achieving a likeness to God. Such participation in the divine nature is, according to Augustine, the ultimate human destiny.

Despite his vision of humanity's exalted destiny, Augustine is not confident that most individuals will attain a likeness to God. For, in keeping with his theodicy, he believes that Adam's sin obscured the image of God in his descendants; as a result, not only have they lost paradise, but they are also born with their essential nature deformed. While Adam could diminish the image of God created within him, humanity cannot, Augustine argues, restore this image to its original condition nor perfect it into a likeness to God without divine intervention. Only through a process of sanctification, enabled by Christ's atonement and enacted by grace, can humanity be re-created in the image of God and perfected to his likeness. Thus, becoming whole again, according to Augustine's view of selfhood, means becoming holy. His theology of sanctification, including his doctrines of grace and justification, presents a schema for self-development that Peter

Lombard summarizes in the formula often repeated in the thirteenth and fourteenth centuries: "Triplex est imago: *imago scilicet creationis, imago recreationis, imago similitudinis*";[9] [Threefold is the image: namely, the image of election, the image of restoration, the image of resemblance].

Although Augustine's definition of the self as the *imago Dei* pervades the medieval ideology of sin and salvation, the human capacity for deification gains particular prominence in mystical theology.[10] Despite the fact that Augustine does not explicitly develop a theory of mysticism, *De trinitate* presents concepts that influence, either directly or indirectly, the later medieval practice of contemplation. Speaking of the mind, Augustine writes: "By . . . [the] image of God in itself [the mind] is so powerful that it is able to cleave to Him whose image it is. . . . Finally, when it shall cleave to Him completely, it will be one spirit, and the Apostle bears witness to this when he says: 'But he who cleaves to the Lord is one spirit.'"[11] Although the context makes it clear that the participation in God which Augustine anticipates can occur only in eternity, his medieval successors entertain the possibility of achieving a brief foretaste of that union on earth through the practice of contemplation. Through introspection, they believe, the contemplative could gradually and sporadically perfect the inherent image of God into a likeness and attain, though only momentarily, self-fulfillment by participating in the divine nature.

In this tradition, contemplation is metaphorically spatialized as a paradoxical movement of the mind both upward and inward, "since to ascend in the scale of being is to enter more deeply into oneself, into the centre of one's being."[12] Though his investigation in *De trinitate* is psychological and analogical, Augustine's examination of his own psyche in the second part of this treatise influences the theory of contemplation in the high Middle Ages. During the twelfth through fourteenth centuries, both the Prescholastics and the Scholastics develop his dynamic model of the self as a deformed image with the capacity for likeness to God into the epistemology, ontology, and anthropology of introspective mysticism.

In Revelation Fourteen of *A Book of Showings* Julian of Norwich invokes a model of the self derived from this tradition of introspective mysticism to confirm the theodicy she proposes in Revelation Thirteen. Variously developed by the Victorines and the Cistercians in the twelfth century, the Franciscans and the Dominicans in the thirteenth, and the Rhineland mystics in the fourteenth, the mystical theology of the *imago Dei* is so ubiquitous and the transmission and dissemination of its central texts so difficult to trace in late fourteenth-century England that it is impossible to identify any single source for Julian's ideas.[13] What is clear, though, is that she comprehends the tradition in precise detail and extends it with creative integrity. Her discussion, particularly in chapters 53 through 63, evinces her mastery of a technical vocabulary and her assimilation of an erudite theology strongly influenced by Neoplatonism. Julian ingeniously imports the concept of the self from contemplative mysticism into the final section of her theodicy in order to supplement the historical resolution to the problem of evil she offers in chapter 51. In addition to the typological relation between humankind and Christ within historical time that makes salvation possible for all, she explains an ontological relation between the elect and the Trinity for all eternity that precludes their damnation. Julian of Norwich thus verifies her original solution to the problem of evil, the concept of the godly will, by astutely integrating the doctrines of predestination and the *imago Dei*.

Julian bases her conjunction of these two doctrines on Rom. 8:29: "For whom he foreknew, he also predestinated to be made conformable to the image of his Son; that he might be the first born amongst many brethren." Not by coincidence the scriptural justification for Julian's argument that God does not blame humankind for sin (chapters 45 through 52 of Revelation Fourteen) is Rom. 8:1 and 33–34: "There is now therefore no condemnation to them that are in Christ Jesus. . . . Who shall accuse against the elect of God? God is he that justifieth. Who is he that shall condemn? Christ Jesus that died; yea that is risen also again, who is at the right hand of God, who also maketh intercession for us." These verses provide Julian with the distinction she makes in chapter 45 between the judgment of God and the judgment of humankind. Having explained in the subsequent chapters why God does not blame humans for sin, Julian now returns to develop the first sentence of chapter 45: "God demyth vs vpon oure kyndely substance, whych is evyr kepte one in hym, hole and safe, without ende; and this dome is of his ryghtfulhede" (14.45.486); ["God judges us in our natural substance, which is always kept one in him, whole and safe, without end; and this judgment is out of his justice" (256)]. Rom. 8:29 provides the scriptural nexus between the theology of predestination and the concept of the self as *imago Dei*.

Julian uses Paul's text not only to validate her original theory of the godly will but also as an organizing principle for chapters 53 through 63 in Revelation Fourteen. Regarding predestination as the process by which those who will be saved realize their inherent likeness to the divine, Julian coordinates the chronology of election identified in Rom. 8:30—predestining, calling, justifying, and glorifying—with the three possible states of the *imago Dei*, as created, re-created, and perfected by God. Her conflation of these two traditional sequences of spiritual development accounts for her arrangement of topics in chapters 53 through 63 as she traces the process of God's operation in human salvation. Julian begins chapter 53 with an explanation of predestination and then concentrates on the created *imago Dei* through chapter 56; in chapter 57 she considers the re-creative act of Christ initiated by the Incarnation that makes possible the calling and the justifying of the predestined; after a summary of her views in chapters 58 and 59, she concludes with an examination of the process of renewal wrought by grace in chapters 60 through 63.

From these two traditional schemata of salvation Julian also develops a third, more innovative, thematic and organizational principle for chapters 53 through 63. For in the course of tracing the integrated sequences of predestination and reformation, she identifies a series of ontological bonds among the persons of the Trinity and humankind. Using analogies drawn from human relationships, particularly familial ties, she strikingly articulates these various unions, either actual or potential.[14] Anticipating this principle at the beginning of chapter 52, she writes of God as Father, Mother, and Spouse and of Christ Jesus as Brother and Savior (14.52.546). In the last ten chapters of Revelation Fourteen Julian develops these familial analogies by distinguishing among the three persons of the Trinity whom the soul encloses and by whom, simultaneously, the soul is enclosed. She implies five different vectors of connection between the three persons of God and the individual; these affiliations emanate from the divine acts of creating, restoring, and rewarding, and they affect humanity, respectively, through nature, mercy, and grace. As her summary of this series of analogies in chapter 58 reveals, these relationships are manifold and dynamic.

> In oure fader almyghty we haue oure kepyng and oure blesse, and a nemptys oure kyndely substannce whych is to vs by oure makyng fro without begynnyng; and in the seconde person in wytt and wysdom we haue oure k(e)pyng, and anemptys oure sensuallyte, oure restoryng and oure savyng, for he is oure moder, broder and savyoure; and in oure good lorde the holy gost we haue oure rewardyng and oure yeldyng for oure lyvyng and oure traveyle, and endlessly ovyrpassyng alle that we desyer in

his mervelous curtesy of his hye plentuous grace. For alle oure lyfe is in thre: in the furst (we haue) oure beyng, and in the seconde we haue oure encresyng, and in the thyrde we haue oure fulfyllyng. The furst is kynde, the seconde is mercy, the thyrde is grace. (14.58.584–85)

[In our almighty Father we have our protection and our bliss, as regards our natural substance, which is ours by our creation from without beginning; and in the second person, in knowledge and wisdom we have our perfection, as regards our sensuality, our restoration and our salvation, for he is our Mother, brother and saviour; and in our good Lord the Holy Spirit we have our reward and our gift for our living and our labour, endlessly surpassing all that we desire in his marvellous courtesy, out of his great plentiful grace. For all our life consists of three: In the first we have our being, and in the second we have our increasing, and in the third we have our fulfillment. The first is nature, the second is mercy, the third is grace. (293–94)]

In the last two sentences of this passage Julian recapitulates from the human perspective the three states of the *imago Dei* (in creation, re-creation, and perfection) as well as the means by which God maintains each state (nature, mercy, and grace). But by extending the traditional familial analogies for the Trinity as Father and Son to include Jesus as Mother as well as Brother, Julian modifies the ontology and anthropology implied by this Augustinian commonplace into an original theory of an androgynous God who creates the soul in an asexual image. Humans, both male and female, can know themselves by knowing God because, as children of God the Father and Jesus the Mother, and siblings of Christ, all individuals, regardless of their sex, have the potential for participating in the divine nature.

II

Julian resumes her explanation of the godly will of the elect in chapter 53 by repeating with only minor variations the definition of the phrase she first presents in chapter 37: "in ech a soule that shall be safe is a godly wylle that nevyr assentyd to synne ne nevyr shall, whych wyll is so good that it may nevyr wylle evyll, but evyr more contynn(u)ly it wyllyth good and werkyth good in the syght of god" (14.53.555); ["in each soul which will be saved there is a godly will which never assented to sin nor ever will, which will is so good that it can never will evil, but always constantly it wills good and it does good in the sight of God"

(283)]. Julian's confidence about the impeccability of the elect rests on her belief that "ech kynde that hevyn shall be fulfyllyd with behovyd nedys of goddys rygh(t)fulnes so to be knytt and onyd in [Jesus Christ] that there in were kepte a substannce whych myght nevyr nor shulde be partyd from hym, and that thorow his awne good wyll in his end-lesse forse(ing) purpose" (14.53.556) ["every nature with which heaven will be filled had of necessity and of God's rightfulness to be so joined and united in him that in it a substance was kept which could never and should never be parted from him, and that through his own good will in his endless prescient purpose" (283)]. Julian thus locates the in-tegrity of the godly will in a substantial union between each of those who will be saved and the second person of the Trinity.

The first of three ontological relationships that she traces between Jesus Christ and humankind, this "ryghtfull knyttyng" is identified by Julian's insistence on its atemporality as the predestination of the elect in Christ from all eternity. "For I saw that god began nevyr to loue mankynde; for ryghte the same that mankynd shall be in endlesse blesse, fulfyllyng the joy of god as anemptis his werkys, ryghte so the same mankynd hath be in the forsyghte of god knowen and lovyd fro without begynnyng in his ryghtfull entent" (14.53.557); ["For I saw that God never began to love mankind; for just as mankind will be in end-less bliss, fulfilling God's joy with regard to his works, just so has that same mankind been known and loved in God's prescience from with-out beginning in his righteous intent" (283)]. In the vocabulary of me-dieval theology, predestination in Christ refers to the Trinity's eternal comprehension of those elected to glory. Summarizing the exegetical tradition of Rom. 8:30, Peter Lombard, for example, identifies the four steps by which God directs the destiny of those who will be saved: "praedestinando non existentes, vocando aversos, justificando pecca-tores, glorificando mortales";[15] [by appointing beforehand the nonex-istent, by calling those turned away, by justifying sinners, and by glori-fying mortals]. Using *praedestinatio* in a more technical and limited sense than usual, Peter differentiates the term from *vocatio*: God must first destine individuals to exist before calling them to election. The notion of predestination in Christ reflects the strong Neoplatonic in-fluence on medieval theology through both Augustine and the Eastern Fathers, for the term refers to the idea or form of the creature in the mind of the Creator prior to its creation. God knows the elect even before the beginning of time as they exist *in potentia* in Christ, the archetype for all created being.

Julian of Norwich understands this Neoplatonic interpretation of Rom. 8:29–30, for she situates the godly will in the eternal union of the elect with their archetype, Christ. In addition to the substantial union between God and human beings forged in the act of creation, which Julian explains in greater detail in chapters 54 through 56, she claims that those who will be saved are joined to Christ from all eternity through the Trinity's predestination of their future glory: "this deerwurthy soule was preciously knytt to hym in the makyng, whych knott is so suttell and so myghty that it is onyd in to god. In whych onyng it is made endlesly holy. Farthermore . . . all the soulys þat shalle be savyd in hevyn with out ende be knytt in this knott, and onyd in this oonyng, and made holy in this holynesse" (14.53.560); ["this beloved soul was preciously knitted to him in its making, by a knot so subtle and so mighty that it is united in God. In this uniting it is made endlessly holy. Furthermore . . . all the souls which will be saved in heaven without end are knit in this knot, and united in this union, and made holy in this holiness" (284)]. According to Julian, the creation, re-creation, and glorification of the elect occur in time as the fulfillment of the plan eternally established in Christ. "And by the endlesse entent and assent and the full acorde of all the trynyte, þe myd person wolde be grounde and hed of this feyer kynde out of whom we be all come, in whom we be alle enclosyd, in to whom we shall all goo . . . by the forseyeng purpose of alle the blessyd trynyte fro without begynnyng" (14.53.557–58); ["And by the endless intent and assent and the full accord of all the Trinity, the mediator wanted to be the foundation and the head of this fair nature, out of whom we have all come, in whom we are all enclosed, into whom we shall all go . . . by the prescient purpose of all the blessed Trinity from without beginning" (283)]. This statement confirms Julian's recognition of the circular trajectory of self-development implied by the medieval theories of predestination and perfection. As Robert Javelet puts it, "Le problème—ou mystère—de la prédestination se situe entre ces deux termes: l'Archétype et l'édification par la vie spirituelle de la future éternité. C'est partir de l'éternel pour y revenir: le futur est enclos dans le passé originel";[16] [The problem—or the mystery—of predestination is situated between these two terms: the Archetype and the establishment through the spiritual life of the future eternity. It is to part from the eternal for the purpose of returning there: the future is enclosed in the original past]. In keeping with this Neoplatonic mythos of predestination as the reunion with an archetype, Julian grounds the godly will in the atemporal act of divine imagination that is ultimately actualized by the participation of the elect in God.

Although her mention in chapter 53 of the Trinity's predestination of "þe myd person . . . [as] grounde and hed of this feyer kynde" (154.53.557) ["the mediator . . . [as] the foundation and the head of this fair nature" (283)] anticipates her later development of the theme of Jesus as Mother both in the creation of the physical body and in the re-creation of the Mystical Body, Julian uses the analogy of brotherhood for this first ontological union between Christ and those who will be saved. Paul's reference to the Son in Rom. 8:29 as "the first born amongst many brethren" explains her association of brotherhood with predestination. But again Julian interprets the Pauline text in a Neoplatonic context, for, as her subsequent discussion of Christ's role in creation reveals, she thoroughly comprehends the theological distinction between the second person of the Trinity, begotten of the Father as the true *imago Dei*, and a humankind made, not born, in the *imago imaginis Dei*.

Julian of Norwich's association of the the godly will with predestination suggests that her conception of the *imago Dei* may be influenced, either directly or indirectly, by that of Bernard of Clairvaux. He moves the *imago Dei* from the mind, where Augustine had situated it, to the will in order to indicate, as Bernard McGinn explains, that "freedom, understood in its most general form as the absence of external coercion, is the inalienable characteristic of the human person as human."[17] Bernard of Clairvaux distinguishes three different states of this freedom in humankind: (1) *liberum arbitrium* (free choice) is freedom from necessity, the essential condition of humankind both before and after the Fall; (2) *liberum consilium* (free counsel), lost by Adam but restored by Christ, enables the elect to refrain from sin; and (3) *liberum complacitum* (free pleasure) is the freedom from sorrow achieved only in heaven.[18] As Bernard explains:

> The first freedom . . . might be termed freedom of nature, the second of grace, the third of life or glory. For in the first place, we were created with free will and willing freedom, a creature noble in God's eyes. Secondly, we are re-formed in innocence, a new creature in Christ: and thirdly, we are raised up to glory, a perfect creature in the Spirit.[19]

In the process of creation, re-creation, and restoration of the *imago Dei*, the powers of the will increase from free choice to free counsel to free pleasure.

116

Most important for an understanding of Julian's conception of the different states of the will is Bernard's notion of free counsel. He divides this power into two parts: "The higher freedom of counsel consists in not being able to sin, the lower in being able not to sin." Although Bernard acknowledges that the higher degree can be attained only in heaven, he assigns the lower degree to Adam prior to the Fall. Through his sin, however, Adam lost even this lower degree of free counsel and was left with free choice alone: "In losing completely his freedom of counsel, he fell from being able not to sin to not being able not to sin."[20] Christ, though, restores the lower degree of free counsel and the subsequent ability to resist sin to the elect in this life; as Bernard observes, "every righteous man enjoys [freedom of counsel], in part again, but in no small part."[21] Of itself, free choice, the inalienable *imago Dei* in humankind, is free only to sin.[22]

Julian's distinction between the beastly will and the godly will seems to be analogous to Bernard's separation of free choice from free counsel. According to Julian, "Ryght as there is a bestely wylle in the lower party that may wylle no good, ryght so there is a godly wyll in the hygher party, whych wylle is so good that it may nevyr wylle evylle, but evyr good" (13.37.443); ["Just as there is an animal will in the lower part which cannot will any good, so there is a godly will in the higher part, which will is so good that it cannot ever will any evil, but always good" (242)]. In this world grace acts as the intermediary between these two parts of the will for the elect. Interpreting the showing of the lord and servant in chapter 52, Julian acknowledges that "we may nott in this lyfe kepe vs fro synne alle holy, in full clenesse as we shall be in hevyn. But we may wele by grace kepe vs fro the synnes whych wolde lede vs to endlesse payne, as holy chyrch techyth vs, and eschewe venyall resonably vppe oure myght" (14.52.551) ["we cannot in this life keep ourselves completely from sin, in the perfect purity that we shall have in heaven. But we can well by grace keep ourselves from the sins which would lead us to endless torment, as Holy Church teaches us, and eschew venial sin, reasonably, to the extent of our power" (281)]. Julian's intermediary state of grace resembles the lower degree of free counsel that Bernard claims can be restored to the elect in this life. "True, we cannot be completely without sin or sorrow here on earth," he writes, "but we can, with the help of grace, avoid being overcome either by sin or by sorrow."[23] According to Julian, then, the godly will, like Bernard's higher degree of free counsel, is not able to sin; the will informed by grace, like Bernard's lower degree of free counsel, is able not to sin; and the beastly will, like Bernard's free choice, is not able not to sin. The anchorite agrees with the abbot that the elect can attain the medial degree of freedom, the ability to resist sin, in this life, even though they will achieve the highest degree only after death.

If indeed Julian derives her analysis of the different states of the will from Bernard of Clairvaux, she nonetheless interprets his ideas in her own distinctive manner. While his "notion of union with God [is] primarily an affective, operational union of willing and loving, an *unitas spiritus*," hers is an "essential or ontological union between God and the soul ... remarkably close to ... Neoplatonic notions of the union of identity or indistinction."[24] In chapters 54 through 56 of Revelation Fourteen Julian focuses on these substantial connections between God and the soul forged through the second stage in the cycle of predestination, the creation of humankind. Her analysis of the roles of God the Father and Jesus the Mother in this act of substantiation attests to her familiarity with medieval theology, for she distinguishes between the first person or Father as the "grounde in whome oure soule standyth" and the second person or Mother as the "mene that kepyth þe substannce and the sensualyte to geder" (14.56.571). Julian's distinction between the Father as ground and the Mother as mean indicates that she interprets Gen. 1:27 in terms of a Christian Neoplatonism ultimately derived from Augustine.

In adapting Neoplatonic theories of emanation and exemplarity to a creationist theology, Augustine makes two crucial changes. First, he transforms Plotinus's assumption that human beings are identical in nature to the One into the Christian axiom that humans participate in God's nature. While Plotinus assumes that all things share in varying degrees the identical essence emanating from the One, Augustine believes that God confers being rather than the divine essence in the act of creation.[25] According to his doctrine of participation, to exist means to exist in God; all of creation, by virtue of existence, shares in God's Being without being God. Second, Augustine identifies the Neoplatonic archetypes not as realities existing outside the divine mind but as the ideas eternally subsisting in the second person of the Trinity.[26] Rejecting Plotinus's concept of the *Nous* distinct from the First Principle, Augustine locates the Neoplatonic Ideas in the Logos. According to Christian exemplarism, then, Christ is the form for all phemonena and the agent of their creation.

From such theories of participation and exemplarism, known either from Augustine or through his influence on later medieval theologians,

Julian develops the two phases of human creation: God the Father's formation of the substance and Jesus the Mother's embodiment of the substance in the sensuality. Participating in God's Being by virtue of their existence, human creatures are enclosed in the Trinity. But by placing the *imago Dei* in the human soul through the agency of the exemplary Logos, the Trinity encloses itself in human creatures. As Julian expresses it, "Hyely owe we to enjoye þat god dwellyth in oure soule; and more hyly we owe to enjoye that oure soule dwellyth in god. Oure soule is made to be goddys dwellyng place, and the dwellyng of oure soule is god, whych is vnmade" (14.54.561–62); ["Greatly ought we to rejoice that God dwells in our soul; and more greatly ought we to rejoice that our soul dwells in God. Our soul is created to be God's dwelling place, and the dwelling of our soul is God, who is uncreated" (285)]. Julian's listing actually reverses the order in which these two phases of creation occur, both temporally and in her own explanation of the process. The Mother's act of informing matter with the *imago Dei*, the phase of creation Julian here refers to first, actually follows the Father's bringing of the human substance into existence, the topic that Julian explores in chapter 54.

The influence of Neoplatonism on medieval Christianity's conception of creation accounts for Julian's assertion of a substantial union between the Creator and human creatures. She claims, paradoxically, that she "sawe no dyfference betwen god and oure substance, but as it were all god; and yett my vnderstandyng toke that oure substance is in god, that is to sey that god is god and oure substance is a creature in god" (14.54.562–63) ["saw no difference between God and our substance, but, as it were, all God; and still my understanding accepted that our substance is in God, that is to say that God is God, and our substance is a creature in God" (285)]. Like Augustine, Julian uses the term *substance* as a synonym for existence.[27] Because creatures are made from nothing, however, they only participate in God's substance. Augustine interprets God's words in Exodus, "I am that I am," as a statement of creaturely subsistence in the Creator: "For since God is the supreme existence, that is to say, supremely is, and is therefore unchangeable, the things that He made He empowered to be, but not to be supremely like Himself."[28] Julian of Norwich makes precisely this point as she explicates the account of creation from Gen. 2:7. Distinguishing between the body, made from earth, and the soul, made in the image of God, she writes: "But to the makyng of mannys soule he wolde take ryght nought, but made it. And thus is the kynde

119

made ryghtfully onyd to the maker, whych is substanncyall kynde
vnmade, þat is god. And therfore it is that ther may ne shall be ryght
nought betwene god and mannis soule" (14.53.559); ["But to the making
of man's soul he would accept nothing at all, but made it. And so is
created nature rightfully united to the maker, who is substantial uncreated nature, that is God. And so it is that there may and will be
nothing at all between God and man's soul" (284)]. The last sentence
further indicates the influence of Augustine, either directly or indirectly, on Julian's interpretation of Gen. 2:7, for in *De trinitate* he insists on the immediacy of the union between humankind and their
Creator: "Certainly, not everything in creatures, which is in some way
or other similar to God, is also to be called His image, but that alone
to which He Himself alone is superior; for the image is only then an
expression of God in the full sense, when no other nature lies between
it and God."[29] The human soul, created as an *imago Dei*, participates in
the essence of God. The divine act of conferring being places the soul
in Being. Julian indicates her understanding of this first phase of creation by stating that "oure soule that is made dwellyth in god in substance, of whych substance by god we be that we be" (14.54.562) ["our
soul, which is created, dwells in God in substance, of which substance,
through God, we are what we are" (285)]. Although she clearly believes
that the entire Trinity is involved in the process of creation, Julian attributes this initial phase to the first person, traditionally referred to as
the Father.

God the Father's formation of the human substance is complemented, according to Julian, by Jesus the Mother's incorporation of
that substance in a material manifestation. Explaining the union of
spirit with matter, soul with body, in humankind, Julian refers to the
first of the three maternities of Jesus, his motherhood in creation.
"Oure substannce is þe hyer perty, whych we haue in oure fader god
almyghty; and the seconde person of the trynyte is oure moder in kynd
in oure substanncyall makyng, in whom we be groundyd and rotyd"
(14.58.585–86); ["Our substance is the higher part, which we have in our
Father, God almighty; and the second person of the Trinity is our
Mother in nature in our substantial creation, in whom we are founded
and rooted" (294)]. Julian's association of Jesus with the embodiment
of the human soul again indicates the influence of Christian Neoplatonism. According to medieval exemplarism, the second person of the
Trinity as Logos is both the thought and the word of God,[30] both the
formal and the efficient cause of creation. Augustine justifies this
Christian exemplarism by distinguishing between Christ as the true

imago Dei and humankind as the *imago imaginis Dei*. Calling attention to the fact that the verb used in Gen. 1:27 is *fecit* (made) rather than *genita* (begotten), Augustine differentiates the second person of the Trinity, begotten of the same substance and in the image of the Father, from humankind, participating in God's substance but only made to the image and likeness of God.[31] The Trinity creates humans in the divine image and likeness through the agency of the second person, the uncreated *imago Dei*. As Augustine states, "the Son is the first species by which, so to speak, all things are specified, and the form by which all things are formed."[32] Christ as Logos is the Father's creative word impressing form upon matter. The Father, or God *sicuti est*, is simple; his attributes are identical with his Being. But in the act of creation, through the mediation of the Logos, the *natura simplex* of God is communicated to the plurality that is the universe. Christ's role in the creative process is analogous to a prism. "By him and through him, the undifferentiated Light of the Father is split up into its component parts, and the sequential experience of these component parts is what is referred to in the mystical tradition as the *via affirmativa* or *via positiva*."[33] According to the tradition of Christian exemplarism, then, the second person or Logos, as both the formal and the efficient cause of material creation, is both transcendent and immanent.

This Christian exemplarism explains Julian's conception of the role of the second person of the Trinity in the work of creation. As the begotten image of the same substance as the Father, the Logos is the archetype of the *imago imaginis Dei* within each individual. This Word also unites that created image of God, the soul, with the body, thus giving the human substance a sensible expression. Differentiating the contributions of the persons of the Trinity to creation, Julian distinguishes between humankind's participation in the Being of the first person and the presence of the second person as the *imago Dei* within each individual:

> For I saw full suerly that oure substannce is in god, and also I saw that in oure sensualyte god is, for in the same poynt that oure soule is made sensuall, in the same poynt is the cytte of god, ordeyned to hym fro without begynnyng. In whych cytte he comyth, and nevyr shall remeve it, for god is nevyr out of the soule, in whych he shalle dwell blessydly without end. (14.55.566–67)

> [For I saw very surely that our substance is in God, and I also saw that God is in our sensuality, for in the same instant and place in which our soul is made sensual, in that same instant and place exists the city of

God, ordained for him from without beginning. He comes into this city
and will never depart from it, for God is never out of the soul, in which
he will dwell blessedly without end. (287)]

Human beings exist within God the Father, but only the Logos resides
within human beings.

The tradition of Christian exemplarism not only explains the function that Julian of Norwich attributes to the second person of the Trinity in the creation of humankind, but also provides the first clue to her
characterization of Jesus as a "moder in kynd in oure substanncyall
makyng" (14.58.586) ["Mother in nature in our substantial creation"
(294)] in its association of the Logos with the sapiential literature of
the Old Testament.[34] Theologians of the third century, such as Origen
and Tertullian, used the account of creation presented by the personified Wisdom in Prov. 8:22–31 to establish the divinity of Jesus as eternal Logos, implicit in John 1:1–14.[35] This identification of the figure of
Wisdom was further substantiated by Paul's reference to Christ in 1
Cor. 1:24 as "the power of God and the wisdom of God."

Such an association of the second person of the Trinity with sapiential literature suggested a female manifestation of God. The personification of Wisdom or Sophia as a woman is presented intermittently in
Proverbs 1 through 9, Ecclesiasticus (Sirach) 1, 4, 6, 14, 15, and 24, and
the Wisdom of Solomon 6 through 10. Of these Old Testament texts,
the most important for the exemplarist tradition are Prov. 8:22–31 and
Ecclesiasticus 24, both of which assert Sophia's eternal presence with
God and her participation in the act of creation. Speaking in her own
voice in Prov. 8:22 and 30, for example, Sophia claims: "The Lord pos-
sessed me in the beginning of his ways, before he made any thing from
the beginning.... I was with him forming all things: and was de-
lighted every day, playing before him at all times." On two occasions
Sophia is identified specifically as a mother: "And she will meet him
as an honourable mother; and will receive him as a wife married of
a virgin" (Ecclus. 15:2); "And I rejoiced in all these: for this wisdom
went before me, and I knew not that she was the mother of them all"
(Wisd. 7:12).

Although the grammatical gender of Sophia is feminine, she becomes, in the exemplarist tradition, a manifestation of the masculine
Christ. As Peter Dronke observes, "The figure who in specific theological contexts will be called *verbum dei* and seen as the masculine *son* of
God has always, in another *integumentum*, been identified with Sapi-

entia or Providentia—a feminine hypostasis."[36] In the twelfth century, for example, Hildegard of Bingen combined an exemplarist cosmogony with a sapiential theology; although she did not depict Christ as female, Hildegard used feminine symbols to "evoke God's interactions with the cosmos insofar as they are timeless or perpetually repeated."[37] In the thirteenth century two influential theologians, one Dominican and the other Franciscan, voiced the idea of Wisdom as mother in creation that Julian echoes, in her own distinctive fashion, a century later. Commenting on Isaiah, Albert the Great says, "The wisdom of God is the first mother in whose womb we have been formed." Later, referring to the concept of predestination, he has Christ claim, "I am more than mother, who formed and carried you in the light of my foreknowledge."[38] In his *Collationes in Hexaemeron* (*Collations on the Six Days*), Bonaventure writes that Wisdom can be compared to a good woman because "there is a principle of fecundity tending to the conceiving, the bearing and the bringing forth of everything that pertains to the universality of the laws. For all the exemplar reasons are conceived from all eternity in the womb or uterus of eternal wisdom. [This is true] most of all [of the exemplary reasons] of predestination."[39] In the fourteenth century, Meister Eckhart also associates Sophia with the archetypal Logos. "Wisdom is a name for a mother. The characteristic of a motherly name is passivity, and in God both activity and passivity must be thought. The Father is active, and the Son is passive because of his function as the one being born. For the Son is Wisdom born from eternity in which all things are distinct."[40] As these examples reveal, theologians in the exemplarist tradition often identify Wisdom as the feminine manifestation of the deity responsible for the predestination of souls and the incorporation of form in matter.

Although the personification of the Logos as a mother was undoubtedly suggested to Julian and her predecessors in the exemplarist tradition by the sapiential literature of the Old Testament, it also conformed to the association of the female with the material and corporeal in the scientific and theological discourse of the Middle Ages. Invoking the authority of Aristotle's natural philosophy, for example, Thomas Aquinas asserts that the male is the active and efficient cause in procreation while the female is the passive and material cause. "In human generation, the mother provides the matter of the body which, however, is still unformed, and receives its form only by means of the power which is contained in the father's seed. And though this power cannot create the rational soul, it nevertheless prepares the matter of the body for receiving a form of that kind."[41] This assimilation of woman and matter was embedded, of course, in the Latin vocabulary of medieval clerics by the phonological similarity among the Latin terms *mater*, *matrix*, and *materia*.[42]

Analogous to this literal identification of the female with the corporeal in medieval scientific theory is her figurative construction as carnality in theological discourse. Patristic allegoresis of Genesis 3, influenced by the dualism of Neoplatonism, construed woman as a metaphor of the flesh. Originating with Philo, this interpretation reads Eve, created from Adam's body, as the sensory and sensual. Explaining the serpent's temptation of Eve, Philo writes: "Pleasure does not venture to bring her wiles and deceptions to bear on the man, but on the woman, and by her means on him. This is a telling and well-made point: for in us mind corresponds to man, the senses to woman."[43] Repeated by Ambrose and Augustine, this interpretation of the physical difference between male and female in terms of the dualism between soul and body persists in the writings of medieval theologians. "Although the Latin traditions in general insisted on the equality of both men and women in their possession of the image [of God]," as McGinn acknowledges, "actual practice frequently regarded women as somehow inferior in conformity with the symbolic values assigned to the female."[44]

The identification of Christ as the feminine Wisdom in exemplarist cosmogony, along with the cultural construction of woman as the body in medieval science and theology, elucidates Julian's characterization of Jesus as "oure moder in kynd in oure substanncyall makyng" (14.58.586) ["our Mother in nature in our substantial creation" (294)]. As Wisdom, the mother of all good things, the second person of the Trinity unites form with matter. Like a human mother in whose body the semen of the father grows into a creature of both soul and body, Jesus is the "mene that kepyth þe substannce and the sensualyte to geder" (14.56.571) ["mean which keeps the substance and the sensuality together" (289)]. Although Julian's extensive development of the maternity of Jesus in creating—and, as we shall see later, in re-creating and perfecting—the *imago Dei* is unique, it is not eccentric.

Despite these scriptural and philosophical justifications for Julian's analogy between creation and maternity, though, her development of the idea of Jesus as Mother interrogates the dominant medieval attitude about gender by calling attention to the ambivalence toward woman in the clerical ideology. Given the ascetic dualism of medieval theology and the valorization of soul over body, the consolidation of

woman with the corporeal was often an articulation of and rationaliza-
tion for misogyny.[45] Julian of Norwich challenges this devaluation of
both the feminine and the bodily by situating her concept of Jesus as
generative Mother in the gap resulting from the contradiction between
the church's insistence on the literal identity of male and female souls
and the symbolic difference of their bodies. Although women were acknowledged to be equivalent to men in the order of salvation, they
were regarded as inferior in the order of creation.[46] The theological
endorsement of women's spiritual equality enables Julian to reject the
contradictory ratification of their corporeal inequality. As I will show,
she creates God as both Father and Mother to emphasize the creation
of all human beings, both male and female, in the image of God.

The complexity and contradictions of the Christian ambivalence toward women crystallize in Augustine's analysis of the structure of the
essential self in book 12 of *De trinitate*. Since the rhetoric and sequence
of Augustine's argument are crucial to an understanding of the tension
in the subsequent medieval attitude, it is necessary to examine his discussion in some detail. In book 12 Augustine distinguishes between
two parts of the soul (*mens*), the higher and lower reason; the former,
engaged in the contemplation of eternal things, can achieve wisdom
(*sapientia*); the latter, oriented toward action in the temporal world,
can achieve only knowledge (*scientia*).[47] He accounts for this division of
labor within the *mens* using the analogy of Eve's creation. Just as the
first woman was formed as Adam's helpmate because no suitable com-
panion could be found for him among the animals, so, Augustine
argues,

> a certain part of our reason, not separated so as to sever unity, but di-
> verted, as it were, so as to help fellowship, is set aside for the performing
> of its own proper work. And just as in man and woman there is one flesh
> of two, so the one nature of the mind embraces our intellect and action,
> or our council and execution, or our reason and reasonable appetite, or
> whatever other more significant terms there may be for expressing them,
> so that as it was said of those: "They shall be two in one flesh," so it can
> be said of these: "Two in one mind."[48]

Despite the distinctive functions of its two parts, Augustine initially
insists that the mind remains a unity, with the hierarchical terms indicating the direction of attention rather than any essential difference
between the higher and lower reason.

Augustine inadvertently betrays his ambivalence about the equality
of the two aspects of the mind and of the two sexes with his allusion

125

to the marriage of male and female. For, seduced by his own metaphoric language, he creates a gendered model of the mind that identifies the higher reason as masculine and the lower reason as feminine.
In the chapter immediately following this claim that the two parts are
one mind as the wedded couple are two in one flesh, Augustine begins
to deconstruct the integrity of the *mens* by privileging the higher reason as the locus of the divine image in humankind: "in that part alone,
to which belongs the contemplation of eternal things, there is not only
a trinity but also an image of God; but in that which has been diverted
to the action upon temporal things, even if a trinity can be found, yet
it cannot be an image of God."[49] Augustine thus situates the *imago Dei*
exclusively in that part of the mind which he metaphorically construes
as male.

Conscious of the dangers of confusing the literal with the figurative,
Augustine insists on the spiritual equality of women notwithstanding
the inferiority of the lower or feminine reason. To counter Paul's contention that man "is the image and glory of God. But the woman is the
glory of the man" (1 Cor. 11:7), he cites the equally authoritative but
contradictory statement of Gen. 1:27: "God made man, to the image of
God he made him; male and female he made them and blessed them."
Augustine tries to reconcile the discrepancy between these two scriptural texts by claiming that Genesis uses *man* literally to refer to the
entire species while Paul uses *man* metaphorically to refer not to one
of the two sexes but rather to one of the two parts of the mind, the
higher reason.

> For [Genesis] says that human nature itself, which is complete in both
> sexes, has been made to the image of God, and [it] does not exclude the
> woman from being understood as the image of God. . . . In what sense,
> therefore, are we to understand the Apostle. . . ? The solution lies, I
> think, in what I already said when discussing the nature of the human
> mind, namely, that the woman together with her husband is the image
> of God, so that that whole substance is one image. But when she is as-
> signed as a help-mate, a function that pertains to her alone, then she is
> not the image of God; but as far as man is concerned, he is by himself
> alone the image of God, just as fully and completely as when he and the
> woman are joined together into one.[50]

Woman, according to Augustine, is literally created in the image of
God insofar as she is identical to man in spirit; but insofar as she is
different in body, she is a metaphor for the lower reason. "Therefore,

in their minds a common nature is recognized; but in their bodies the division of this one mind itself is symbolized."[51] Augustine thus distinguishes between *woman* as metonymy for *human* and as metaphor for *body*.

Augustine's equivocation between the metonymic and the metaphoric significance of *woman* proved extremely influential and authorized both the empowerment and the subordination of women throughout the Middle Ages. In his subsequent discussion in book 12 of *De trinitate* Augustine demonstrates how easy it is to ignore his own distinction between the spiritual equality and physical inequality of the sexes by expressing two contradictory attitudes toward women. On the one hand, to defend women against those who would exclude them from full membership in the church, he interprets 1 Cor. 11:7 as an allegory of the mind and argues that all human beings of both sexes possess both the higher and the lower reason. Citing Paul's statement that "there is neither male nor female" in Christ (Gal. 3:28), he asserts that women are "with us co-heirs of grace."[52] On the other hand, in his analysis of the psychology of temptation, Augustine identifies the female not just as a metaphor of temporality and physicality but as the literal embodiment of them. The historical Eve, deceived by the serpent, lured Adam into eating the forbidden fruit, just as the feminine part of the mind, the lower reason, in contact with the body, seduces the higher or masculine reason to sin. Augustine's earlier insistence that the female is only the metaphor for the lower reason in all human beings thus dissolves into a suggestion that the minds of literal females are constituted solely by the lower reason.[53]

Augustine's references to Eve in book 12 of *De trinitate* chart this tension between his avowed defense of women and his implicit condemnation of them. From the analogy between the lower reason and Eve as the helpmate and equal of Adam (chapter 3) he moves to an identification of the lower reason with Eve as the temptress to sin (chapter 12). Augustine thus reverses his own assertion about the integrity of the higher and lower reason by transforming his metaphor of marriage as a union of equals, two in one flesh, into a metaphor of marriage as the adversarial struggle for dominance between hierarchically valorized principles. Thus Augustine's *De trinitate* both gives voice to women and silences them. Created in the image of God, females are equal to males spiritually; but as a sign of the lower reason, the feminine must be subordinated to the masculine in the self and in the society.

Augustine's medieval successors continued his characterization of the higher reason as masculine and his representation of sanctity as the subjugation of the lower or feminine self.[54] For example, in his *Epistola ad fratres de Monte Dei* (Letter to the brethren of Mont Dieu or *Golden Epistle*, 1144–1145) the twelfth-century Cistercian William of St. Thierry reinscribes this distinction between the masculine and feminine in the mind with a rhetoric more virulently antifeminist than Augustine's own; using *anima* (translated as *soul*) for the lower and *animus* (translated as *spirit*) for the higher reason, William writes:

> The soul [*anima*] is something incorporeal, capable of reason, destined to impart life to the body. It is this which makes men animal, acquainted with the things of the flesh, cleaving to bodily sensation. But when it begins to be not only capable but also in possession of perfect reason, it immediately renounces the mark of the feminine and becomes spirit [*animus*] endowed with reason, fitted to rule the body, spirit in possession of itself. For as long as it is soul it is quick to slip effeminately into what is of the flesh; but the spirit thinks only on what is virile and spiritual.[55]

Walter Hilton, a contemporary of Julian of Norwich in the tradition of *imago Dei* mysticism, also attests to the vigor of the gendered model of the essential self in fourteenth-century England. In book 2 of *The Scale of Perfection*, completed shortly before Hilton's death in 1396, he distinguishes two parts of the soul, sensuality and reason. He also divides the reason into two parts, the higher or male and the lower or female.

> The higher part is compared to a man, for it should be master and sovereign, and that is properly the image of God, for by that alone the soul knows God and loves him. The lower part is compared to a woman, for it should be obedient to the higher part of reason as woman is obedient to man, and that lies in the knowledge and rule of earthly things, to use them discerningly according to need and to refuse them when there is no need; at the same time always to have an eye raised to the higher part of reason, with reverence and fear, in order to follow it.[56]

As these examples demonstrate, Augustine's identification of the feminine with the sensory and sensual aspect of the mind remains a dominant concept in medieval contemplative mysticism.

Julian of Norwich's characterization of Jesus as Mother takes advantage of the medieval ambivalence derived from the discrepancy between Augustine's literal and figurative constructions of woman. His contention that women are literally created in the image of God empowers her to create an image of God as woman. But by representing Jesus as Mother, Julian reconceives the Augustinian *imago Dei*. In the act of individual creation, Jesus the Mother unites the *imago Dei* with a material body; as the efficient cause of incorporation, "he is mene that kepyth þe substannce and the sensualyte to geder, so that it shall nevyr departe" (14.56.571) ["he is the mean which keeps the substance and the sensuality together, so that they will never separate" (289)]. Using the Middle English terms *substance* and *sensualite*,[57] Julian insists that both parts of the soul are integral to it: "and as anemptis oure substannce it may ryghtly be callyd oure soule; and anemptis oure sensualite it may ryghtly be callyd oure soule, and that is by the onyng that it hath in god" (14.56.572); ["as regards our substance, it can rightly be called our soul, and as regards our sensuality, it can rightly be called our soul, and that is by the union which it has in God" (289)]. Although she maintains the hierarchical division of the essential self into substance and sensuality, she refuses to attribute gender to either part.

Furthermore, Julian values the sensuality, the nexus between the spiritual and the corporeal, because, like other theologians of the thirteenth and fourteenth centuries, she regards the human person as a union of body and soul.[58] Julian expresses her respect for the sensuality or lower reason by making it the locus of Christ's presence within the individual: "That wurschypfull cytte þat oure lorde Jhesu syttyth in, it is oure sensualyte, in whych he is enclosyd; and oure kyndly substance is beclosyd in Jhesu, with þe blessyd soule of Crist syttyng in rest in the godhed" (14.56.572); ["The honourable city in which our Lord Jesus sits is our sensuality, in which he is enclosed; and our natural substance is enclosed in Jesus, with the blessed soul of Christ sitting in rest in the divinity" (289)]. Alluding to this statement, Riehle observes that "Julian's understanding of the image of God is that it embraces the whole man, including his bodiliness. . . . It is thus possible to speak of God taking up his dwelling in man's *sensualite*." Riehle regards Julian's respect for the sensuality as her most important contribution to the theology of the *imago Dei* and as evidence of her great familiarity with Latin theology.[59]

Julian may well have derived her metaphor of the sensuality as a "wurschypfull cytte" from sapiential theology. At the culmination of her account of creation in Ecclus. 24:14–16, Wisdom says:

> From the beginning, and before the world, was I created, and unto the world to come I shall not cease to be: and in the holy dwelling-place I have ministered before him.

And so was I established in Sion, and in the holy city likewise I rested: and my power was in Jerusalem.

And I took root in an honourable people, and in the portion of my God his inheritance: and my abode is in the full assembly of saints.

Ecclus. 24:14–16 may have authorized Julian's tropological identification of the souls of the saved as the earthly Jerusalem, the dwelling place of Wisdom in time. These verses accord in a particularly interesting manner with Paul's mention of the anagogical Jerusalem in Gal. 4:26: "But that Jerusalem which is above is free; which is our mother." This concordance confirms Julian's idea that the sensuality is the locus of Mother Jesus' indwelling in humankind.

According to Julian's exemplarist cosmogony, then, Jesus as Mother in human creation is both transcendent and immanent, residing simultaneously as *imago Dei* in the heavenly Trinity and as *imago imaginis Dei* in the saints on earth. Conceiving of creation as the cooperative act of the first person or Father and the second person or Mother enables Julian to reconceive the *imago Dei* and to reject the traditional division of the soul into masculine and feminine. Her distinction between substance and sensuality, though derived from Augustine's differentiation between the higher and lower reason, not only rejects the gendered model of the soul but also ennobles the lower reason by identifying it as an integral part of the human being. Her exemplarist cosmogony thus entails a radical revision of the prevailing androcentric anthropology. By enhancing the status of the sensuality or lower reason in the human soul, Julian also elevates the bodily and the feminine. Just as male and female constitute the human race and soul and body constitute the human person, so substance and sensuality, stripped of any identification by gender, constitute the human soul.

In contrast to many of her predecessors in the discourse of contemplative mysticism, who regard sanctification as the process of suppressing the feminine or bodily aspect of the self, Julian envisions holiness as the wholeness of the soul, the sensuality reunited with the substance. Although she insists on the inviolability of the godly will in the substantial union between the Creator and those predestined for salvation, Julian regards sin as a division between the two parts of the soul as well as a temporary separation from God. Through the motherhood of re-creation Jesus reunites the divided soul. "And thus in oure substannce we be full and in oure sensualyte we feyle, whych feylyng god wylle restore and fulfyll by werkyng of mercy and grace, plentuously flowyng in to vs of his owne kynde goodnesse" (14.57.576–77); ["And so in our substance we are full and in our sensuality we are lacking, and this lack God will restore and fill by the operation of mercy and grace, plentifully flowing into us from his own natural goodness" (291)]. Julian thus reaffirms the original integrity of self, the sacredness of sensuality as well as substance, with the second maternity she attributes to Jesus, the motherhood of re-creation or redemption.[60]

Julian's conception of redemption as reunification of the self explains her representation of Jesus as Mother in humankind's re-creation. While all three persons of the Trinity are substantially united to humankind, only the second person achieves union with the creaturely sensuality. In addition to Christ's special role in enlivening the body in the first act of creation, Julian calls attention to the second person's unique function in taking on a body in the Incarnation. According to the soteriology of Anselm's *Cur Deus homo*, Christ had to become human to make appropriate atonement for the original human transgression. Julian concurs in this conception of redemption.

> And for the worschypfull oonyng þat was thus made of god between the soule and þe body, it behovyd nedys to be þat mankynd shuld be restoryd fro doubyll deth, whych restoryng myȝt nevyr be in to the tyme that þe seconde person in the trynyte had takyn þe lower party of mankynd, to whome that hyest was onyd in the furst makyng. And theyse two pertyes were in Crist, the heyer and þe lower, whych is but one soule. The hyer perty was evyr in pees with god in full joy and blysse. The lower perty, whych is sensualyte, sufferyd for the saluacion of mankynd. (14.55.568–69)

> [And because of the glorious union which was thus made by God between the soul and the body, mankind had necessarily to be restored from a double death, which restoration could never be until the time when the second person in the Trinity had taken the lower part of human nature, whose highest part was united to him in its first creation. And these two parts were in Christ, the higher and the lower, which are only one soul. The higher part was always at peace with God in full joy and bliss. The lower part, which is sensuality, suffered for the salvation of mankind. (287–88)]

Because human sensuality is responsible for this rupture with the divine, Christ must take on flesh to make reparation. Through the Incarnation, Jesus as Mother makes possible the restoration of the human sensuality to its original partnership with the divine substance. As Mother in creation Jesus establishes the original union between the human substance and sensuality, and as Mother in re-creation, Jesus assumes a body in the Incarnation to reestablish that integral self. Conceiving of these embodiments enacted by Christ as motherhood, Julian of Norwich transforms the Augustinian denigration of woman as sign of the body. By envisioning a God who is both Father and Mother, she affirms that both literally and symbolically woman is created and re-created in the *imago Dei*.[61]

Jesus' motherhood in the creation and re-creation of humanity culminates in the third maternity that Julian attributes to Christ, the motherhood of working. As she summarizes: "I vnderstode thre manner of beholdynges of moderhed in god. The furst is grounde of oure kynde makyng, the seconde is takyng of oure kynde, and ther begynnyth the moderhed of grace, the thurde is moderhed in werkyng" (14.59.593); ["I understand three ways of contemplating motherhood in God. The first is the foundation of our nature's creation; the second is his taking of our nature, where the motherhood of grace begins; the third is the motherhood at work" (297)]. This third motherhood of Jesus, as Julian explains in chapter 60, refers to the process of restoring the obscured *imago Dei* in the soul, made possible by Christ's incarnation and motherhood of mercy, through the "forth spredyng" of grace;[62] or, as she puts it, "how that we be brought agayne by the motherhed of mercy and grace in to oure kyndly stede, where þat we ware in, made by þe moderhed of kynd loue, whych kynde loue nevyr leevyth vs" (14.60.594) ["how we are brought back by the motherhood of mercy and grace into our natural place, in which we were created by the motherhood of love, a mother's love which never leaves us" (297)]. A number of scholars have already demonstrated that Julian draws her discussion of the motherhood of working from Scripture and devotional writings rather than from theological discourse; her analysis is affective rather than metaphysical.[63] In this third instance, Jesus' maternity is associated not with a physical body but with the Mystical Body, the spiritual incorporation of those who will be saved into Christ through the church. Julian resembles other medieval writers in attributing to Christ the maternal acts of giving birth to the renewed soul in his passion, nourishing it with the sacraments, and disciplining the soul in order to teach virtue (14.60).

Julian directs most of her attention, however, to relating Jesus' motherhood in working to her theodicy. Using the analogy of a mother allowing a child to be injured in order to learn a valuable lesson, Julian contends that God allows sin "for it nedyth vs to falle, and it nedyth vs to see it; for yf we felle nott, we shulde nott knowe how febyll and how wrechyd we be of oure selfe, nor also we shulde not so fulsomly know þe mervelous loue of oure maker" (14.61.603) ["for we need to fall, and we need to see it; for if we did not fall, we should not know how feeble and how wretched we are in ourselves, nor, too, should we know so completely the wonderful love of our Creator" (300)]. Reiterating the metaphors of falling and rising she first enunciated in chapters 36 through 39 of Revelation Thirteen, Julian presents sin as a *felix culpa* not only for the human race in general, but also for each individual who will be saved. Although Julian draws on the devotional tradition in depicting this third maternity of Jesus, she presents the image in a distinctive manner that reflects the optimistic tone of her theodicy.[64] Her emphasis in chapter 61, for example, on the tender response of the mother to the fearful tears of the child conforms to her insistence throughout Revelations Thirteen and Fourteen that God feels no wrath toward sinful humankind. The concrete description of the shamed child crying for its mother's help (14.41.605–6) also suggests that Julian enlivens the devotional metaphor of Jesus as Mother with details derived from personal observation, perhaps of her own experience as a daughter or a mother.

Julian of Norwich ends the Fourteenth Revelation with a refrain that resonates through much of Revelation Thirteen: "Alle shalle be welle, and thou shalt see it thy selfe, that alle manner thyng shall be welle. And than shalle þe blysse of oure moderheed in Crist be new to begynne in the joyes of oure fader god, whych new begynnyng shall last, without end new begynnyng" (14.63.618); ["All will be well, and you will see it yourself, that every kind of thing will be well. And then will the bliss of our motherhood in Christ be to begin anew in the joys of our Father, God, which new beginning will last, newly beginning without end" (305)]. As this echo suggests, Julian develops the threefold maternity of Christ in chapters 53 through 63 to confirm and conclude the theodicy she initiates in Revelation Thirteen. Through her comparison between Jesus and a protective but enabling mother in chapter 61, she explains again that "synne is behouely" ["sin is necessary"] in order for human beings to achieve knowledge of themselves and of God. However, as Julian confidently reasserts, "alle shalle be welle." For Jesus as a Mother in working will perfect his children with the grace released through his suffering as Mother of mercy and so reunite the substance and sensuality to the original integrity established by his motherhood in creation. At the end of Revelation Fourteen, Julian recapitulates the ways in which Jesus is a Mother in creation, re-creation, and restoration of the divine image in humanity.

> Thus in oure very moder Jhesu oure lyfe is groundyd in the forseeyng wysdom of hym selfe fro with out begynnyng, with þe hye myght of the fader and þe souereyne goodnesse of the holy gost. And in the takyng of oure kynd he quyckyd vs, and in his blessyd dyeng vppon the crosse he bare vs to endlesse lyfe. And fro þat tyme, and now and evyr shall in to domysday, he fedyth vs and fordreth vs, ryght as þe hye souereyne kyndnesse of moderhed wylle, and as þe kyndly nede of chyldhed askyth. (14.63.616–17)

> [So in our true Mother Jesus our life is founded in his own prescient wisdom from without beginning, with the great power of the Father and the supreme goodness of the Holy Spirit. And in accepting our nature he gave us life, and in his blessed dying on the Cross he bore us to endless life. And since that time, now and ever until the day of judgment, he feeds us and fosters us, just as the great supreme lovingness of motherhood wishes, and the natural need of childhood asks. (304)]

Having given birth to the godly will from all eternity, Jesus as Mother in creation incorporates that *imago Dei* in a physical body. Through his assuming a human body in the motherhood of mercy, Jesus' sacrificial death makes possible the re-creation and perfection of the sinful sensuality through the self-awareness and perseverance engendered in each one who will be saved by the motherhood of grace. According to Julian of Norwich, then, Jesus is thrice a mother, closely associated with the human body as the principal life giver in creation, redemption, and restoration. By creating God in the androgynous images of Father and Mother, Julian thus reconceives the essential self as the complete humanity of male and female, body and soul.

Re-Visions and *A Book of Showings*

AFTER THE series of revelations of 13 May 1373, Julian of Norwich experienced no subsequent showings. Rather, she devoted almost a quarter of a century to acts of re-vision, exploring the implications of the revelations and composing at least two different accounts of them, the short and long texts. Just as she matured as a moral and mystical theologian during the twenty years separating her two texts, so she also developed as a writer.

The showings were obviously Julian's impetus to authorship. As the first English woman known to have written a book, she was keenly aware of the criticism that might be leveled against her for violating St. Paul's prohibition against women's teaching about spiritual matters. Given the conservatism of English spirituality and the fact that the writings of Continental women visionaries did not begin to become available in England until the 1390s, Julian had no tradition of female authority upon which to build.[1] In the short text she defends herself and explains the concern for her fellow Christians that compels her to write.

> Botte god for bede that ȝe schulde saye or take it so that I am a techere, for I meene nouȝt soo, no I mente nevere so; for I am a womann, leued, febille and freylle. Botte I wate wele, this that I saye, I hafe it of the schewynge of hym tha(t) es souerayne techare. Botte sothelye charyte styrres me to telle ȝowe it, for I wolde god ware knawenn, and mynn evynn crystene spede, as I wolde be my selfe to the mare hatynge of synne and lovynge of god. Botte for I am a womann, schulde I therfore leve that I schulde nouȝt telle ȝowe the goodenes of god, syne that I sawe in that same tyme that is his wille, that it be knawenn? (1:222)

> [But God forbid that you should say or assume that I am a teacher, for that is not and never was my intention; for I am a woman, ignorant, weak and frail. But I know very well that what I am saying I have received by the revelation of him who is the sovereign teacher. But it is truly love which moves me to tell it to you, for I want God to be known and my fellow Christians to prosper, as I hope to prosper myself, by hating sin

more and loving God more. But because I am a woman, ought I therefore to believe that I should not tell you of the goodness of God, when I saw at that same time that it is his will that it be known? (135)]

The showings, Julian contends, give her both the motivation and the authority to write. Despite her awareness of her vulnerability to criticism, she persists in her attempt to communicate the lessons of the revelations to others.

However, Julian herself did not initially understand the full meaning of the showings. As she explains in the long text, she progressed through three different stages of comprehension.

The furst is the begynnyng of techyng that I vnderstode ther in in the same tyme. The secunde is the inwarde lernyng that I haue vnderstonde there in sythen. The thyrd is alle the hole revelation fro the begynnyng to the ende whych oure lorde god of his goodnes bryngyth oftymes frely to the syght of my vnderstondyng. And theyse thre be so onyd, as to my vnderstondyng, that I can nott nor may deperte them. (14.51.519–20)

[The first is the beginning of the teaching which I understood from it at the time. The second is the inward instruction which I have understood from it since. The third is all the whole revelation from the beginning to the end, which our Lord God of his goodness freely and often brings before the eyes of my understanding. And these three are so unified, as I understand it, that I cannot and may not separate them. (269)]

Her illumination came gradually because Julian found the showings rich in implications: "I sawe and vnderstode that euery shewyng is full of pryvytes" (14.51.519); ["I saw and understood that every showing is full of secrets" (269)]. It took her fifteen years to reach the third stage of comprehension, the awareness of the revelation's unity.

And fro the tyme þat it was shewde, I desyerde oftyn tymes to wytt in what was oure lords menyng. And xv yere after and mor, I was answeryd in gostly vnderstondyng, seyeng thus: What, woldest thou wytt thy lordes menyng in this thyng? Wytt it wele, loue was his menyng. Who shewyth it the? Loue. (What shewid he the? Love.) Wherfore shewyth he it the? For loue. Holde the therin, thou shalt wytt more in the same. But thou schalt nevyr witt therin other withoutyn ende. (16.86.732–33)

[And from the time that it was revealed, I desired many times to know in what was our Lord's meaning. And fifteen years after and more, I was answered in spiritual understanding, and it was said: What, do you wish

136

to know your Lord's meaning in this thing? Know it well, love was his meaning. Who reveals it to you? Love. What did he reveal to you? Love. Why does he reveal it to you? For love. Remain in this, and you will know more of the same. But you will never know different, without end. (342)]

Julian needed an additional five years before she perceived the meaning of the "mysty example" of the lord and servant in which the "pryvytes of the reuelacyon be yet moch hyd" (14.51.519) ["secrets of the revelation were deeply hidden" (269)]. She explains the method by which she read this example, paying attention to each detail until she finally came to recognize the significance of this most subtle "inwarde goostely shewyng."

> For twenty yere after the tyme of the shewyng saue thre monthys I had techyng inwardly as I shall sey: It longyth to the to take hede to alle þe propertes and the condescions that were shewed in the example, though þe thyngke that it be mysty and indefferent to thy syght. I assen- tyd wylfully with grett desyer, seeing inwardly with avysement all the poyntes and the propertes that were shewed in the same tyme, as ferforth as my wytt and my vnderstandyng wylle serve. (14.51.520–21)

> [For twenty years after the time of the revelation except for three months, I received an inward instruction, and it was this: You ought to take heed to all the attributes, divine and human, which were revealed in the example, though this may seem to you mysterious and ambiguous. I willingly agreed with a great desire, seeing inwardly with great care all the details and the characteristics which were at that time revealed, so far as my intelligence and understanding will serve. (270)]

Julian regarded the process of coming to understand the revelations as a lifelong endeavor. She opens her long text's last chapter by indicating that her effort to attain the contemplative union with God disclosed by the showings will continue after she concludes this written account: "This boke is begonne by goddys gyfte and his grace, but it is nott yett performyd, as to my syght" (16.86.731); ["This book is begun by God's gift and his grace, but it is not yet performed, as I see it" (342)]. In other words, Julian considers her *Showings* a record of an as yet incomplete experience. Her account can achieve closure only in the ineffable beatific vision that she anticipates in the future.

The two different versions of *A Book of Showings* document Julian of Norwich's theological and literary maturation over a quarter of a century. A useful heuristic for analyzing the different stages in her comprehension of the revelations and the various phases in the composition of her book is Moore's distinction among three categories: the visionary experience itself (including both raw experience and incorporated interpretation as defined in chapter 1), and two different types of interpretation, reflexive and retrospective. Of these two interpretive modes, the former is the "interpretation spontaneously formulated either during the experience itself or immediately afterwards"; it corresponds to what Julian terms "the begynnyng of techyng." The latter is the "doctrinal interpretations formulated after the experience is over";[2] it corresponds to "the inwarde lernyng that I haue vnderstonde there in sythen." To exemplify these different layers of a mystical text Moore uses a passage from the final version of *A Book of Showings*.

> And I sawe no dyfference between god and oure substance, but as it were all god; and yett my vnderstandyng toke that oure substance is in god, that is to sey that god is god and oure substance is a creature in god. For the almyghty truth of the trynyte is oure fader, for he made vs and kepyth vs in hym. And the depe wysdome of þe trynyte is our moder, in whom we be closyd. And the hye goodnesse of the trynyte is our lord, and in hym we be closyd and he in vs. (14.54.562–63)

> [And I saw no difference between God and our substance, but, as it were, all God; and still my understanding accepted that our substance is in God, that is to say that God is God, and our substance is a creature in God. For the almighty truth of the Trinity is our Father, for he made us and keeps us in him. And the deep wisdom of the Trinity is our Mother, in whom we are enclosed. And the high goodness of the Trinity is our Lord, and in him we are enclosed and he in us. (285)]

Moore cites this passage as an example of the difference between experience and interpretation and between reflexive and retrospective interpretation. "The first part of the first sentence," he observes, "states what Julian saw ('And I sawe no dyfference . . .'), the second how she immediately understood it ('and yett my vnderstandyng toke . . .'), and the third with the following sentences, her more elaborate theological interpretation ('that is to sey . . .'). "[3] Moore's categories for analysis call attention to the fact that the long text of *A Book of Showings* is built up in three or more layers and that a comparison of these different interpretive moments reveals Julian in the process of maturing as a theologian and author. The short text, comprising her account of her visionary experience itself and her preliminary response to it, is the baseline against which her intellectual development over the quarter-century of completing the long text can be measured.

As I demonstrated in chapter 1, Julian's visionary experience as recorded in the short text of *A Book of Showings* presents three themes related to the three progressive stages of affective spirituality: compassion, contrition, and union with God. The first part of the short text, chapters 1 through 13, concentrates on compassion, and the second part, chapters 14 through 25, on contrition; the theme of union, less fully developed than the other two, is interspersed throughout. In the long text Julian maintains this basic "plot"[4] but increases the length of her book sixfold by expanding her accounts of certain showings, most notably Revelation Fourteen, and by including the retrospective interpretation she achieved over twenty years of meditation, particularly in Revelations Thirteen, Fourteen, and Sixteen. As Colledge and Walsh point out, Revelation Fourteen constitutes a third of the entire long text and only brief sections of chapters 41 and 43 and a phrase in chapter 47 appear in the short text.[5] That Julian so expanded *A Book of Showings* in the course of two decades or more, incorporating both new aspects of the original experience and substantial portions of retrospective interpretation, is not unusual. As Moore indicates, the relationship between visionary experience and interpretation is reciprocal: "for just as interpretation may change or develop in response to new features of experience or in light of new doctrinal understanding, so too may experience itself develop in accordance with changes in a mystic's beliefs, expectations, and intentions."[6] However, these stages in Julian's re-visions of her revelations and in her revision of the short text radically alter the genre and the design of the final version of *A Book of Showings*.

While the short text provides a relatively straightforward autobiographical account of her visionary experience, the long text combines this narration with discursive analysis. The extensive additions to the short text, particularly in Revelation Fourteen, seem to threaten the structure of Julian's book, for the story of the visionary experience is overwhelmed by the report of the subsequent meditation upon it. As Windeatt observes of the long text:

> A sense of its own narrative continuity no longer controls the book, for the first text has been turned inside out by those pressures in the implications which have impelled Julian's development as a mystical writer. In-

stead, the narrative of the original one-day's visionary experience is held in fractured form within what is now the real continuum of the meditations on the visions.[7]

Windeatt's statement calls attention to the hybrid quality of the final version of *A Book of Showings*. The tension between the narrative "plot" and the metanarrative commentary intensifies the strain Julian acknowledges between the unity of her vision's message and the diversity of her reflexive and retrospective interpretations. Revising her short text, she had to accommodate the different chronological and cognitive perspectives of the original vision and the twenty years of re-vision.

In disclosing her revelations in the long text, Julian not only sought to describe her initial experience, but also to communicate her understanding of that experience as it developed in time. She wished to convey simultaneously to her readers the three different moments of revelation: the immediacy of the showing, the gradual unfolding of its meaning through meditation and contemplation, and the realization of the unity of her vision. The attempt to re-create these moments in written language, however, posed difficult problems of structure and strategy for Julian. How does a writer engender in the regularly paced flow of words the incremental and erratic process of clarification that occurred over two decades? And how does she express in the sequential and differentiating medium of language the oneness of vision?

Julian of Norwich solves these problems through the design of the final version of *A Book of Showings*, for, as my analysis will demonstrate, she maintains the balance between the centrifugal force of expansion and the centripetal impulse of contraction through the explicit and implicit structuring of her material. To distinguish the immediate mystical engagement from her own retrospective interpretation, Julian divides the long text into sixteen showings, describing near the beginning of each section the sight, bodily or ghostly, or the words revealed to her. While preserving the integrity of the original revelations, this *ordinatio* demonstrates Julian's realization of the meaning of each showing in the new material incorporated throughout the long text. The sight or locution sets a theme for each showing that is reiterated and developed throughout that division. Julian conveys the gradual enhancement of her inward understanding by returning to this initial motif or theme throughout the showing, each time elaborating on it in more detail. Through this recursive, cumulative method of developing the revelations, she imitates the ruminative process of meditation.[8]

At the same time that Julian's meditation incites her to elaborate on her first version of the *Showings*, though, she also realizes that the long text belies the unity and simplicity of her revelations. To indicate this essential integrity of meaning within the apparent diversity of the long text, Julian draws connections among the sixteen showings through frequent cross-references. Colledge and Walsh observe that this technique reflects a deliberate strategy of her revision: "So long as she adheres to the sequence of the subject-matter of the short text, she does not employ cross-references; it is significant how many of such cross-references . . . occur in passages which have no correspondence with the first version." Julian's editors therefore conclude that the extensive cross-referencing in the long text "testifies to the meditative processes which had endowed Julian with her perception of the unity of the revelations and the relevance of each to the others, so that finally she can write of the last that it is 'conclusyon and confirmation to all the xv' (632.4)."[9] Through this method of recalling and anticipating showings, Julian invokes the unity of the "hole revelation fro the begynnyng to the ende" and affirms the oneness of her vision. Both within and among the sixteen showings Julian uses the woof of verbal echoes or cross-references to weave together the warp of her three themes—compassion, contrition, and union with God—into the interlace pattern of her *Book of Showings*.

The revisions that I will examine in this chapter indicate that over the years Julian paid more attention to the explicit and intrinsic structure of the long text as she came to conceive of it as a book and of herself as an author. Analyzing the differences between the two versions of *A Book of Showings*, Windeatt concludes that the final one is "a consciously 'presented' and arranged text, a literary redaction of the original account of experience, which through its expansions set the shewings within a wider frame of reference."[10] Julian's awareness of the "bookishness" of her long text is indicated by the apparatuses she includes—not only the clearly articulated divisions and cross-references already mentioned, but also a table of contents and frequent summaries in which she enumerates the points just covered or comments on her organization or techniques in a particular section. Her attention to literary effects is also revealed by her willingness to change the original sequence of events to achieve greater consistency or to add passages to anticipate themes developed in more detail later. By analyzing the strategy informing her revision and reorganization of the short text, I will demonstrate the magnitude of Julian's literary achievement in her final version of *A Book of Showings*.

I

The first clue to Julian's conception of her long text as a book is the table of contents with which this final version begins. This textual apparatus, which Colledge and Walsh believe to be of Julian's own composition,[11] provides an overview of the content and structure of *A Book of Showings* and functions as a map for her readers by shaping their expectations about this text's direction. By summarizing the showings in this opening chapter, Julian also indicates her conscious arrangement of material in the long text. The short text, divided into twenty-five chapters, provides only one level of organization; moreover, the chapters often include several visionary phenomena and only four of them correspond to the inception of a revelation in the long text.[12] Julian's division of the long text into sixteen revelations and the subdivision of each into one or more chapters indicate her desire to clarify the themes and structure of her showings for her readers. Each revelation begins with a description of a discrete visionary event and develops its implications through the course of her retrospective interpretation. This *ordinatio* enables Julian not only to highlight the visionary phenomena themselves, but also to elaborate upon them.[13]

This preliminary *capitulatura* also indicates the balance Julian must sustain between the book's unity of meaning and its diversity of manifestation. Her summary of the first showing exemplifies the organization of the whole.

> This is a reuelacion of loue that Jhesu Christ our endles blisse made in xvi shewynges, of which the first is of his precious crownyng of thornes; and ther in was conteined and specified the blessed trinitie with the incarnacion and the vnithing betweene god and mans sowle, with manie fayer schewynges and techynges of endelesse wisdom and loue, in which all the shewynges that foloweth be grovndide and ioyned. (1.281)

> [This is a revelation of love which Jesus Christ, our endless bliss, made in sixteen showings, of which the first is about his precious crowning of thorns; and in this was contained and specified the blessed Trinity, with the Incarnation and the union between God and man's soul, with many fair revelations and teachings of endless wisdom and love, in which all the revelations which follow are founded and connected. (175)]

On the one hand, Julian differentiates the sequential series of revelations contained in what she numbers as chapters 4 through 8. On the other, she insists—in both the first and last clauses of the sentence—on the identity of this series and all subsequent showings. Implying the enfolded layers of revelation with such words as *contained*, *specified*, *grounded*, and *joined*, Julian emphasizes that the multiplicity of the showings must not obscure the simplicity of their meaning.

An analysis of Julian's transformation of the short text's first seven chapters into Revelation One of the long text serves as a paradigm for the techniques she uses to enhance the design of her *Book of Showings*.[14] Revelation One consists of chapters 4 through 9 and includes material found in the short text in chapters 3 through 7. Several examples will demonstrate Julian's various efforts to revise the organization of the short text in order to achieve a more emphatic or logical arrangement in the long. To call attention to the visionary phenomena, for example, she changes the point at which several chapters begin. The first revelation opens with the description of Christ's bleeding head; in the short text this material is embedded in the first paragraph of chapter 3 rather than highlighted at its inception. Likewise, Julian moves her account of the three modes of showings from the beginning of chapter 7 in the short text to the end of chapter 9 in the long so that Revelation Two will open with the description of the second bodily showing, Christ's tortured face.

Julian is also willing to depart from the historical sequence of events for literary reasons. In chapters 4 and 5, for example, she changes the original order of the revelations, placing the showing of Mary at the time of the Annunciation before the "gostly sight of [God's] homely louyng" ["spiritual sight of [God's] familiar love"], because this new arrangement avoids the redundancy necessitated by a return to the theme of love at the end of chapter 4 in the short text. Another example of such reorganization occurs at the end of Revelation One. In order to move logically from what she has learned to what she will teach, Julian transfers the words she spoke to those around her bed from chapter 7 of the short text to chapter 8 of the long text. In the first version this account of her words to those around her comes after she discusses her responsibilities to her fellow Christians at large; in the revised version, this address to the immediate audience precedes her address to the wider audience of her book. This penultimate paragraph of chapter 8 also serves as transition to the concluding paragraph in which Julian presents herself as an intermediary between God and her "evyn cristen." In their revised order the three final paragraphs of chapter 8 demonstrate how the lessons of Revelation One flow from Julian herself to her acquaintances and then to her readers. Such rearrangement supports Windeatt's observation "that Julian was prepared to make radical changes in the presentation of material in [the long text], changes which altered the sequence of historical events to improve the effect of the over-all account."[15] Julian's attention to the inception of the chapters and her rearrangement of chronology reveal her concern with the structural and rhetorical effectiveness of her final version of *A Book of Showings*.

Since, as she claims in the table of contents, "all the shewynges that foloweth be grovndide and ioyned" ["all the revelations which follow are grounded and connected"] in Revelation One, the retrospective interpretation Julian incorporates into the long text parallels her revision at large by amplifying the theme of union with God and anticipating her later development of this theme in Revelation Fourteen. The added material consists of the first part of the second paragraph in chapter 4, the last paragraph of chapter 5, and chapters 6 and 7. Julian introduces the topic of union with God in her celebration in chapter 4's second paragraph of the unity of the Trinity and its persons' functions as maker, keeper, and lover. This addition amplifies her brief acknowledgment in the short text that her vision of Christ's bleeding head was accompanied by an understanding of the godhead: "With this syght of his blyssede passyonn, with the godhede that I saye in myn vndyrstandynge, I sawe that this was strengh ynow₃e to me, ₃e, vnto alle creatures lyevande that schulde be saffe agaynes alle the feendys of helle and agaynes alle gostelye enmyes" (1:211); ["With this sight of his blessed Passion and with his divinity, of which I speak as I understand, I saw that this was strength enough for me, yes, and for all living creatures who will be protected from all the devils of hell and from all their spiritual enemies" (131)]. In the long text Julian amplifies this remark about Christ's dual nature in the second paragraph of chapter 4.

> And in the same shewing sodeinly the trinitie fulfilled my hart most of ioy, and so I vnderstode it shall be in heauen without end to all that shall come ther. For the trinitie is god, god is the trinitie. The trinitie is our maker, the trinitie is our keper, the trinitie is our everlasting louer, the trinitie is our endlesse ioy and our bleisse, by our lord Jesu Christ, and in our lord Jesu Christ. And this was shewed in the first syght and in all, for wher Jhesu appireth the blessed trinitie is vnderstand, and to my sight. (1.4.294–96)

> [And in the same revelation, suddenly the Trinity filled my heart full of the greatest joy, and I understood that it will be so in heaven without end to all who will come there. For the Trinity is God, God is the Trin-

ity. The Trinity is our maker, the Trinity is our protector, the Trinity is our everlasting lover, the Trinity is our endless joy and our bliss, by our Lord Jesus Christ and in our Lord Jesus Christ. And this was revealed in the first vision and in them all, for where Jesus appears the blessed Trinity is understood, as I see it. (181)]

Julian's comprehension that Jesus is a member of the Trinity provides a doctrinal gloss on her reflexive interpretation of the vision of Christ's bleeding head: "Right so, both god and man, the same that sufferd for me" (1.4.294); ["he who just so, both God and man, himself suffered for me" (181)]. And her triad of *maker, keeper,* and *lover* echoes throughout the other additions to Revelation One and foreshadows the full exploration of the Trinity's union with humankind in Revelation Fourteen.

Julian's second addition to Revelation One, occurring at the end of chapter 5, expands her consideration of the second of the two examples she presents to articulate her ghostly sight of God's homely love, the analogy of the hazelnut. Her reiteration of *maker, keeper,* and *lover* in the middle of chapter 5 and, with only slight variation, in the new material at its end indicates its thematic connection to her first addition to the long text. The message of this ghostly showing of the hazelnut, as Julian hints in the middle of chapter 5, anticipates her explanation of the ontological union between the Trinity and humankind in Revelation Fourteen: "For till I am substantially vnyted to him I may never haue full reste ne verie blisse; þat is to say that I be so fastned to him that ther be right nought that is made betweene my god and me" (1.5.300); ["For until I am substantially united to him, I can never have perfect rest or true happiness, until, that is, I am so attached to him that there can be no created thing between my God and me" (183)]. In the retrospective interpretation concluding chapter 5, Julian amplifies the hazelnut analogy and its lesson about the meagerness of the universe with a discussion of the mutual longing of God and humankind. To her testimony that true rest can be found only in God, not in created things, Julian appends a prayer expressing her desire for union with the divine: "God of thy goodnes geue me thy selfe, for thou art inough to me, and I maie aske nothing that is lesse that maie be full worshippe to thee. And if I aske anie thing that is lesse, ever me wanteth; but only in thee I haue all" (1.5.302); ["God, of your goodness give me yourself, for you are enough for me, and I can ask for nothing which is less which can pay you full worship. And if I ask anything which is less, always I am in want; but only in you do I have everything" (184)]. Through this added prayer Julian enacts the love-longing that is one of the three wounds she desired of God prior to her visionary experience.

In chapter 6, new to the long text, Julian develops the first example of God's homely love presented in chapter 5, the metaphor of God as our clothing. The repetition of *the goodnes of god* throughout chapter 6 echoes Julian's reflexive interpretation of the first example in chapter 5: "he is all thing that is good" (1.5.299) ["he is everything which is good" (183)]; and the imagery of enclosure in the fourth paragraph recalls the preceding metaphor of clothing. By explaining that the goodness of God validates intercessary prayer, Julian prepares for the extended discussion of the types of and motives for prayer in chapters 41 through 44 of Revelation Fourteen. And just as chapter 6's discussion of prayer is followed by a consideration of Mary as an exemplar of contemplation in chapter 7's first paragraph, so chapter 44 includes a cross-reference to the showing of "the blessydfull soule of our lady sent Mary" ["the blessed soul of our Lady St. Mary" (256)] in the first revelation (14.44.483).

After expanding the description of the vision of Christ's bleeding head in the second through fourth paragraphs of chapter 7, Julian concludes with allusions to the motifs she will employ to explain the typological and tropological resolutions to the problem of evil following her discussion of prayer in Revelation Fourteen: the relationship between the lord and servant and the various unions between the Trinity and humankind. As it is introduced in chapter 7, the "open example" of the lord and servant provides further evidence of God's homely love, the topic of the ghostly sight of chapter 5. The lord's kindness to the servant, despite the great disparity in their ranks, is an allegory of Jesus' love for humankind and of the typological relationship between Adam and Christ that provides the historical solution to the problem of evil in chapter 51. Julian then introduces the familial metaphors that inform her explanation of the ontological bonds between the persons of the Trinity and humankind: "thys marvelous curtesy and homelynesse of oure fader, that is oure maker, in oure lorde Jhesu Crist, that is oure broder and oure sauior" (1.7.315); ["this wonderful courtesy and familiarity of our Father, who is our Creator, in our Lord Jesus Christ, who is our brother and our saviour" (189)]. Although she has not yet mentioned the analogy of Jesus as Mother, it will be incorporated into this familial pair by chapter 58 of Revelation Fourteen.

As this thematic analysis of the expansion of Revelation One demonstrates, Julian revises the introductory chapters of her long text so that they may serve as a prologue to *A Book of Showings*. Through these additions she prepares her readers for the subsequent development of the theme of union with God, particularly in Revelation Fourteen.[16] Not only do these accretions in Revelation One prefigure the themes and motifs presented later in the long text, they also demonstrate the intrinsic design of the final version of *A Book of Showings*. Julian retrospectively interprets, in reverse order of their initial presentation, the three visionary phenomena of Revelation One. The bodily sight of Christ's bleeding head (A) and the showing of Mary ghostly in bodily likeness (B) occur in chapter 4 and recur in chapter 7, with paragraph one considering Mary as an example of union with God (B) and paragraphs two through four expanding the description of the vision of the tortured Christ (A). The intervening paragraph in chapter 4 about the Trinity and Julian's reaction to her vision (C) anticipates the ghostly sight of homely love presented in chapter 5. Julian articulates this ghostly showing in two figures: she uses the metaphor of God as clothing to indicate that "he is all thing that is good" (C1) and the analogy of the hazelnut to represent the meagerness of the created universe (C2). The rest of chapter 5, including the two paragraphs appended to its end, examines this analogy (C2), and the discussion of prayer and the example of the lord and servant in chapter 6 further explore the goodness of God implied in the clothing metaphor (C1). The organization of Revelation One can be diagrammatically represented as a thematic triptych:

Chapters	4	5	6	7
Themes	A (C) B	C1 C2	C1	B A

By presenting the same topics (A, B, C1) in reverse order in the chapters surrounding the central discussion of the hazelnut analogy (C2) in chapter 5, Julian structures Revelation One to exemplify the enfolded layers of meaning within *A Book of Showings*.

As my analysis of other showings will reveal, such intricate interweaving occurs not only within a particular revelation, but also, with the system of cross-references, throughout the entire *Book of Showings*. This intrinsic design renders it difficult to read Julian's long text in a linear, chronological fashion; rather, it requires that the reader engage in the process of meditation, tracing the thematic strands throughout their various interlacings both within and among the sixteen revelations. The recursive structure of *A Book of Showings* thus enacts Julian's own process of composition and involves its readers in reenacting the gradual illumination achieved through meditation. By rereading the long text and ruminating on its themes, the reader should come to recognize the unity of meaning in Julian's diversity of articulation.

Although Julian's revision of Revelation One of the long text encapsulizes the various techniques she uses to enhance the literary qualities of her book, a brief analysis of several other showings will confirm the deliberateness of her strategy. Revelation Two, composed of chapter 10, epitomizes Julian's characteristic methods of organizing her material. Colledge and Walsh praise it as "a truly remarkable and wholly professional performance," as indeed it is. Comparing the versions of this showing in the short and long texts demonstrates, as her editors observe, Julian's "reflective and meditative processes at work."[17] The short text includes, at the end of chapter 7, only the first thirteen lines of the long text's version, the description of the vision of the tortured Christ's face and Julian's call for more light. In her revision, Julian expands her account of the second bodily showing more than sevenfold to ninety-six lines by incorporating the understanding she gradually acquired of this revelation and her reaction to it. Her meditation on Jesus' disfigured face brings to her mind the *imago Dei* in each individual disfigured by sin and the act of atonement through which Christ makes possible each one's restoration to the original state of likeness to God. Her reflection on her own reaction to the darkness engulfing her vision elicits Julian's thoughts about the prayerful response necessary for the individual to participate in this restoration. She elaborates on these two themes—restoration and prayer—throughout the *Showings*, but most extensively in Revelation Fourteen, where, as Paul Molinari has shown, she again conjoins them.[18]

The key term Julian explores in chapter 10 is *sight* as she learns to see beyond the literal, physical image to its spiritual reality. Both the bodily sight of Jesus' disfigured face and her response to it become the subjects of her meditation, and she alternately considers Christ's and the individual's roles in the redemption. The vision of Jesus' tortured countenance haunts Julian throughout the second revelation; at the center of chapter 10, in lines 33 through 67, she discloses her ultimate understanding of its significance. After affirming the validity of her bodily sight of Christ's disfiguration by its resemblance to the veronica, Julian transforms her literal vision into an allegorical one. Through the

course of her meditation, she comes to recognize the theological significance of Christ's discolored face as "a fygur and a lyknes of our
fowle blacke dede, which that our feyre bryght blessed lord bare for our
synne" (2.10.327–28) [a symbol and a likeness of our foul, black death,
which our fair, bright, blessed Lord bore for our sins (my translation)].
Playing on the divergence between the physical and spiritual realities,
Julian explains that the literal image of Christ's disfigured face is a
figurative likeness of the literal disfiguration, caused by sin, of God's
image in the human soul, but only through Christ's literal disfiguration
can the *imago Dei* be restored to its original likeness.

> And ryght as we were made lyke to the trynyte in oure furst makyng, our
> maker would þat we should be lyke to Jhesu Cryst oure sauiour in hevyn
> withouȝt ende by the vertu of oure (geyn) makyng. Then betwene thes
> two he would for loue and for worshipe of man make hym selfe as lyke
> to man in this deadly lyfe in our fowlhede and in our wretchednes as man
> myght be without gylt; wherof it menyth, as is before sayd, it was the
> ymage and the lyknes of owr fowle blacke dede where in our feyer bryght
> blessyd lorde hyd his godhede. (2.10.330)

> [And just as we were made like the Trinity in our first making, our Cre-
> ator wished us to be like Jesus Christ our saviour in heaven forever,
> through the power of our making again. Then, between these two, Jesus
> wished, for his love and for man's honour, to make himself as much like
> man in this mortal life, in our foulness and our wretchedness, as a man
> could be without sin; and this is meant where it is said before that the
> revelation symbolized and resembled our foul, black mortality, in which
> our fair, bright, blessed Lord concealed his divinity. (194–95)]

Her retrospective interpretation of the second bodily showing in Revelation Two introduces the concept central to the soteriology of Julian's
affective spirituality: Christ's willingness to take on the image, though
not the reality, of human sinfulness is what makes possible the restoration, through grace, of humankind's original resemblance to God. She
returns to this process of restoring the *imago Dei* in her discussion of
the second motherhood of Jesus, the motherhood of re-creation, in
Revelation Fourteen.

Julian's discussion of the atonement made possible through Christ's
human suffering is coupled with her reflection on the human response
necessary to actuate such restoration. Her own reaction to the bodily

sight provides a model for those who wish to be saved. After calling for
more light so that she can better see the disfigured face during her
visionary experience, she recognizes that Christ is her metaphoric light
and that seeing him through prevenient grace leads her to seek him by
cooperating with the initial gift of grace.

> For I *saw* him and *sought* him, for we be now so blynde and so vnwyse
> that we can never *seke* god till what tyme þat he of his goodnes shewyth
> hym to vs. And whan we *see* owght of hym graciously, then are we steryd
> by the same grace to *seke* with great desyer to *see* hym more blessedfully.
> And thus I *saw* him and *sought* him, and I had hym and wantyd hym; and
> this is and should be our comyn workyng in this life, as to my *sight*.
> (2.10.325–26, italics mine)[19]

> [For I *saw* him and *sought* him, for we are now so blind and so foolish
> that we can never *seek* God until the time when he in his goodness shows
> himself to us. And when by grace we *see* something of him, then we are
> moved by the same grace to *seek* with great desire to *see* him for our
> greater joy. So I *saw* him and *sought* him, and I had him and lacked him;
> and this is and should be our ordinary undertaking in this life, as I *see* it.
> (193, italics mine)]

Julian's paradox of simultaneously seeing and seeking expresses the
Augustinian theology of grace: the individual cannot cooperate with
grace until it first operates, through God's gift, in her. Julian reiterates
this paradox throughout chapter 10 by ringing verbal changes on the
terms *seeing* and *seeking* to indicate the stages in the individual's response to grace.

Julian's first amplification of the key terms occurs in paragraph three
as she explains how she achieved an understanding of what it means to
have a spiritual rather than a physical sight of God's presence. As she
pondered her call for more light during the second bodily showing at
some later, unspecified time, she visualized herself on the "sea
grounde" ["bottom of the sea"]. Through this imaginative experience,
Julian realizes that God wishes her to trust in his presence in all perils.
"For he will that we beleue that we *see* hym contynually, thow that vs
thynke that it be but litle; and in the beleue he maketh vs evyr more to
gett grace, for he will be *seen*, and he will be *sought*, and he will be
abyden, and he will be *trustyd*" (2.10.326–27, italics mine); ["For it is
God's will that we believe that we *see* him continually, though it seems
to us that the sight be only partial; and through this belief he makes us

always to gain more grace, for God wishes to be *seen*, and he wishes to be *sought*, and he wishes to be *expected*, and he wishes to be *trusted*" (194, italics mine)]. Through this rhetorical extension of her original phrase, Julian indicates the individual's need to respond to the gift of prevenient grace by cooperating through faith and prayer.

Julian rings further changes on the quartet of *seeing, seeking, abiding*, and *trusting* when she returns to the topic of prayer at line 68 of chapter 10. Continuing her discussion of the "comyn workyng" of grace in the individual, she distinguishes seeking from finding, the latter the result of a "speciall grace" granted when God so wills. But Julian immediately deconstructs her distinction by stating that "*sekyng* is as good as *beholdyng* for the tyme that he wille suffer the sowle to be in traveyle," for "a sowle that only resynyth hym (to) god with very *truste* eyther in *sekyng* or *beholdyng*, it is the most worshippe that he may do" (2.10.332–34, italics mine) ["*seeking* is as good as *contemplating*, during the time that he wishes to permit the soul to be in labour," for "the greatest honour which a soul can pay to God is simply to surrender itself to him with *true confidence*, whether it be *seeking* or *contemplating*" (195–96, italics mine)]. Julian again reiterates the divisions of this process of spiritual sight, first introduced at the end of her account of the imaginative vision of the sea floor, in the final paragraph of chapter 10, as she elaborates on the sequence of seeking, abiding, and trusting—all of which lead, in God's time, to beholding.

> It is gods wil that we haue iij thynges in our sekyng of his ȝefte. The furst is that we *seke* wyllfully and besyly withouȝte slowth ... ; the seconde þat we *abyde* hym stedfastely for his loue.... The iij is that we *truste* in hym myghtely, of fulle and tru feyth, for it is his wille þat we know that he shall aper sodenly and blyssydefully to all his lovers. (2.10.334–35, italics mine)

> [It is God's will that we receive three things from him as gifts as we seek. The first is that we *seek* willingly and diligently without sloth.... The second is that we *wait* for him steadfastly, out of love for him.... The third is that we have great *trust* in him, out of complete and true faith, for it is his will that we know that he will appear, suddenly and blessedly, to all his lovers. (196, italics mine)]

Through these verbal echoes Julian explains the process of gradual revelation that her own experience in coming to understand this second bodily showing enacts. In the course of chapter 10 she transforms her call for literal light—a response to the dimness of the bodily sight of Christ's disfigured face—into an explanation of the procedure of spiritual seeing that leads, ultimately, to a literal beholding, through either a mystical or a beatific vision, of God.

This analysis of Revelation Two demonstrates not only the meditative process by which Julian derived "inwarde lernyng" from the immediate visionary phenomena of the showings, but also her characteristic mode of presenting both the sight and the insight through the interlacing of themes in each revelation. In the single chapter that constitutes the second revelation, Julian uses a simple pattern of alternation to sketch the process of restoring the *imago Dei* as an interaction between God and humankind.

Paragraphs	1	2	3	4	5 to 68	5 from 68	6	7
Themes	A	B	B	A	A	B	B	B

She develops the first theme, Christ's act of atonement (A), in association with the description of the disfigured face of Jesus in paragraphs one, four, and five to line 68. She develops the second theme, the individual's cooperation with grace (B), in association with her own call for light in paragraphs two, three, five from line 68, six, and seven. The paragraphs in Revelation Two, diagramed thematically, thus follow an interlace pattern.

The same careful teasing out of the implications of the visionary phenomena and intertwining of themes is apparent in one of the longest of the showings, Revelation Thirteen. In its fourteen chapters, expanded from chapters 13 through 18 in the short text, Revelation Thirteen records the dialogue between Julian and God concerning the dilemma of evil. It proceeds as a conversation, with Julian either reporting or paraphrasing God's responses to the questions and doubts she expresses. Interlocution structures the fourteen chapters diachronically as Julian moves logically from general questions about the nature of evil and the reason God allowed it to more specific questions about individual salvation.

This sequential pattern is intersected at regular intervals, however, by synchronic commentaries that structure the revelation thematically and provide the transitions as Julian moves from one topic to another. Through such a metanarrative gloss in chapter 30, Julian indicates that this thirteenth revelation consists of three related themes: the two parts of the showing open to all Christians about the Savior and their salvation, and the secret of the great deed at the end of time by which the Trinity will resolve the problem of evil. Revelation Thirteen develops these three topics in a structural *emboîtement*, with the open showings of the Savior and salvation proceeding along parallel lines and framing the Lord's privy counsel hidden in the central chapters 32 through 34.[20]

In answer to her concern about evil, Julian receives an aural showing in chapter 27: "Synne is behouely, but alle shalle be wele, and alle shalle be wele, and alle maner of thynge shalle be wele" (13.27.405); ["Sin is necessary, but all will be well, and all will be well, and every kind of thing will be well" (225)]. She divides this locution into two parts, first defining sin as a defect that causes pain and then identifying Christ's passion as a comfort for this pain. In chapters 35 and 40, Julian returns to this association of sin with pain. First, she completes her analysis of the role God plays in evil. Alluding to Revelations One and Three, she concludes in chapter 35:

Alle þat oure lorde doyth is ryghtfull(e), and alle that he sufferyth is wurschypfulle; and in theyse two is comprehendyd good and evylle. For alle that is good oure lorde doyth, and þat is evyll oure lord sufferyth. I say nott that evylle is wurschypfulle, but I sey the sufferannce of oure lorde god is wurschypfulle, wher by hys goodnes shalle be know withouȝt ende, and hys mervelous mekenesse and myldhed by thys werkyng of mercy and grace. (13.35.433‾34)

[For our Lord does everything which is good, and our Lord tolerates what is evil. I do not say that evil is honourable, but I say that our Lord God's toleration is honourable, through which his goodness will be known eternally, and his wonderful meekness and mildness by this working of mercy and grace. (237)]

Although God allows and endures evil, such sufferance results in a higher good, the demonstration of divine mercy. But lest her readers should presume to test this mercy by sinning deliberately, Julian repeats in chapter 40 her warning about the pain caused by sin: "And to me was shewed none harder helle than synne, for a kynd soule hatyth no payne but synne; for alle is good but syn, and nought is yvell but synne" (13.40.458); ["And no more cruel hell than sin was revealed to me, for a loving soul hates no pain but sin; for everything is good except sin, and nothing is evil except sin" (247)]. Julian thus concludes Revelation Thirteen by persuading her readers that they must strive to avoid the hell on earth of sin above all else.

Since God allows evil in order to achieve a greater good, Julian is assured in the second part of the locution of chapter 27 that "alle shalle be wele, and alle shalle be wele, and alle maner of thynge shalle be wele" (13.27.405). Through most of Revelation Thirteen she explores this theme of consolation. In chapter 28 she clarifies the two types of compassion the Savior offers: "That one was the blysse that we be brought to, wher in he wille that we enioye. That other is for comfort in oure payne, for he wille that we wytt that it alle shalle be turned vs to wurschyp and to profyʒte by the vertu of hys passyon, and þat we wytte that we sufferyd ryght nought aloone, but with hym, and see hym oure grownde" (13.28.410–11); ["One was the bliss that we are brought to, in which he wants us to rejoice. The other is for consolation in our pain, for he wants us to know that it will all be turned to our honour and profit by the power of his Passion, and to know that we suffered in no way alone, but together with him, and to see in him our foundation" (227)]. In tribulation the Christian has the dual consolation of knowing Christ suffers with her in the present and will transform her pain to honor in the future bliss of heaven.

After turning in chapter 35 to the second open revelation, the individual's salvation, Julian reconsiders these two comforts in terms of the process of justification in chapters 37 and 38. In chapter 37 she comforts those who will be saved in their present tribulation with Christ's words, "I kepe the fulle suerly" ["I protect you very safely" (241)], and introduces the concept of the "godly wylle" (13.37.442, 43). Then in chapter 38 she reiterates, through the examples of sinners who have been saved like Mary Magdalen and John of Beverley, that the pain of sin will be transformed into future bliss and its shame into honor, and she explains the stages in the sacrament of penance that will enact this transformation of tribulation into glory in the present. For, as Julian recognizes in chapter 29, just as Christ has made amends for the greatest evil imaginable, the sin of Adam, so, she realizes in chapter 38, God can likewise render an individual's sin a *felix culpa* through the sacrament of penance. In chapter 40, the conclusion of Revelation Thirteen, Julian is assured that through this process of justification, Jesus' "goostly thyrst," first alluded to in chapter 31, will be sated and all will indeed be well for those who are saved as they are "onyd in blysse" ["made one in bliss" (246)] with the Trinity for all eternity. Revelation Thirteen thus begins and ends with the consolation that "alle shalle be wele" for those who will be saved. Chapters 28, 29, and 31 present this comfort in terms of the Savior's actions, and chapters 36 through 40 trace the stages of an individual's salvation. The framing structure of this showing can be diagramed as a series of embedded boxes:

Chapters				Chapters
30	Savior		salvation	36
28		present comfort in tribulation		37
		future bliss in heaven		38
29	Adam	*felix culpa* the contrite		39
31		Christ's spiritual thirst		40

Julian presents this first consolation about the Savior and salvation, apparent to "alle mankynde that is of good wylle" (13.30.414) ["all men who are of good will" (228)], in mirror images on both sides of Revelation Thirteen.

Despite the clear consolation offered for those who will be saved, Julian nonetheless wonders how "alle shalle be wele" for those who are not among the predestined. Her skepticism, she confesses, disrupts her contemplation: "ther be many dedys evyll done in oure syght and so gret harmes take that it semyth to vs that it were vnpossible that evyr it shuld com to a good end. And vp on thys we loke, sorow and morne therfore so that we can nott rest vs in the blyssedfulle beholding of god as we shuld do" (13.32.422–23); ["there are many deeds which in our eyes are so evilly done and lead to such great harms that it seems to us impossible that any good result could ever come of them. And we contemplate this and sorrow and mourn for it so that we cannot rest in the blessed contemplation of God as we ought to do" (232)]. In the innermost section of Revelation Thirteen, chapters 32 through 34, Julian explores the intimations she has received of "oure lordes prevy conncelle," a secret comfort that assuages her concern for the damned. The full revelation of this hidden consolation will not occur until the end of time: "There is a deed the whych the blessydfulle trynyte shalle do in the last day, as to my syght, and what the deed shall be and how it shall be done, it is vnknowen of alle creaturys whych are beneth Crist, and shall be tylle when it shalle be done" (13.32.423–24); ["There is a deed which the blessed Trinity will perform on the last day, as I see it, and what the deed will be and how it will be performed is unknown to every creature who is inferior to Christ, and it will be until the deed is done" (232)]. Although this revelation contradicts the church's teachings about the damnation of sinners, Julian receives no additional details about the apocalyptic deed.

Rather, she can only reconcile her showing with orthodox doctrine by maintaining faith in the authority of both these apparently contradictory statements of truth.

> And stondyng alle thys, me thought it was vnpossible that alle maner of thyng shuld be wele, as oure lorde shewde in thys tyme. And as to thys I had no other answere in shewyng of oure lorde but thys: That þat is vnpossible to the is nott vnpossible to me. I shalle saue my worde in alle thyng, and I shalle make althyng wele. And in thys I was taught by the grace of god that I shuld stedfast(l)y holde me in the feyth as I had before vnderstond, and ther with þat I shulde stonde and sadly beleue that alle maner thyng shall be welle, as oure lorde shewde in that same tyme. (13.32.425–26)

> [And all this being so, it seemed to me that it was impossible that every kind of thing should be well, as our Lord revealed at this time. And to this I had no other answer as a revelation from our Lord except this: What is impossible to you is not impossible to me. I shall preserve my word in everything, and I shall make everything well. And in this I was taught by the grace of God that I ought to keep myself steadfastly in the faith, as I had understood before, and that at the same time I should stand firm and believe firmly that every kind of thing will be well, as our Lord revealed at that same time. (233)]

In the short text Julian alludes to this apocalyptic deed only briefly in a paragraph that corresponds to her introduction of the topic in chapter 30. That all but three sentences of chapters 32 and 33 are new to the long text and that she takes great care in chapters 33 and 34 to affirm her faith in the Christian doctrine of damnation indicates that Julian realizes how much controversy the revelation of this "prevy conncelle" might stir up. Given this danger and the enigmatic nature of this showing, it is indeed appropriate that the third consolation be hidden at the center of Revelation Thirteen.

Chapters				*Chapters*
30	Savior		salvation	36
28		present comfort in tribulation		37
		future bliss in heaven		38
29	Adam	*felix culpa*	the contrite	39
31		Christ's spiritual thirst		40
32–35		"oure lordes prevy conncelle"		

156

Julian's design of the thirteenth revelation thus recapitulates its message, for the reader is carefully led to a glimpse of the Lord's secret locked in its structural *emboîtement*. Such a correspondence between meaning and presentation corroborates Julian's maturation as an author in the long text of *A Book of Showings*.

II

The technique of interlocking themes that Julian employs within the revelations is also the method she uses to connect the discrete showings to each other and to manifest the essential unity of her vision. In revising the short text, Julian numbered the revelations and, as mentioned above, included anticipatory and retrospective cross-references to indicate the relationships between and among the sixteen showings. These cross-references disclose the figures in the tapestry of themes that she develops in the long text. Tracing through the strands in the design of Revelation Thirteen, for example, demonstrates not only the recursive and cumulative process of meditation, as Julian elaborates on particular ideas in subsequent showings, but also the unity of her vision, as the discrete showings are woven together in thematic knots throughout the text.

As the cross-references indicate, Revelation Thirteen bears significant relation to Revelation Three. Julian begins chapter 27 by recalling her question about evil first posed in the third showing: "And after this I saw god in a poynte, that is to say in my vnderstandyng, by which syght I saw that he is in althyng. . . . [and] that he doth alle that is done. I merveyled in that syght with a softe drede, and thought: What is synne?" (3.11.336); ["And after this I saw God in an instant of time, that is to say in my understanding, by which vision I saw that he is present in all things. . . . [and] that he does everything which is done. I marvelled at that vision with a gentle fear, and I thought: What is sin?" (197)]. Although Julian defers further consideration of the problem of evil until Revelation Thirteen, she introduces in chapter 11 the phrase that becomes the refrain unifying the later showing: "alle thynges that is done is welle done" (3.11.338). Acknowledging in chapter 27 the reality of the pain caused by sin, Julian nonetheless confirms that all is well by elaborating on the three comforts God provides: the Savior, salvation, and the secret deed that will resolve the problem of evil at doomsday. Throughout the thirteenth showing she cites Revelation Three as proof for her optimism. In chapter 34, for example, she asserts: "Alle thys that I haue now seyde, and more as I shalle sey aftyr, is comfortyng ageynst synne; for in the thyrde shewyng, whan I saw that god doyth all that is done, I saw nott synn, and than saw I that alle is welle. But whan god shewyde me for synne, than sayde he: Alle schalle be wele" (13.34.431); ["All this which I have now said, and more which I shall presently say, is a solace against sin; for in the third revelation, when I saw that God does everything which is done, I did not see sin, and then I saw that all is well. But when God did show me about sin, then he said: All will be well" (236)]. In chapter 35 she invokes the third and the first revelations to support her conclusion about divine providence:

> For by the same blyssyd myght, wysdom and loue þat he made alle thyng, to þe same end oure good lorde ledyth it contynually, and ther to hym selfe shalle bryng it, and when it is tyme we shalle see it. And the ground of thys was shewyd in the furst [chapter 5], and more openly in þe thyrde, wher it seyth: I saw god in a poynt. (13.35.433)

> [For by the same blessed power, wisdom and love by which he made all things, our good Lord always leads them to the same end, and he himself will bring them there, and at the right time we shall see it. And the foundation of this was shown in the first revelation [chapter 5], and more plainly in the third, where it says: I saw God in an instant of time. (237)]

Through these references, Julian links together her discussion of the problem of evil in Revelations Three and Thirteen and confirms the latter through the former.

While Julian refers to the third revelation to affirm her confidence in divine providence, she cites other showings as proof of the specific comforts God provides for sinners. Chapter 31 is a nexus of such proof, for Julian alludes to three other showings to support the validity of this revelation about the heavenly union between the Trinity and the saved. Amplifying her brief allusion to Jesus' ghostly thirst in Revelation Eight, chapter 17, as she had promised, Julian explains the divine love-longing for humanity that will last until all those who are to be saved are gathered together in heaven at the end of time. She endorses her explication of Jesus' ghostly thirst with the proof of his dual claim to heaven as God, given in Revelation Twelve, and as man, given in Revelation Nine. Through these cross-references she knots together three preceding showings to confirm Christ's promise of eternal bliss for the saved as one of the ways in which all shall be well. Just as a medieval theologian cites scriptural verses to prove assertions or to resolve apparent contradictions, so Julian refers to her own revelations both to support and to explain her retrospective interpretations of her visionary experience.

Julian's care in developing this complex network of cross-references and verbal echoes becomes apparent in her efforts to reconcile the revelation of the Lord's privy counsel with the church's teachings about the damnation of sinners, for she resolves this apparent contradiction through a subtle thematic interlace linking Revelations Three, Five, Thirteen, and Fourteen. Obviously troubled by the discrepancy between her showing and orthodox doctrine, Julian requests a vision of hell or purgatory in chapter 33. Although this request is not granted, she cites Christ's reproof of the Devil in Revelation Five to affirm her faith in the doctrine of divine retribution for sin.

And for ought þat I culde desyer, I ne culde se of thys ryght nouȝt but as it is before seyde in þe fyfte shewyng, wher that I saw þe devylle is reprovyd of god and endlessly dampned. In whych syȝt I vnderstond þat alle the creatures þat be of the devylles condiscion in thys lyfe and ther in endyng, ther is no more mencyon made of them before god and alle his holyn then of the devylle, notwythstondyng that they be of mankynde, wheder thay haue be cristend or nought; for though the reuelation was shewde of goodnes, in whych was made lytylle mencion of evylle, ȝett I was nott drawen ther by from ony poynt of the feyth þat holy chyrch techyth me to beleue. (13.33.427–28)

[But for all that I could wish, I could see nothing at all of this except what has already been said in the fifth revelation, where I saw that the devil is reproved by God and endlessly condemned. By this sight I understand that every creature who is of the devil's condition in this life and so dies is no more mentioned before God and all his saints than is the devil, notwithstanding that they belong to the human race, whether they have been baptized or not; for although the revelation was shown to reveal goodness, and little mention was made in it of evil, still I was not drawn by it away from any article of the faith which Holy Church teaches me to believe. (234)]

159

Julian further substantiates her orthodoxy by referring to the visions of Christ's passion in Revelations One, Two, Four, and Eight. Although the condemnation of the Jews was not mentioned in these showings, she argues, it is nonetheless a point of faith that she accepts. Despite the discrepancy between the showing of the Lord's "prevy conncelle" and the church's teachings, Julian attempts to affirm both in Revelation Thirteen.

However, Julian returns to the problem in Revelation Fourteen. Still puzzled by the contradiction between these two authorities, she reconsiders the issue from the divine rather than the human perspective in chapters 45 through 52. Julian signals the recurrence of this issue by alluding to her previous discussion in Revelation Thirteen. Distinguishing between God's judgment and humankind's in chapter 45, she refers to the relevant chapters in the preceding showing through verbal echoes:

> The furst dome, whych is of goddes *ryghtfulnes*, and that is of his owne hygh endlesse loue, and that is that feyer swete dome that was *shewed in alle the feyer revelation in whych I saw hym assign(e) to vs no maner of blame*. And though theyse were swete and delectable, ȝytt only in the beholdyng of this I culde nott be fulle esyd, and that was for the *dome of holy chyrch*, whych I had before vnderstondyn and was contynually in my syght. And therfore by this dome me thought that me behovyth nedys *to know my selfe a synner*. And by the same dome I vnderstode that *synners be sometyme wurthy blame and wrath*, and theyse two culde I nott see in god. (14.45.487, italics mine)

> [The first judgment, which is from God's *justice*, is from his own great endless love, and that is that fair, sweet judgment which was *shown in all the fair revelations in which I saw him assign to us no kind of blame*. And though this was sweet and delectable, I could not be fully comforted only by contemplating it, and that was because of the *judgment of Holy Church*, which I had understood before and which was continually in my sight. And therefore it seemed to me that by this judgment I must necessarily *know myself a sinner*. And by the same judgment I understood that *sinners sometimes deserve blame and wrath*, and I could not see these two in God. (257, italics mine)]

Although Julian does not refer to Revelation Thirteen by number, she repeats crucial phrases that recall her previous discussion. The phrase "no maner of blame" appears in chapters 27, 28, and 39. However, it seems to contradict the doctrine about the damnation of sinners confirmed in chapter 33 by a cross-reference to Christ's reproof of the Devil in Revelation Five and in chapter 37 by Julian's recognition of her own sinfulness.

Following the allusion to God's wrath back to its origin in Revelation Five indicates how early in the long text Julian anticipates this nexus in Revelation Fourteen, for she adds a passage to the revised chapter 13 insisting on God's lack of anger in reproving the Devil:

> But in god may be *no wrath*, as to my syght, for our good lorde endelessly havyng regard to his awne worshyppe, and to the profyghte of all them that shal be savyd, with myght and ryght he withstondyth the reprovyd, the which of malyce and of shrewdnes besye them to contrary and do against goddes wyll. (5.13.347–48, italics mine)

> [But in God there can be *no anger*, as I see it, and it is with power and justice, to the profit of all who will be saved, that he opposes the damned, who in malice and malignity work to frustrate and oppose God's will. (201, italics mine)]

Although God continually thwarts the Devil's plots against his will, he does so without wrath. Julian's next reference to God's lack of anger in Revelation Eight introduces another distinction crucial to her resolution of the problem of sin in the fourteenth showing, for she attributes to her "outwarde party" her own momentary regret for having asked to suffer with Christ.

> And though I as a wrech hath repentyd me, as I seyde before, yff I had wyst what payne it had be, I had be loth to haue prayde it, heer I saw werely that it was grugyng and dawnger of the flessch without assent of the soule, *in whych god assignyth no blame*. Repentyng and wylfulle choyse be two contrarytes, whych I felt both at that tyme; *and tho be two partes, that oon outward, that other inwarde. The outwarde party is our dedely flessh, whych is now in payne and now in woo. . . . The inward party is a hygh and a blessydfulle lyfe, which is alle in peece and in loue.* (8.19. 371–72, italics mine)

> [And though like a wretch I had regretted what I had asked, as I have said—if I had known the pain for what it was I should have been loath to pray for it—now I saw truly that this was the reluctance and domination of the flesh, to which my soul did not assent, and *to which God imputes no blame*. Reluctance and deliberate choice are in opposition to

one another, and I experienced them both at the same time; and these are two parts, one exterior, the other interior. *The exterior part is our mortal flesh, which is sometimes in pain, sometimes in sorrow. . . . The interior part is an exalted and blessed life which is all peace and love.* (212, italics mine)]

In Revelation Fourteen, Julian relates these two parts of herself to the soul's substance and sensuality and to the difference between the divine and human perspectives.

God's judgment differs from humankind's, Julian contends, because "*God demyth vs vpon oure kyndely substance,* whych is evyr kepte one in hym, hole and safe, without ende; and this dome is *of his ryghtfulhede.* And *man demyth vppon oure channgeable sensualyte,* whych semyth now oone and now a nother" (14.45.486, italics mine) ["*God judges us in our natural substance,* which is always kept one in him, whole and safe, without end; and this judgment is *out of his justice.* And *man judges us in our changeable sensuality,* which now seems one thing and now another" (256, italics mine)]. That God's dispassionate judgment of sinners must be distinguished from humankind's harsh and variable one is an observation Julian first makes in Revelation Three:

> *Alle [God's] domys be esy* and swete, and to grett ees bryngyng the sowle that is turned fro the beholdyng of the *blynd demyng of man* in to the feyer swette demyng of our lorde god. *For man beholdyth some dedys wele done and some dedys evylle, and our lorde beholdyth them not so,* for as alle that hath beyng in *kynde* is of gods makyng, so is alle thyng that is done in properte of gods doyng. (3.11.339, italics mine)

> [*All [God's] judgments are easy* and sweet, bringing to great rest the soul which is converted from contemplating men's blind judgments to the judgments, lovely and sweet, of our Lord God. *For a man regards some deeds as well done and some as evil, and our Lord does not regard them so,* for everything which exists in *nature* is of God's creation, so everything which is done has the property of being of God's doing. (198, italics mine)]

Julian places this distinction between divine and human judgment in Revelation Three after a brief discussion of God's righteousness and mercy. "And thus as it myghte be for the tyme, the *ryghtfulnes* of gods workyng was shewyd to the sowle. . . . *And in a other tyme he shewde for beholdyng of synne nakedly, as I shall say after, when he vsyth workyng of mercy and grace*" (3.11.338–39, italics mine); ["And thus the *rightfulness*

162

of God's dealing was shown to the soul. . . . *And on another occasion he did show sin, undisguised, for my contemplation, as I shall tell afterwards, when he performs works of mercy and grace*" (198, italics mine)]. This anticipation of chapter 35 of Revelation Thirteen is reinforced, as was shown earlier, by a cross-reference invoking this point of Revelation Three in chapter 35, where Julian expands the topic of God's righteousness and mercy. And when she further elaborates on these topics in Revelation Fourteen, she initiates her discussion with allusions to Revelation Thirteen.

Chapter 45 provides a paradigm of the recursive, accumulative method Julian employs to develop her retrospective interpretation in the long text. Returning to the same issues, each time enhancing and expanding them, she marks the connections between and among her widely dispersed analyses through cross-references or verbal echoes. As Julian commences her resolution of the problem of evil in chapter 45, for example, she gathers together the relevant threads of her previous discussions of this topic through her reference to Revelation Thirteen and her repetition of the key phrase *no maner of blame*. Following this phrase, or its cognate, *no wrath*, back to their initial appearances in Revelations Five and Eight shows that Julian already anticipates in these earlier showings the distinction between substance and sensuality so crucial to her resolution to the problem of evil in Revelation Fourteen. And in pointing to the difference between divine and human judgments and between God's righteousness and Jesus' mercy when she first articulates the dilemma of evil in Revelation Three, she provides the very terms needed for its solution in Revelation Fourteen. That Julian added all these enchained passages in revising the short text confirms the deliberateness with which she develops the interlace structure of the long text.

Intricate as they are, Julian's cross-references and verbal echoes demonstrate her method of "reading" her revelations and directing her audience's reading. Over the course of two decades of meditation, she was able to comprehend both the complexity and the unity of her visionary experience. Although constrained by the sequential medium of language, she tries to present in *A Book of Showings* her own process of illumination and to balance the centrifugal impulse of analytical articulation against the centripetal force of contemplative quietude. Through the recursive interlace structure of her long text, Julian engages her audience in a meditative procedure that forces them to comprehend for themselves the unity in diversity of the showings.

The first woman known to have written in English, Julian of Norwich composed the two versions of her *Book of Showings* during the period when Chaucer, Gower, Langland, and the *Pearl* poet were forging a literary idiom from the vernacular Middle English.[21] Whether or not she knew their works, her prose bears some resemblance to their poetry. Though it did not circulate widely during her lifetime or achieve canonical status as literature, Julian's long text exhibits, as I have demonstrated in this chapter, much the same comprehensiveness and complexity as the literary texts of her more widely admired male contemporaries. Despite many obvious differences of subject matter, genre, and style, Julian, like these Ricardian poets, exhibits "a strongly literary sense of form and structure in [her] handling of text-divisions" and she eschews linear form in favor of a more recursive structure.[22] *A Book of Showings* therefore deserves to be acknowledged as the prose masterpiece of Ricardian literature.

✳ *Conclusion* ✳

JULIAN of Norwich's *Book of Showings* has achieved a larger audience during this century than at any other time in the six hundred years since her completion of the long text around 1393. This interest in Julian's book was originally incited by Grace Warrack's translation of it into modern English in 1901.[1] By midcentury Warrack's rendition was in its thirteenth edition, and several other translations became available during the next decades. Recognizing the importance of Julian's *Showings*, the Paulist Press chose to publish both the short and long texts in its Classics of Western Spirituality series. Judging by the number of editions or adaptations of *A Book of Showings* now in print, Julian's reputation has never been greater.

The compelling resonance of Julian's thought for a contemporary audience derives from her theological range and originality. More than thirty years ago, Thomas Merton, the foremost contemplative of the twentieth century, recognized Julian's preeminence:

> There can be no doubt that Lady Julian is the greatest of the English mystics. Not only that, but she is one of the greatest English theologians. . . . Actually, in Julian of Norwich, we find an admirable synthesis of mystical experience and theological reflection, ranging from "bodily visions" of the passion of Christ to "intellectual visions" of the Trinity, and from reflections on the creation and providence to intuitions penetrating the inmost secret of the redemption and divine mercy. . . .
>
> In a word, Julian of Norwich gives a coherent and indeed systematically constructed corpus of doctrine, which has only recently begun to be studied as it deserves.[2]

Although the preceding study has focused on the medieval context of her ideas, I wish to amplify Merton's observation by pointing to the ways in which the long text of *A Book of Showings* presages certain directions in contemporary religious thought.

The assurance that "alle shalle be wele" is undoubtedly the phrase most often associated with Julian's name in the twentieth century. Epitomizing her teleological solution to the problem of evil, this statement may well have gained renown because of the currency "soul-making" theodicies have achieved during the last two hundred years. First articulated by Irenaeus and the Hellenistic Fathers in the early Christian era, and introduced again by the Protestant theologian Friedrich

Schleiermacher at the beginning of the nineteenth century, such theodicies rest on the assumption that humankind "is in process of becoming the perfected being[s] whom God is seeking to create."[3] Although the details with which the theologians in this tradition develop their ideas are influenced by their differing religious cultures, they, like Julian, concentrate on the reparation for sin rather than the transgression itself and emphasize humankind's growth in goodness rather than their guilt. Similarly, more recent thinkers like Schleiermacher and Pierre Teilhard de Chardin, though using the vocabulary of their respective eras, interpret Genesis 3 not as a literal narrative about humanity's fall from perfection, but, like Julian, as a myth of embodiment, of humanity's entry into a material world in which individuals can attain consciousness of God.[4] The remarkable resemblance of her solution to the problem of evil to the "soul-making" theodicies of the last two centuries attests the validity and originality of Julian's thought.

The other aspect of the long text of *A Book of Showings* that has particularly captured the attention of her current audience is, of course, Julian's analogy of Jesus as Mother. Although this analogy has a long and distinguished medieval heritage, she develops it with greater precision than any of her predecessors. As feminist theologians search for ways to modify the prevailing patriarchal assumptions of Christianity, Julian's discussion of Jesus' maternal functions serves as a paradigm for creating God in a truly human image. As she explains, human persons, whether female or male, are created by both God the Father and Jesus the Mother as a union of body and soul incorporating qualities associated with both sexes. In rejecting the Augustinian model that attributes the *imago Dei* to the masculine reason alone, Julian cautions about the dangers of reiterating the traditional identification of woman exclusively with the body. Instead, her analogy of Jesus as Mother provides an androgynous ideal of personhood to displace the dominant binary opposition of sexual difference.

Finally, as the first English woman identified as an author, Julian of Norwich sacrificed much in order to gain "a room of her own" in which to write.[5] Choosing to live in an anchorhold for at least the last part of her life, Julian was immured to symbolize her death to the world. Despite these constraining conditions, she achieved a learning and a creativity that otherwise would not have been possible for her as a woman in medieval society. As we strive over the next decades to reclaim the mothers of Christian culture, let us celebrate the indomitable spirit of women like Julian of Norwich.

* *Notes* *

*Unless another source is cited, the translations
in the text are my own.*

Introduction

1. *A Book of Showings to the Anchoress Julian of Norwich*, ed. Edmund Colledge, O.S.A., and James Walsh, S.J., 2 vols., Studies and Texts 35 (Toronto: Pontifical Institute of Mediaeval Studies, 1978), 1:201. Quotations in Middle English from the short text are documented parenthetically by 1 preceding the page number, indicating their location in Part One, the first volume of this edition. Quotations in Middle English from the long text are documented parenthetically by revelation, chapter, and page number from Part Two, the second volume of this edition. Modern English translations are documented parenthetically by page number from Julian of Norwich, *Showings*, trans. Edmund Colledge, O.S.A., and James Walsh, S.J., Classics of Western Spirituality (New York: Paulist Press, 1978). For a critique of Colledge and Walsh's choice of the Paris manuscript of the long version as their copy-text, see Marion Glasscoe, "Visions and Revisions: A Further Look at the Manuscripts of Julian of Norwich," *Studies in Bibliography* 42 (1989): 103–20.

2. Colledge and Walsh, "Introduction," *A Book of Showings*, 1:33–38.

3. *The Book of Margery Kempe*, ed. Sanford B. Meech and Hope Emily Allen, Early English Text Society, o.s., 212 (London: Early English Text Society, 1940), 42; *The Book of Margery Kempe*, trans. B. A. Windeatt (Harmondsworth, England: Penguin Books, 1985), 77.

4. My discussion of the extant manuscripts and the relationship between the short and long texts summarizes the more thorough explanation in Colledge and Walsh, "Introduction," *A Book of Showings*, 1:1–25.

5. Colledge and Walsh indicate all of the differences between the short and the long texts in the notes to their edition of *A Book of Showings*. I discuss the themes of the short text in greater detail at the end of chapter 1 and analyze some examples of Julian's revisions in chapters 2 and 6.

6. In "The Composition of Julian of Norwich's *Revelation of Love*," *Speculum* 68 (1993): 637–83, published after the completion of my study, Nicholas Watson argues that the short text was composed between 1382 and 1388 and the long text completed in the early fifteenth century. If Watson's dating is accepted, it would allow for the influence on Julian of Continental mystics like Bridget of Sweden, Catherine of Siena, Mechtild of Hackeborn, Suso, and Ruusbroec, whose writings began to circulate in England during the 1390s (653–57). I am grateful to Professor Watson for providing me with a copy of his essay prior to its publication.

167

7. Watson explains the constraints that Julian of Norwich faced as an English woman writer, ibid., 642–57.

8. Karma Lochrie identifies this feature of mystical discourse and discusses its relationship to gender in *Margery Kempe and Translations of the Flesh*, New Cultural Studies (Philadelphia: University of Pennsylvania Press, 1991), chapter 2.

9. Recent books about Julian of Norwich are addressed to believers; these include Grace Jantzen, *Julian of Norwich: Mystic and Theologian* (New York: Paulist Press, 1988); Brant Pelphrey, *Christ Our Mother: Julian of Norwich*, The Way of the Christian Mystics 7 (Wilmington, Del.: Michael Glazier, 1989); Sheila Upjohn, *In Search of Julian of Norwich* (London: Darton, Longman and Todd, 1989); Joan Nuth, *Wisdom's Daughter: The Theology of Julian of Norwich* (New York: Crossroad, 1991); and Ritamary Bradley, *Julian's Way: A Practical Commentary on Julian of Norwich* (London: HarperCollins *Religious*, 1992).

10. Peter Moore, "Mystical Experience, Mystical Doctrine, Mystical Technique," in *Mysticism and Philosophical Analysis*, ed. Steven T. Katz (London: Sheldon Press, 1978), 111. See also idem, "Christian Mysticism and Interpretation: Some Philosophical Issues Illustrated in the Study of the Medieval English Mystics," in *The Medieval Mystical Tradition in England: Exeter Symposium 4*, ed. Marion Glasscoe (Cambridge: D. S. Brewer, 1987), 154–76.

11. Nicholas Watson, *Richard Rolle and the Invention of Authority*, Cambridge Studies in Medieval Literature 13 (Cambridge: Cambridge University Press, 1991), proposes that a literary-critical reading of mystical texts should concentrate on "a mystical writer's 'predicament' in formulating doctrinal positions, articulating an appropriately didactic discourse and describing mystical experience," and should look "at the specifically *mundane* pressures that beset a mystical text, impelling it towards complex and ambiguous claims for its own status as an embodiment of truth" (2). Watson provides an excellent example of this approach to Julian of Norwich in "'A Good Lord, How Myte Al Ben Wele?' Julian of Norwich's Self-Invention as a Theologian," a paper he delivered at a conference entitled "The Roles of Women in the Middle Ages," sponsored by the Binghamton Center for Medieval and Early Renaissance Studies in October 1992. I thank Professor Watson for sharing this paper with me.

12. For information on the education of women, see Nicholas Orme, *English Schools in the Middle Ages* (London: Methuen, 1973), 52–55; and idem, "The Education of the Courtier," in *Education and Society in Medieval and Renaissance England* (London: Hambledon Press, 1989), 153–75, especially 170–71. In *Medieval English Nunneries, c. 1275–1535* (1922; reprint, New York: Biblo and Tannen, 1964), Eileen Power contends that fourteenth-century nuns had

no better acquaintance with Latin than lay women of equivalent social rank (237–60) and that they provided a scanty education for only a small number of upper- and wealthy middle-class girls (260–84, 568–81). Power shows that Carrow Abbey, which may have owned Julian's anchorhold, educated children in the thirteenth and fourteenth centuries (267–68).

13. Bella Millett demonstrates that anchoresses, especially in the twelfth and thirteenth centuries, ranged the spectrum from learned to illiterate, in "Women in No Man's Land: English Recluses and the Development of Vernacular Literature in the Twelfth and Thirteenth Centuries," in *Women and Literature in Britain, 1150–1500*, ed. Carol Meale, Cambridge Studies in Medieval Literature 17 (Cambridge: Cambridge University Press, 1993), 86–103. Judging by Rolle's and Hilton's treatises, it was not unusual in the fourteenth century for anchoresses who had been nuns to read at least the vernacular.

14. Josephine Koster Tarvers, "'Thys ys my mystrys boke': English Women as Readers and Writers in Late Medieval England," in *The Uses of Manuscripts in Literary Studies: Essays in Memory of Judson Boyce Allen*, ed. Charlotte Morse, Penelope Doob, and Marjorie Woods, Studies in Medieval Culture 31 (Kalamazoo, Mich.: Medieval Institute Publications, 1992), 305–27. Three essays in *Women and Literature in Britain, 1150–1500*, ed. Carol Meale, Cambridge Studies in Medieval Literature 17 (Cambridge: Cambridge University Press, 1993), are also of interest: Felicity Riddy, "'Women talking about the things of God': A Late Medieval Sub-Culture," 104–27; Carol Meale, "'. . . alle the bokes that I haue of latyn, englisch, and frensch': Laywomen and Their Books in Late Medieval England," 128–58; and Julia Boffey, "Women Authors and Women's Literacy in Fourteenth- and Fifteenth-Century England," 159–82.

15. See *The Book of Margery Kempe* 1:62, in Meech and Allen, 54; in Windeatt, 192–93. For discussions of Margery's knowledge of religious culture, see Clarissa Atkinson, *Mystic and Pilgrim: The Book and the World of Margery Kempe* (Ithaca: Cornell University Press, 1983); and Lochrie, *Margery Kempe and Translations of the Flesh*, chapter 3. For an overview of the means of transmission of religious culture to the laity of all classes in fifteenth-century England, see Eamon Duffy, *The Stripping of the Altars: Traditional Religion in England c. 1400–c. 1500* (New Haven: Yale University Press, 1992), especially chapters 2, 6, and 7; and Jonathan Hughes, *Pastors and Visionaries: Religion and Secular Life in Late Medieval Yorkshire* (Woodbridge, Suffolk: The Boydell Press, 1988).

16. Jantzen, *Julian of Norwich*, 15–20, surveys the different assessments offered of Julian's learning and speculates about the kind of education she might have received.

17. Brant Pelphrey argues that Julian was uneducated in *Love Was His Meaning: The Theology and Mysticism of Julian of Norwich*, Salzburg Studies in

English Literature, Elizabethan & Renaissance Studies (Salzburg: Institut für Anglistik und Amerikanistik, Universität Salzburg, 1982), 18–28; see also idem, *Christ Our Mother*, 15.

18. Colledge and Walsh, "Introduction," *A Book of Showings*, 1:44 and 43–59; see also their discussion of Julian's learning in "Editing Julian of Norwich's *Revelations*: A Progress Report," *Mediaeval Studies* 38 (1976): 404–27; and Sister Anna Maria Reynolds, C.P., "Some Literary Influences in the *Revelations* of Julian of Norwich (c. 1342–post-1416)," *Leeds Studies in English and Kindred Languages*, nos. 7 and 8 (1952): 18–28.

19. M. T. Clanchy, *From Memory to Written Record: England, 1066–1307* (Cambridge: Harvard University Press, 1979), 183.

20. Alexander Murray, *Reason and Society in the Middle Ages* (Oxford: Clarendon Press, 1978), 300.

21. Clanchy, *From Memory to Written Record*, 185.

22. Richard Rolle, *The Fire of Love*, trans. Clifton Wolters (London: Penguin Books, 1972), 46–47. Hope Emily Allen argues that Rolle began writing the *Incendium amoris* around 1343, in *Writings Ascribed to Richard Rolle, Hermit of Hampole*, The Modern Language Association Monograph Series (New York: D. C. Heath, 1927), 228; but Watson contends it is an earlier work, in *Richard Rolle and the Invention of Authority*, 277–78.

23. Nicholas Love, *Nicholas Love's* Mirror of the Blessed Life of Jesus Christ: *A Critical Edition*, ed. Michael G. Sargent, Garland Medieval Texts 18 (New York: Garland Publishing, 1992), 10.

24. Riddy, "'Women talking about the things of God,'" 111–17, discusses this phrase as a sign of the "feminised space" and oral culture of nuns and devout lay women in contrast to the Latin literacy of the male clergy.

25. In "Religion as a Cultural System," in *Anthropological Approaches to the Study of Religion*, ed. Michael Banton (New York: Frederick A. Praeger, 1966), Clifford Geertz provides the definition of culture to which I refer: "an historically transmitted pattern of meanings embodied in symbols, a system of inherited conceptions expressed in symbolic forms by means of which men communicate, perpetuate, and develop their knowledge about and attitudes toward life" (3).

26. Moore, "Mystical Experience, Mystical Doctrine, Mystical Technique," 108.

27. Ibid., 109.

28. Ibid., 113; see his argument against excluding visions and locutions from serious consideration as mystical experiences, on 119–20.

29. Julian reiterates this division in the corresponding passage in the long text, 1.9.323, and at 16.73.666. Paul Molinari, S.J., *Julian of Norwich: The Teaching of a Fourteenth Century English Mystic* (1958; reprint, n.p.: The Arden Library, 1979), 60–70, contends that Julian's three types of phenomena do not correspond to the traditional scheme of supernatural apprehensions derived

from Augustine; however, Nicholas Watson, "The Trinitarian Hermeneutic in Julian of Norwich's *Revelation of Love*," in *The Medieval Mystical Tradition in England, Exeter Symposium 5*, ed. Marion Glasscoe (Cambridge: D. S. Brewer, 1992), 85–86, argues that Julian uses the Augustinian terminology although it is not always adequate to her purposes.

30. Watson demonstrates that it is both impossible and unnecessary to distinguish Julian's raw experience from her incorporated interpretation, in "The Trinitarian Hermeneutic in Julian of Norwich's *Revelation of Love*."

31. See John P. H. Clark, "Late Fourteenth-Century Cambridge Theology and the English Contemplative Tradition," in *The Medieval Mystical Tradition in England: Exeter Symposium 5*, ed. Marion Glasscoe (Cambridge: D. S. Brewer, 1992), 1–16, especially 12–13; Jantzen also speculates about these opportunities in *Julian of Norwich*, 17–20; for an overview of Julian's milieu, see Norman P. Tanner, *The Church in Late Medieval Norwich, 1370–1532*, Studies and Texts 66 (Toronto: Pontifical Institute of Mediaeval Studies, 1984).

CHAPTER 1
AFFECTIVE SPIRITUALITY AND THE GENESIS OF
A BOOK OF SHOWINGS

1. In advising Julian to take comfort in the passion of Christ, the curate follows the service of visitation of the dying as described by Duffy, *The Stripping of the Altars*, 314–16.

2. Ibid., chapter 7.

3. Jaroslav Pelikan, *The Christian Tradition: A History of the Development of Doctrine* (Chicago: University of Chicago Press, 1978), 3:134–39, also uses "The Dream of the Rood" as an example of the early medieval theory of redemption.

4. R. K. Gordon, ed. and trans., *Anglo-Saxon Poetry*, rev. ed. (New York: Dutton, 1954), 235.

5. Gertrud Schiller, *Iconography of Christian Art*, vol. 2, *The Passion of Jesus Christ*, trans. Janet Seligman (1968; Greenwich, Conn.: New York Graphic Society, 1972), 145–47.

6. Ibid., 152–54.

7. R. W. Southern, *The Making of the Middle Ages* (New Haven: Yale University Press, 1953), 219–57; Colin Morris, *The Discovery of the Individual 1050–1200*, Medieval Academy Reprints for Teaching 19 (1972; reprint, Toronto: University of Toronto Press, 1987), 139–57. See also the caveat about Morris's use of the word *individual* expressed by Caroline Walker Bynum, "Did the Twelfth Century Discover the Individual?" in *Jesus as Mother: Studies in the Spirituality of the High Middle Ages* (Berkeley and Los Angeles: University of California Press, 1982), 82–109.

8. *Why God Became Man* 1.7, in *A Scholastic Miscellany: Anselm to Ockham*, ed. and trans. Eugene Fairweather, Library of Christian Classics 10 (Philadelphia: Westminster Press, 1956), 107–8; for the Latin text, see S. Anselmi, *Opera omnia*, ed. Francis Schmitt, O.S.B., 6 vols. (Edinburgh: Thomas Nelson and Sons, 1938–1961), 2:55–56.

9. Southern, *The Making of the Middle Ages*, 235.

10. *Why God Became Man* 1.3, in Fairweather, 104–5; Schmitt, *Opera omnia*, 2:51. For a thorough discussion of Anselm's soteriology and its significance, see Pelikan, *The Christian Tradition*, 3:129–44.

11. *The Prayers and Meditations of St. Anselm with the Proslogion*, trans. Sister Benedicta Ward, S.L.G. (London: Penguin Books, 1973), 95; "Oratio ad Christum, cum mens vult eius amore fervere," in Schmitt, *Opera omnia*, 3:7.

12. Translated in Morris, *The Discovery of the Individual*, 144; for Latin text, see *Petri Abaelardi opera theologica*, vol. 1, *Commentaria in epistolam Pauli ad Romanos*, ed. Eligius M. Buytaert, O.F.M., Corpus christianorum, Continuatio mediaevalis 11 (Turnhout: Brepols, 1969), 112–13.

13. Thomas Aquinas, *Summa theologiae* 3.46, 3, Blackfriars ed., vol. 54, ed. and trans. Richard T. A. Murphy, O.P. (New York: McGraw-Hill, 1965), 13. The Latin of this dual-text edition is based on Sancti Thomae Aquinatis, *Opera omnia iussu impensaque, Leonis XIII P. M. edita* (Rome: Ex typographia polyglotta s. c. de propaganda fide, 1882–1919), 11:438.

14. S. Bonaventurae, *Opera omnia*, ed. studio et cura pp. Collegii a S. Bonaventura, 10 vols. (Florence: Ad Claras Aquas [Quarachhi] ex typographia Collegii S. Bonaventurae, 1882–1902), 3:428. This example and the previous two are cited and translated in Rosemary Woolf, "The Theme of Christ the Lover-Knight in Medieval English Literature," *Review of English Studies*, n.s., 13 (1962): 2; reprinted in *Art and Doctrine: Essays on Medieval Literature*, ed. Heather O'Donoghue (London: The Hambledon Press, 1986), 100. As Woolf notes, Bonaventure is quoting Hugh of St. Victor's *De arrha animae*.

15. Erich Auerbach traces the changing meaning of the word *passio* from the late classical period through the high Middle Ages, in "Excursus: *Gloria Passionis*," in *Literary Language and Its Public in Late Latin Antiquity and in the Middle Ages*, trans. Ralph Manheim, Bollingen Series 74 (1958; reprint, New York: Pantheon Books, 1965), 67–81; see also Ewert Cousins, "The Humanity and the Passion of Christ," in *World Spirituality: An Encyclopedic History of the Religious Quest*, vol. 17, *Christian Spirituality: High Middle Ages and Reformation*, ed. Jill Raitt with Bernard McGinn and John Meyendorff (New York: Crossroad, 1987), 375–91.

16. Translated by Morris, *The Discovery of the Individual*, 143, from *The Oxford Book of Medieval Latin Verse*, ed. F.J.E. Raby, 2d ed. (Oxford: Clarendon Press, 1959), no. 171.

17. *The Works of Bernard of Clairvaux*, vol. 2, *Song of Songs I*, trans. Kilian Walsh, O.C.S.O., Cistercian Fathers Series 4 (Kalamazoo, Mich.: Cistercian

Publications, 1981), 152; for the Latin text, see S. Bernardi, *Opera*, vols. 1 and 2, *Sermones super Cantica Canticorum*, ed. J. Leclercq, C. H. Talbot, and H. M. Rochais (Rome: Editiones Cistercienses, 1957–1958), 1:118.

18. Bernard of Clairvaux, *Song of Songs I*, 150; Leclercq, Talbot, and Rochais, *Opera*, 1:117.

19. Julia Kristeva, *Tales of Love*, trans. Leon S. Roudiez (New York: Columbia University Press, 1987), 154.

20. Jantzen discusses the influence of affective spirituality and the relationship among these three requests in *Julian of Norwich*, 53–73.

21. Richard Kieckhefer, *Unquiet Souls: Fourteenth-Century Saints and Their Religious Milieu* (Chicago: University of Chicago Press, 1984), 105; imitation of Christ could be accomplished through either devotional or ascetic practices, as Kieckhefer demonstrates on 113–21.

22. *Aelred of Rievaulx's De institutione inclusarum: Two English Versions*, ed. John Ayto and Alexandra Barratt, Early English Text Society, o.s., 287 (London: Oxford University Press, 1984), 39. This Middle English translation of Aelred's treatise comes from the late fourteenth-century Vernon manuscript; in their introduction, Ayto and Barratt conclude, based on their examination of dialectal strata, that this translation "existed in at least two other versions, the language of which had marked SE and Northern features (and possibly existed also in EMid and even SW versions)" (liv); it is thus possible that Julian of Norwich had access to a Middle English translation of Aelred's treatise. For the Latin text, see *Aelredi rievallensis opera omnia*, vol. 1, *Opera ascetica*, ed. A. Hoste, O.S.B., and C. H. Talbot, Corpus christianorum, Continuatio mediaevalis 1 (Turnhout: Brepols, 1971), 662.

23. *Aelred of Rievaulx's De institutione inclusarum*, 39; Hoste and Talbot, *Opera omnia*, 1:662.

24. *The Prickynge of Love*, ed. Harold Kane, 2 vols., Elizabethan & Renaissance Studies 92:10 (Salzburg: Institut für Anglistik und Amerikanistik, Universität Salzburg, 1983), 1:26. Margery Kempe's inclusion of the *Stimulus amoris* in the list of books read to her attests the popularity of this free translation of it, possibly by Walter Hilton, in late medieval England. For the number of extant manuscripts, see Michael Sargent, "Bonaventura English: A Survey of the Middle English Prose Translations of Early Franciscan Literature," in *Spätmittelalterliche Geistliche Literatur in der Nationalsprache*, Analecta Cartusiana 106 (Salzburg: Institut für Anglistik und Amerikanistik, Universität Salzburg, 1984), 2:158–61.

25. James Marrow, *Passion Iconography in Northern European Art of the Late Middle Ages and Early Renaissance*, Ars Neerlandica 1 (Kortrijk, Belgium: Van Ghemmert, 1979), 14–17.

26. W. Simons and J. E. Ziegler, "Phenomenal Religion in the Thirteenth Century and Its Image: Elisabeth of Spalbeek and the Passion Cult," in *Women in the Church*, ed. W. J. Sheils and Diana Wood, Studies in Church

History 27 (Oxford: Basil Blackwell for The Ecclesiastical History Society, 1990), 117–26, especially 124.

27. *Prickynge of Love*, 1:6.

28. Elizabeth Alvilda Petroff, *Medieval Women's Visionary Literature* (Oxford: Oxford University Press, 1986), 40.

29. For discussions of the tradition of metaphors of love in mysticism, see Wolfgang Riehle, *The Middle English Mystics*, trans. Bernard Standring (1977; London: Routledge & Kegan Paul, 1981), chapter 3, especially 42–43; E. Ann Matter, *The Voice of My Beloved: The Song of Songs in Western Medieval Christianity* (Philadelphia: University of Pennsylvania Press, 1990), chapter 5; and Ann Astell, *The Song of Songs in the Middle Ages* (Ithaca: Cornell University Press, 1990), chapter 3.

30. *The Works of Bonaventure*, trans. José de Vinck, 5 vols. (Patterson, N.J.: St. Anthony Guild Press, 1960–1970), 1:127; for the Latin text, see S. Bonaventurae, *Opera omnia*, 8:79.

31. For studies of the development of systematic meditation on the passion, see Marrow, *Passion Iconography in Northern European Art*, 7–27; Elizabeth [Zeeman] Salter, *Nicholas Love's "Myrrour of the Blessed Lyf of Jesu Christ,"* Analecta Cartusiana 10 (Salzburg: Institut für Englische Sprache und Literatur, Universität Salzburg, 1974), chapter 4; and Michael Sargent, "Introduction," *Nicholas Love's* Mirror of the Blessed Life of Jesus Christ, ix–xx.

32. Bernard of Clairvaux, *Song of Songs I*, 152; Leclercq, Talbot, and Rochais, *Opera*, 1:118.

33. Bernard of Clairvaux, *Song of Songs I*, 154; Leclercq, Talbot, and Rochais, *Opera*, 1:120.

34. "On Loving God" 4.12, in Bernard of Clairvaux, *Selected Works*, trans. G. R. Evans, Classics of Western Spirituality (New York: Paulist Press, 1987), 183–84; for the Latin text, see "De diligendo Deo," in S. Bernardi, *Opera*, vol. 3, *Tractatus et opuscula*, ed. J. Leclercq and H. M. Rochais (Rome: Editiones Cistercienses, 1963), 129.

35. Etienne Gilson, *The Mystical Theology of Saint Bernard*, trans. A.H.C. Downes (New York: Sheed and Ward, 1940), 81–82. For Bernard's theory of memory, see also Janet Coleman, *Ancient and Medieval Memories: Studies in the Reconstruction of the Past* (Cambridge: Cambridge University Press, 1992), chapter 11.

36. "On Loving God" 3.10, in Bernard of Clairvaux, *Selected Works*, 181–82; Leclercq and Rochais, *Opera*, 3:127.

37. "On Loving God" 4.11, in Bernard of Clairvaux, *Selected Works*, 182; Leclercq and Rochais, *Opera*, 3:127.

38. *The Works of Bonaventure*, 1:239; S. Bonaventurae, *Opera omnia*, 8:120.

39. *The Works of Bonaventure*, 1:97; S. Bonaventurae, *Opera omnia*, 8:68.

40. Salter, *Nicholas Love's "Myrrour of the Blessed Lyf of Jesu Christ,"* 143.

41. *The Works of Bernard of Clairvaux*, vol. 3, *On the Song of Songs II*, trans. Kilian Walsh, O.C.S.O., Cistercian Fathers Series 7 (Kalamazoo, Mich.: Cistercian Publications, 1983), 221; Leclercq, Talbot, and Rochais, *Opera*, 2:42. Marsha Dutton, "The Cistercian Source: Aelred, Bonaventure, and Ignatius," in *Goad and Nail*, ed. E. Rozanne Elder, Studies in Medieval Cistercian History 10 (Kalamazoo, Mich.: Cistercian Publications, 1985), 151–78, demonstrates the influence of Aelred of Rievaulx's *De institutione inclusarum* on Bonaventure's *Lignum vitae*, including their mutual citation of this verse.

42. *The Works of Bonaventure*, 1:6; S. Bonaventurae, *Opera omnia*, 5:295.

43. Salter, *Nicholas Love's "Myrrour of the Blessed Lyf of Jesu Christ,"* 135–36; and André Wilmart, "Eve et Goscelin (II)," *Revue Bénédictine* 50 (1930): 42–83.

44. Aelred recommends three topics of meditation—past events from the life of Christ; the present condition of the meditator; and the Four Last Things that the future holds: death, judgment, hell, and heaven. Although the last two subjects are unique to Aelred's program and never achieve the popularity of the first during the late Middle Ages, these three topics correspond to the three stages of affective development formulated by Bernard and Bonaventure. Meditation on the life of Christ incites compassion; meditation on the present self, particularly one's state of sinfulness, stirs contrition; and meditation on the future disposition of the soul elicits a desire for union with God. See Marsha Dutton, "Christ Our Mother: Aelred's Iconography for Contemplative Union," in *Goad and Nail*, ed. E. Rozanne Elder, Studies in Medieval Cistercian History 10 (Kalamazoo, Mich.: Cistercian Publications, 1985), 21–45.

45. Michael Sargent, "Introduction," *Nicholas Love's* Mirror of the Blessed Life of Jesus Christ, xv–xix, indicates that many scholars now identify the author of the *Meditationes* as Johannes de Caulibus, about whose life virtually nothing is known; since most of the sources I refer to use the earlier attribution of Pseudo-Bonaventure, I continue to do so in my text.

46. Daniel R. Lesnick, *Preaching in Medieval Florence* (Athens: University of Georgia Press, 1989), 159.

47. *Meditations on the Life of Christ*, trans. Isa Ragusa and ed. Isa Ragusa and Rosalie Green (Princeton: Princeton University Press, 1961), 246. The influence on Margery Kempe of the meditative program presented by Pseudo-Bonaventure is demonstrated by Gail M. Gibson, *The Theater of Devotion: East Anglian Drama and Society in the Late Middle Ages* (Chicago: University of Chicago Press, 1989), chapter 3.

48. Salter, *Nicholas Love's "Myrrour of the Blessed Lyf of Jesu Christ,"* 134.

49. Love, *Nicholas Love's* Mirror of the Blessed Life of Jesus Christ, 10.

50. Walter Hilton, *The Scale of Perfection*, trans. John P. H. Clark and Rosemary Dorward, Classics of Western Spirituality (New York: Paulist

Press, 1991), 80; see also Clark's introduction, 39–40, for the influence of Bernard of Clairvaux on Hilton.

51. Ibid., 81.

52. Ibid., 82.

53. Ibid.

54. Ibid., 105.

55. Ibid., 106. In his discussion of the second stage of contemplation in chapter 5, Hilton also implies the spiritual progression from contrition to compassion to contemplation through the examples he presents.

> Sometimes a man or woman meditating on God feels a fervor of love and spiritual sweetness in the remembrance of his passion, or any of his works in his humanity; or he feels great trust in the goodness and mercy of God for the forgiveness of his sins, and for his great gifts of grace; or else he feels dread in his affection, with great reverence for those secret judgments of God which he does not see, and for his righteousness; or else in prayer he feels the thought of his heart draw up from all earthly things, streamed together with all its powers as it rises into our Lord by fervent desire and with spiritual delight. (80)

Of the four examples Hilton cites, all but the third correlate with the three wounds of Julian's third request.

56. Because Julian makes no mention of a reclusive life in *A Book of Showings*, most scholars believe that she did not become an anchorite until sometime after her visionary experience. Molinari, *Julian of Norwich*, 9–10, speculates that she was educated by the Benedictine nuns at Carrow Abbey but had not entered religious life. Based on the evidence of Julian's learning, particularly her Latin literacy, Colledge and Walsh argue in "Editing Julian of Norwich's *Revelations*," 416–20, and in "Introduction," *A Book of Showings*, 43–45, that she entered the religious life in her teens and was enclosed in the anchorhold only after completing the long text in 1393. They claim that her association with Carrow Abbey is uncertain although Molinari indicates that the anchorhold at St. Julian Conisford belonged to Carrow. In contrast, Sister Benedicta [Ward], S.L.G., argues that no evidence links the late medieval anchorite with a prior life as a religious or Julian with Carrow Abbey, in "Julian the Solitary," in *Julian Reconsidered* (Fairacres, Oxford: SLG Press, 1988), 11–29.

57. Julian's deletion of both of these references to the contemplative life from her long text indicates that she, like her contemporary Hilton, came to recognize the legitimate interest of lay Christians in affective spirituality.

58. Duffy's discussion of the "reality of the demonic" for late medieval people, especially at the moment of death, in *The Stripping of the Altars*, 266–68 and 317–18, helps to explain Julian's vivid depiction of the Devil.

CHAPTER 2
FROM VISUALIZATION TO VISION:
MEDITATION AND THE BODILY SHOWINGS

1. Richard Kieckhefer, "Major Currents in Late Medieval Devotion," in *World Spirituality: An Encyclopedic History of the Religious Quest*, vol. 17, *Christian Spirituality: High Middle Ages and Reformation*, ed. Jill Raitt with Bernard McGinn and John Meyendorff (New York: Crossroad, 1987), 89.

2. Catherine Jones, "The English Mystic Julian of Norwich," in *Medieval Women Writers*, ed. Katharina M. Wilson (Athens: University of Georgia Press, 1984), 272.

3. Sixten Ringbom, *Icon to Narrative: The Rise of the Dramatic Close-Up in Fifteenth-Century Devotional Painting*, 2d ed. (1965; Doornspijk, The Netherlands: Davaco Publishers, 1984), 18. Pelphrey, *Christ Our Mother*, 67–70, attributes Julian's desire for compassion to religious art.

4. E. W. Tristram, *English Medieval Wall Painting*, vol. 2, *The Thirteenth Century*, with a Catalogue compiled in collaboration with Monica Bardswell (Oxford: Published on behalf of the Pilgrim Trust by Oxford University Press, 1950), 360–61, 554; plate 205 in Catalogue.

5. Sydney Cockerell, *The Gorleston Psalter* (London: Printed at the Chiswick Press, 1907), 32–33 and plate 3; Lucy Freeman Sandler, *Gothic Manuscripts 1285–1385*, 2 vols., A Survey of Manuscripts Illuminated in the British Isles 5 (London: Harvey Miller Publishers in conjunction with Oxford University Press, 1986), 2:56–58; P. Lasko and N. J. Morgan, eds., *Medieval Art in East Anglia 1300–1520* (London: Thames and Hudson in association with Jarrold & Sons, 1974), entry 20 on 18.

6. Ringbom, *Icon to Narrative*, 11–13, distinguishes three types of medieval religious images: didactic, cultic, and devotional. Contrasting the third type with the first two, he writes, "Here the attention is focussed on an attitude in the beholder which consists neither of thirst for information and guidance by means of *historiae*, nor of the revering and adoration of *imagines*, but of a deep emotional experience." Ringbom goes on to discuss the importance of devotional images to medieval piety on 14–39.

7. Sandler, *Gothic Manuscripts*, 1:50; see also Lasko and Morgan, *Medieval Art in East Anglia*, entry 51 on 36–37 and illustration 51 on 39, for the description of the Norwich or Despencer Retable depicting scenes from the Passion and believed to have been made for the high altar of the cathedral ca. 1380–1400.

8. Even though Julian's familiarity with particular works of art cannot be established conclusively, a comparative study at least enables the twentieth-century readers of medieval texts to envision descriptions often alien to their imaginations; see, for example, Francis Wormald's comparison of the Cruci-

fixion in the *Holkham Bible Picture-Book* with a passage from Rolle's *Meditations on the Passion*, in "The Survival of Anglo-Saxon Illumination after the Norman Conquest," in *Collected Writings*, vol. 1, *Studies in Medieval Art from the Sixth to the Twelfth Centuries*, ed. J.J.G. Alexander, T. J. Brown, and Joan Gibbs (London: Harvey Miller Publishers in conjunction with Oxford University Press, 1984), 167.

9. Emile Mâle argues that the practice of affective meditation spurred the revolution in the visual arts in the fourteenth and fifteenth centuries and not vice versa, in chapter 3 of *Religious Art in France: The Late Middle Ages*, trans. Marthiel Mathews from the 5th edition of 1949, Bollingen series 90, 3 (Princeton: Princeton University Press, 1986).

10. Cousins, "The Humanity and the Passion of Christ," 383–86; Cousins terms this form of meditation "a mysticism of the historical event." See also idem, "Francis of Assisi: Christian Mysticism at the Crossroads," in *Mysticism and Religious Traditions*, ed. Steven Katz (New York: Oxford University Press, 1983), 163–90.

11. Lesnick, *Preaching in Medieval Florence*, 161–71.

12. "The Privity of the Passion: Bonaventura de mysteriis passionis Iesu Christi," in *Yorkshire Writers: Richard Rolle of Hampole and His Followers*, ed. C. Horstman, 2 vols. (London: Swan Sonnenschein & Co., 1895), 1:198. As Salter indicates in *Nicholas Love's "Myrrour of the Blessed Lyf of Jesu Christ,"* 103, this is one of seven different Middle English translations of the Passion section (chapters 74 through 92) of the *Meditationes vitae Christi* made during the fourteenth century.

13. "The Privity of the Passion," 198–99.

14. Ibid., 203.

15. *Aelred of Rievaulx's De institutione inclusarum*, 47; Hoste and Talbot, *Opera omnia*, 1:670.

16. "The Privity of the Passion," 203.

17. Lesnick, *Preaching in Medieval Florence*, 165–66. Pseudo-Bonaventure admits in the prologue that many of the episodes he includes are not attested by the Gospels, but he contends that they are nonetheless valid subjects for meditation if they incite devotion; see *Meditations on the Life of Christ*, 5.

18. Colledge and Walsh present evidence of Julian's familiarity with the *Meditationes vitae Christi*, probably in an early English recension, possibly "The Privity of the Passion," in "Editing Julian of Norwich's *Revelations*," 412–14. Previous discussions of the influence of meditation on *A Book of Showings* include Pamela Gradon, *Form and Style in Early English Literature* (London: Methuen, 1971), 311–13; J.A.W Bennett, *Poetry of the Passion: Studies in Twelve Centuries of English Verse* (Oxford: Clarendon Press, 1982), 41–43; Vincent Gillespie, "Strange Images of Death: The Passion in Later Medieval English Devotional and Mystical Writing," in *Zeit, Tod und Ewigkeit in der Renaissance Literatur*, Analecta Cartusiana 117 (Salzburg: Institut für Anglistik

und Amerikanistik, Universität Salzburg, 1987), 2:111–59; and Marion Glasscoe, "Time of Passion: Latent Relationships between Liturgy and Meditation in Two Middle English Mystics," in *Langland, the Mystics, and the Medieval English Religious Tradition: Essays in Honour of S. S. Hussey*, ed. Helen Phillips (Cambridge: D. S. Brewer, 1990), 141–60.

19. Cousins, "The Humanity and the Passion of Christ," 383.

20. See *A Book of Showings*, 1:210, 225, 227, 233–35, 239, 242, 243 for these bodily showings in the short text and the corresponding passages in the long text: 1.4.294 and 1.7.311–13; 2.10.324–25; 4.12.342–43; 8.16 and 17.357–65; 9.21.379; 10.24.394–95; 12.26.402.

21. Marrow, *Passion Iconography in Northern European Art*, 11–12.

22. "The Privity of the Passion," 207.

23. Salter, *Nicholas Love's "Myrrour of the Blessed Lyf of Jesu Christ,"* 53–54, claims that an early English translation of the Passion chapters of the *Meditationes* influenced Julian's showing; she provides the corresponding passage from an unpublished Middle English translation extant in six manuscripts, in "Continuity and Change in Middle English Versions of the *Meditationes vitae Christi*," *Medium Aevum* 26 (1957): 28. The dual interpretation of "I thirst" is widespread in late medieval devotional literature; see, for example, Richard Rolle's "Meditation B," in *Richard Rolle: Prose and Verse*, ed. S. J. Ogilvie-Thomson, Early English Text Society 293 (Oxford: Oxford University Press, 1988), 80–81. However, Julian's emphasis on the drying of Christ's body, hinted at in "The Privity of the Passion" but not by Rolle, is rarer and may derive from popular meditations on the Words of Jesus on the Cross; see Duffy, *The Stripping of the Altars*, 248–56, especially 251–53.

24. The most thorough study of differences between Julian's versions of the visual showings in her two texts is B. A. Windeatt, "Julian of Norwich and Her Audience," *Review of English Studies*, n.s., 28 (1977): 1–17, especially 8–12. In "The Apophatic Image: The Poetics of Effacement in Julian of Norwich," in *The Medieval Mystical Tradition in England: Exeter Symposium 5*, ed. Marion Glasscoe (Cambridge: D. S. Brewer, 1992), 53–77, Vincent Gillespie and Maggie Ross present a detailed analysis of the long text's account of the showings of Christ's passion in order to demonstrate how Julian manipulates the conventions of affective piety.

25. Windeatt, "Julian of Norwich and Her Audience," 2.

26. Ibid., 10.

27. Ibid., 9.

28. Rosemary Woolf, *The English Religious Lyric in the Middle Ages* (Oxford: Clarendon Press, 1968), 183–84.

29. Ibid., 398. Schiller, *Iconography of Christian Art*, 2:219–20, also discusses the conflation of the iconography of the Throne of Grace and Man of Sorrows in the late Middle Ages.

30. Schiller, *Iconography of Christian Art*, 2:124.

31. *Sarum Missal*, ed. J. Wickham Legg (1916; reprint, Oxford: Clarendon Press, 1969), 113. Woolf discusses the lyrics of reproach in *The English Religious Lyric*, 36–52.

32. "On Loving God" 3.7, in Bernard of Clairvaux, *Selected Works*, 179; Leclercq and Rochais, *Opera*, 3:124.

33. Woolf, *The English Religious Lyric*, 49–50 and 187.

34. Schiller, *Iconography of Christian Art*, 2:197 and subsequent discussion to 205. As Schiller explains, "Veneration of the Sacred Heart, which goes back to thirteenth-century mysticism and derives not from concepts of the Passion but from that of the loving union of the soul with Christ, found its first liturgical form in the office for the Feast of the Lance," officially introduced in 1354 (194). For late medieval devotion to the Wounds of Jesus, see Duffy, *The Stripping of the Altars*, 238–48.

35. Emilie Zum Brunn, "Appendix: The Augustinian Exegesis of '*Ego sum qui sum*' and the '*Metaphysics of Exodus*,'" in *St. Augustine: Being and Nothingness*, trans. Ruth Namad, 2d ed. (1978; New York: Paragon House, 1988), 97–119. For a discussion of Augustine's interpretation of Moses and Paul as the prototypes of contemplative union, see Dom Cuthburt Butler, *Western Mysticism*, 3d ed. (1922; New York: Barnes & Noble, 1967), 55–62.

36. Richard of St. Victor, *The Twelve Patriarchs, The Mystical Ark, Book Three of The Trinity*, trans. Grover A. Zinn, Classics of Western Spirituality (New York: Paulist Press, 1979), 4:22, 304; Migne, *PL* 196.165. As Zinn notes, this work is often referred to as *Benjamin Major*.

Chapter 3
"Alle Shalle Be Wele": The Theodicy of Julian of Norwich

1. Two other studies provide detailed analyses of Julian's solution to the problem of evil from perspectives different from mine: Jantzen, *Julian of Norwich*, chapter 9, examines the theodicy in terms of contemporary spirituality; and Watson traces the process by which Julian achieves her resolution, in "'A, Good Lord, How Myte Al Ben Wele?'"

2. Augustine, *Confessions* 7.12, in *Augustine: Confessions and Enchiridion*, ed. and trans. Albert Outler, Library of Christian Classics 7 (Philadelphia: Westminster Press, 1955), 148; for the Latin text, see *Confessionum, Libri XIII*, ed. Lucas Verheijen, *Sancti Augustini opera*, Corpus christianorum, Series latina 27 (Turnhout: Brepols, 1981), 104–5.

3. *The Divine Names* 4.34, in Pseudo-Dionysius, *The Complete Works*, trans. Colm Luibheid, Classics of Western Spirituality (New York: Paulist Press, 1987), 95; for the Greek text, see Migne, *PG* 3.733C. Julian's allusion to Pseudo-Dionysius's *Letter to Polycarp* in Revelation Eight indicates that she

had some familiarity with him; see *A Book of Showings*, 8.18.368, note to line 27.

4. Jeffrey Burton Russell, *Lucifer: The Devil in the Middle Ages* (Ithaca: Cornell University Press, 1984), 189.

5. Augustine, *Confessions* 7.13, in Outler, 148; Verheijen, 105.

6. Pseudo-Dionysius, *The Divine Names* 4.30, in Luibheid, 93; Migne, *PG* 3.732A.

7. Augustine, *On the Literal Interpretation of Genesis: An Unfinished Book* 1.3, in *Saint Augustine On Genesis*, trans. Roland J. Teske, S.J., The Fathers of the Church 84 (Washington, D.C.: Catholic University of America Press, 1991), 146; for the Latin text, see *De Genesis ad litteram, imperfectus liber*, in Migne, *PL* 34.221.

8. Augustine, *Confessions* 7.3, in Outler, 137; Verheijen, 94.

9. The first term is used by John Hick, *Evil and the God of Love* (New York: Harper & Row, 1966), 65–75; the second by Michael Stoeber, *Evil and the Mystics' God* (Toronto: University of Toronto Press, 1992), 14–16. I am indebted to both these studies for an understanding of the premises of Western theodicies. For further discussion of Augustine's theodicy, see also G. R. Evans, *Augustine on Evil* (Cambridge: Cambridge University Press, 1982).

10. Although Julian defers her explanation of soteriology until chapter 51, her brief reference to the "glorious asseeth" that Christ made for Adam's sin (13.29.412) prefigures the theological precision of the latter discussion. As Frances Beer points out in *Women and Mystical Experience in the Middle Ages* (Woodbridge, Suffolk: The Boydell Press, 1992), 145n.1, Julian's term derives from the French *asset*, and ultimately from the late Latin *ad satis*, "satisfaction."

11. *Middle English Dictionary*, ed. Hans Kurath, Sherman Kuhn, Robert Lewis (Ann Arbor: University of Michigan Press, 1954–), s.v. "bihoveli."

12. Beer, *Women and Mystical Experience in the Middle Ages*, 147, also points to the link between human sin and Christ's passion evoked by the word *scourge*.

13. Bede identifies John as a disciple of Hilda of Whitby who later became bishop of Hexham (now Beverley) and York; although he does not refer to the incident to which Julian alludes, he provides an account of John's miracles in *Bede's Ecclesiastical History of the English People*, ed. Bertram Colgrave and R.A.B. Mynors (Oxford: Clarendon Press, 1969), 5.2–6, 457–69. According to Hughes, *Pastors and Visionaries*, chapter 6 passim, there is evidence of a late medieval cult of John of Beverley, particularly at York. A Benedictine of Stanbrook (D.S.H.) cites Henry V's prayer to John of Beverley at Agincourt as evidence of this saint's popularity, in "English Spiritual Writers: XII. Dame Julian of Norwich," *Clergy Review*, n.s., 44 (December 1959): 708.

14. Colledge and Walsh, eds., *A Book of Showings*, attribute the confusion of this phrase to a scribal error; they read *by me* as "with respect to, as concerns," in the note on 2:436.

15. Pelikan, *The Christian Tradition*, 4:13. For a survey of the dominant issues of fourteenth-century theology, see 17–22.

16. William Courtenay, *Schools and Scholars in Fourteenth-Century England* (Princeton: Princeton University Press, 1987), 309; in chapter 10 Courtenay demonstrates that the Augustinian revival was prominent in Oxford theology after 1350. Most of the research on fourteenth-century Augustinianism focuses on Oxford. However, Clark, "Late Fourteenth-Century Cambridge Theology," speculates that the more traditional Augustinianism of Cambridge probably influenced the Middle English mystics, including Julian of Norwich.

17. Courtenay, *Schools and Scholars*, 295.

18. Augustine, *Confessions* 7.16, in Outler, 150; Verheijen, 106.

19. Augustine, *On Free Will* 3.17.48, in *Augustine: Earlier Writings*, trans. John H. S. Burleigh, Library of Christian Classics 6 (Philadelphia: Westminster Press, 1953), 200; for the Latin text, see *De libero arbitrio*, ed. W. M. Green, in *Aurelii Augustini opera*, Part 2, 2, Corpus christianorum, Series latina 29 (Turnhout: Brepols, 1970), 304.

20. John P. H. Clark, "*Fiducia* in Julian of Norwich, II," *Downside Review* 99 (1981): 218; Colledge and Walsh, "Introduction," *A Book of Showings*, 1:109–10.

21. John P. H. Clark, "Introduction," *Walter Hilton: The Scale of Perfection*, 23. In *Richard Rolle and the Invention of Authority*, 132–35, Watson suggests the possible influence of William of St. Thierry on Rolle's distinction in chapter 19 of *Incendium amoris* between two different conceptions of the perfect: those who are predestined (pilgrims) and those who have had the mystical experience of fire, sweetness, and song. Although Rolle refuses to argue that the first group is able to refrain from mortal sin, he asserts that the second group has achieved this indefectibility of love. Rolle provides an interesting contrast to Julian because she makes this claim for the first group: the godly will prevents the predestined from committing mortal sin.

22. My translation of William of St. Thierry, *De natura et dignitate amoris*, in Migne, *PL* 184.389–90: "Notanda vis verborum, *Non*, inquit, *peccatum facit*, quod patitur potius quam facit qui natus est ex Deo: et *non potest peccare*, perseverando scilicet in peccato, dum legi Dei, cui mente servit, etiam carnem festinat subiegere, quae tentatione et peccato incurrent, legi peccati videbatur servire."

23. Translated from Migne, *PL* 184.348, by Colledge and Walsh, "Introduction," *A Book of Showings*, 1:110.

24. For a discussion of this model, see David Bell, *The Image and Likeness:*

The Augustinian Spirituality of William of St. Thierry, Cistercian Studies Series 78 (Kalamazoo, Mich.: Cistercian Publications, 1984).

25. The phrase is Pelikan's; for a history of the interpretation of 1 Tim. 2:4 in medieval debates about predestination, consult the following in his *The Christian Tradition*: 3:24–25, 90, 277; 4:34–35.

26. For discussion of this distinction between God's antecedent and consequent wills and Ockham's views on predestination, see Marilyn McCord Adams, *William Ockham II*, Publications in Medieval Studies 26 (Notre Dame, Ind.: University of Notre Dame Press, 1987), 1168–73.

27. Augustine, *Enchiridion* 27.103, in Outler, 401.

28. Gordon Leff, *Gregory of Rimini: Tradition and Innovation in Fourteenth Century Thought* (Manchester, England: Manchester University Press, 1961), 199–202.

29. Ibid., 204.

30. Augustine, *Admonition and Grace* 13.39, trans. John Courtney Murray, S.J., in *The Writings of Saint Augustine*, vol. 4, The Fathers of the Church 2 (Washington, D.C.: Catholic University of America Press, 1947), 293; for the Latin text, see *De correptione et gratia*, in Migne, *PL* 44.940. Adams, *William Ockham II*, 1299–1347, provides a helpful analysis of fourteenth-century theories of predestination.

31. Hick, *Evil and the God of Love*, 183–84.

CHAPTER 4
THE PARABLE OF THE LORD AND SERVANT AND
THE DOCTRINE OF ORIGINAL SIN

1. Augustine, *On the Literal Interpretation of Genesis: An Unfinished Book* 1.3, in Teske, 146; Migne, *PL* 34.221. See also Elaine Pagels, *Adam, Eve, and the Serpent* (New York: Random House, 1988), chapter 6, especially 135.

2. Augustine, *The Nature of the Good* 7, in *Augustine: Earlier Writings*, trans. John H. S. Burleigh, Library of Christian Classics 6 (Philadelphia: Westminster Press, 1953), 328; for the Latin text, see *De natura boni*, in Migne, *PL* 42.554.

3. Jean Delumeau, *Sin and Fear: The Emergence of a Western Guilt Culture, Thirteenth–Eighteenth Centuries*, trans. Eric Nicholson (1983; New York: St. Martin's Press, 1990), 203. Delumeau's survey of penitential literature in chapter 7 owes much to Thomas Tentler, *Sin and Confession on the Eve of the Reformation* (Princeton: Princeton University Press, 1977). As Tentler explains, "Sacramental confession was designed to cause guilt as well as cure guilt" (xiii). Gavin Langmuir indicates the methodological limitations of *Sin and Fear* in a review in *Speculum* 67 (1992): 657–59.

4. Mâle, *Religious Art in France: The Late Middle Ages*, 318–24.

5. Emile Mâle, *Religious Art in France: The Thirteenth Century*, trans. Marthiel Mathews from the 9th ed. of 1958, Bollingen Series 90, 2 (1898 and 1958; Princeton: Princeton University Press, 1984), 362–84. Mâle shows that the depiction of the torments of the damned becomes even more gruesome in the fourteenth and fifteenth centuries, in the next volume of this work, *Religious Art in France: The Late Middle Ages*, 420–33.

6. Delumeau, *Sin and Fear*, 293.

7. Augustine, *Eighty-Three Different Questions*, trans. David Mosher, The Fathers of the Church 70 (Washington, D.C.: Catholic University of America Press, 1982), 89; for the Latin text, see *De diversis quaestionibus octoginta tribus*, ed. Almut Mutzenbecher, in *Aurelii Augustini opera*, Part 13, 2, Corpus christianorum, Series latina 44A (Turnhout: Brepols, 1975), 83.

8. Thomas Aquinas, *Summa theologiae* 1a2ae.47, 1, Blackfriars ed., vol. 21, ed. and trans. John Patrick Reid, O.P. (New York: McGraw-Hill, 1964), 115; for the Latin text, see Sancti Thomae Aquinatis, *Opera omnia iussu impensaque*, 6:300.

9. Colledge and Walsh, "Introduction," *A Book of Showings*, 1:24–25.

10. Pagels, *Adam, Eve, and the Serpent*, chapter 5.

11. Augustine, *Confessions* 8.10, in Outler, 172; Verheijen, 127.

12. Augustine, *Confessions* 8.10, in Outler, 172; Verheijen, 127.

13. Augustine, *Concerning the City of God against the Pagans* 14.15, trans. Henry Bettenson (Harmondsworth, England: Penguin Books, 1972), 575; for the Latin text, see *De civitate Dei Libri XI–XXII*, ed. Bernard Dombart and Alphonsus Kalb, *Aurelii Augustini opera*, Part 14, 2, Corpus christianorum, Series latina 47 (Turnhout: Brepols, 1955), 437.

14. Augustine, *The City of God* 14.15, in Bettenson, 576; Dombart and Kalb, 437–38. See also *Confessions* 7.3, in Outler, 136–37; Verheijen, 94–95.

15. Norman Powell Williams, *The Ideas of the Fall and of Original Sin* (1927; reprint, London: Longmans, Green and Co., 1938), 133.

16. For further discussion of this free-will defense in Augustinian theodicy, see Hick, *Evil and the God of Love*, 66–75; and Stoeber, *Evil and the Mystics' God*, 14–15.

17. Anselm, *Why God Became Man* 1.24, in Fairweather, 142; Schmitt, *Opera omnia*, 2:92–93. Bradley also presents this example in *Julian's Way*, 101, but she does not comment on it in the same way that I do.

18. Louis Réau, *Iconographie de l'art chrétien*, vol. 1, *Iconographie de la Bible* (1956; reprint, Nendeln, Liechtenstein: Kraus Reprints, 1974), 91–92.

19. Robert Javelet, *Image et ressemblance au douzième siècle de Saint Anselme à Alain de Lille*, 2 vols. (Paris: Éditions Letouzey & Ané, 1967), 1:266–85.

20. Ibid., 273–76.

21. Bernard of Clairvaux, *On the Song of Songs II*, 169–70; Leclercq, Talbot, and Rochais, *Opera*, 1:253.

22. Bernard of Clairvaux, *On the Song of Songs IV*, trans. Irene Edmonds,

Cistercian Fathers Series 40 (Kalamazoo, Mich.: Cistercian Publications, 1980), 174; for the Latin text, see Leclercq, Talbot, and Rochais, *Opera*, 2:294.

23. Javelet, *Image et ressemblance*, 1:276, points out that the medieval theological vocabulary of similitude and dissimilitude corresponds to the modern concepts of immanence and transcendence.

24. Augustine, *Confessions* 7.10, in Outler, 147; Verheijen, 103–4. Pierre Courcelle, "Tradition Neo-Platonicienne et traditions Chrétiennes de la 'region de dissemblance,'" *Archives d'histoire doctrinale et littéraire du moyen âge* 23 (1957): 5–10, identifies this passage from Augustine's *Confessions* as Bernard's source for the allusion to the region of unlikeness in sermon 36 of *On the Song of Songs*.

25. Etienne Gilson, "*Regio dissimilitudinis* de Platon à Saint Bernard de Clairvaux," *Mediaeval Studies* 9 (1947): 126, recognizes that Augustine's concept of original sin as a fall into a region of unlikeness has both Neoplatonic and scriptural precedent.

26. Ibid., 122–23.

27. Ewert Cousins, "Bonaventure's Mysticism of Language," in *Mysticism and Language*, ed. Steven Katz (New York: Oxford University Press, 1992), 239.

28. Bernard of Clairvaux, *On the Song of Songs II*, 178; Leclercq, Talbot, and Rochais, *Opera*, 2:7.

29. Julian's description of the lord as compassionate is another similarity between her examination of original sin and Bernard's sermon 36.

> But if I look up and fix my eyes on the aid of the divine mercy, this happy vision of God soon tempers the bitter vision of myself, and I say to him: "I am disturbed within so I will call you to mind from the land of Jordan." This vision of God is not a little thing. It reveals him to us as listening compassionately to our prayers, as truly kind and merciful, as one who will not indulge his resentment. His very nature is to be good, to show mercy always and to spare. By this kind of experience, and in this way, God makes himself known to us for our good. . . . In this way your self-knowledge will be a step to the knowledge of God; he will become visible to you according as his image is being renewed with you. And you, gazing confidently on the glory of the Lord with unveiled face, will be transformed into that same image with ever increasing brightness, by the work of the Spirit of the Lord.

See Bernard of Clairvaux, *On the Song of Songs II*, 179; Leclercq, Talbot, and Rochais, *Opera*, 2:7–8.

30. Evans, *Augustine on Evil*, 175.

31. Anselm, *Why God Became Man* 1.6, in Fairweather, 106–7; Schmitt, *Opera omnia*, 2:54.

32. Pelikan, *The Christian Tradition*, 3:110.

33. Anselm, *Why God Became Man* 2.6, in Fairweather, 152; Schmitt, *Opera omnia*, 2:101.

34. Anselm, *Why God Became Man* 2.16, in Fairweather, 167; Schmitt, *Opera omnia*, 2:117.

35. Anselm, *Why God Became Man* 1.3, in Fairweather, 104–5; Schmitt, *Opera omnia*, 2:51.

36. Pelikan, *The Christian Tradition*, 4:23.

37. *Piers Plowman: The B Version*, ed. George Kane and E. Talbot Donaldson (London: The Athlone Press, 1975), 14.14–15.

38. Riehle, *The Middle English Mystics*, 161 and 215n.187.

39. A commonplace of medieval theology, the idea that the elect will exceed the original perfection of Adam ultimately derives from Augustine; see *Admonition and Grace* 12.33, in Murray, 285; Migne, *PL* 44.936. The idea is articulated for the Middle Ages in Anselm of Canterbury's *Why God Became Man*, especially 2.16, in Fairweather, 166–67; Schmitt, *Opera omnia*, 2:117.

CHAPTER 5
RECONCEIVING THE *IMAGO DEI*: THE MOTHERHOOD OF JESUS AND THE IDEOLOGY OF THE SELF

1. For surveys of the ancient and medieval interpretations of the Delphic oracle, see Pierre Courcelle, *Connais-toi toi-même de Socrate à Saint Bernard* (Paris: Études Augustiniennes, 1974); Etienne Gilson, "Self-Knowledge and Christian Socratism," in *The Spirit of Mediaeval Philosophy*, trans. A.H.C. Downes (1936; New York: Charles Scribner's Sons, 1940), 209–28; and J.A.W. Bennett, "*Nosce te ipsum*: Some Medieval Interpretations," in *J.R.R. Tolkien, Scholar and Storyteller*, ed. Mary Salu and Robert T. Farrell (Ithaca: Cornell University Press, 1979), 138–58. For differing views of the emphasis on self-consciousness that emerges after 1050, see Morris, *The Discovery of the Individual*; and Caroline Walker Bynum, "Did the Twelfth Century Discover the Individual?" in *Jesus as Mother*, 82–109. As Coleman shows in *Ancient and Medieval Memories*, by the end of the thirteenth century, there were three competing conceptions of human nature: "one that was theological where man was understood as a morally engaged agent in the economy of salvation; another, from the Greco-Arabic tradition, which considered man as an element amongst others comprising the universe; and increasingly, a third in which man was conceived as capable of developing the *habitus* of virtues, a conception drawn from the rhetorical and moral treatises of Cicero and other ancients on the virtues" (169). Julian of Norwich conforms to the theological conception.

2. For analyses of Augustine's contemplative mysticism, see Andrew Louth, *The Origins of the Christian Mystical Tradition* (Oxford: Clarendon Press, 1981), 132–58; P. Fulbert Cayré, *La contemplation augustinienne* (1927; reprint, Paris: Desclée de Brouwer, 1954); and Butler, *Western Mysticism*.

3. In "The Body of Christ in the Later Middle Ages: A Reply to Leo Steinberg," in *Fragmentation and Redemption: Essays on Gender and the Human Body in Medieval Religion* (New York: Zone Books, 1991), 79–117, Caroline Walker Bynum presents evidence that "medieval thinkers used gender imagery more fluidly and less literally than we do" (108). She demonstrates that men as well as women employed the motif of Jesus as Mother in the Middle Ages and that the frequent depiction of Christ as female in devotional literature and art mitigated the misogynistic clerical tradition.

4. M. André Mandouze summarizes the controversy about Augustinian mysticism up through the early 1950s in "Où en est la question de la mystique augustinienne?" in *Augustinus Magister: Congrès international augustinien,* Paris, 21–24 September 1954 (Paris: Études Augustiniennes, 1954), 3:103–63.

5. Gérard Verbeke, "Connaissance de soi et connaissance de Dieu chez saint Augustin," *Augustiniana* 4 (1954): 495–515.

6. In their footnote to 14.56, line 11 of *A Book of Showings* (2:571), Colledge and Walsh cite Peter Erb's and Mary Baldwin's respective attributions of this sentiment to Augustine's *Enarrationes in Psalmos* 74.9, and *Confessiones* 3.7; certainly the editors are correct in stating that the notion "becomes a commonplace in Eckhart and later German spiritual writers."

7. For an introduction to the theology of the *imago Dei*, see Bernard McGinn, "The Human Person as Image of God II: Western Christianity," in *World Spirituality: An Encyclopedic History of the Religious Quest*, vol. 16, *Christian Spirituality: Origins to the Twelfth Century*, ed. Bernard McGinn and John Meyendorff, (New York: Crossroad, 1985), 312–30.

8. Saint Augustine, *The Trinity* 14.8.11, trans. Stephen McKenna, C.SS.R., The Fathers of the Church 45 (Washington, D.C.: Catholic University of America Press, 1963), 426; for the Latin text, see *De trinitate*, ed. W. J. Mountain with Fr. Glorie, in *Aurelii Augustini opera*, Part 16, 1 and 2, Corpus christianorum, Series latina 50 and 50A (Turnhout: Brepols, 1968), 16.2, 436.

9. Peter Lombard, *Commentarius in Psalmos Davidicos*, Ps. 4:7, in Migne, *PL* 191.88.

10. Pelikan, *The Christian Tradition*, 4:66–68.

11. Augustine, *The Trinity* 14.14.20, in McKenna, 438; Mountain and Glorie, 16.2, 448.

12. Louth, *The Origins of the Christian Mystical Tradition*, 147.

13. Aimé Solignac et al., "Image et ressemblance," *Dictionnaire de spiritualité ascétique et mystique, doctrine et histoire*, fasc. 48–49 (Paris: Beauchesne, 1970), 1418–60; Javelet, *Image et ressemblance*. Riehle contrasts the *imago Dei* spirituality of the German and English mystics in *The Middle English Mystics*, 142–64.

14. Valerie Lagorio follows Hope Emily Allen in tracing this familial analogy to Matt. 3:35: "Whoso does the will of God, he is my brother, my sister, and my mother"; she gives examples of this motif from the *Mirror of Simple Souls*, *The Book of Margery Kempe*, and the *Maulde Book*, the short title of the

Middle English translation of Mechtild of Hackeborn's *Liber specialis gratiae*, in "Variations on the Theme of God's Motherhood in Medieval English Mystical and Devotional Writings," *Studia Mystica* 8 (1985): 17. Jennifer Heimmel, *"God Is Our Mother": Julian of Norwich and the Medieval Image of Christian Feminine Divinity*, Elizabethan & Renaissance Studies 92:5 (Salzburg: Institut für Anglistik und Amerikanistik, Universität Salzburg, 1982), 29, cites Mechtild of Hackeborn's report of God's words to her: "Ego sibi pater in creatione; ego mater in redemptione; ego frater in regni divisione; ego soror in dulci societate;" [I am a father to you in creation; I am a mother in redemption; I am a brother in division of the royal power; I am a sister in sweet companionship].

15. Peter Lombard, *In Epistolam ad Romanos* 8.30–32, in Migne, *PL* 191.1451. For a discussion of the meaning of predestination in Christ, see Javelet, *Image et ressemblance*, 1:118–24.

16. Javelet, *Image et ressemblance*, 1:118

17. McGinn, "The Human Person as Image of God, II. Western Christianity," 325; see also Gilson, *The Spirit of Mediaeval Philosophy*, 211–12.

18. For a thorough discussion of Bernard's concept of the *imago Dei* and the traditions on which it is based, see Bernard McGinn, "Introduction," *The Works of Bernard of Clairvaux*, vol. 7, *Treatises III: On Grace and Free Choice*, trans. Daniel O'Donovan, O.S.C.O., Cistercian Fathers Series 19 (Kalamazoo, Mich.: Cistercian Publications, 1977), 3–50. As McGinn observes, this distinction among the three states of freedom is the "most influential contribution of the entire treatise. . . . Due to its inclusion in the *Sentences* of Peter Lombard, it was to remain a familiar topic of discussion in the history of Scholasticism" (18). The abbot introduces a different definition of the *imago Dei* in sermons 80 through 82 of *On the Song of Songs*; see Javelet, *Image et ressemblance*, 1:189–97.

19. *On Grace and Free Choice* 3.7, in O'Donovan, 62–63; Leclercq and Rochais, *Opera*, 3:171.

20. *On Grace and Free Choice* 7.21, in O'Donovan, 79; Leclercq and Rochais, *Opera*, 3:182.

21. *On Grace and Free Choice* 5.15, in O'Donovan, 71; Leclercq and Rochais, *Opera*, 3:177.

22. McGinn, "Introduction," *Treatises III*, 23; as McGinn explains, Bernard derives his terminology from Augustine's *De correptione et gratia* (*Admonition and Grace*) (23).

23. *On Grace and Free Choice* 9.29, in O'Donovan, 85; Leclercq and Rochais, *Opera*, 3:186.

24. Bernard McGinn attributes the first conception of union to the twelfth-century mystics like Bernard of Clairvaux and William of St. Thierry and the second to the thirteenth-century Continental women mystics and Meister Eckhart, in "Love, Knowledge and *Unio Mystica* in the Western

Christian Tradition," in *Mystical Union and Monotheistic Faith: An Ecumenical Dialogue*, ed. Moshe Idel and Bernard McGinn (New York: Macmillan, 1989), 63, 71. As I go on to show, however, Julian of Norwich's conception of an ontological union between God and the soul does not resemble Eckhart's notion of indistinct union in which the substantive difference between the two disappears. Richard Kieckhefer clarifies the different ideas of union available to late medieval mystics in "Meister Eckhart's Conception of Union with God," *Harvard Theological Review* 71 (1978): 203–35.

25. For the differences between Augustine and Neoplatonism, see James F. Anderson, *St. Augustine and Being: A Metaphysical Essay* (The Hague: Martinus Nijhoff, 1965), 1–11, 35; and Bell, *The Image and Likeness*, 22–25.

26. T. J. Kondoleon, "Exemplarism," *New Catholic Encyclopedia* (New York: McGraw-Hill, 1967), 5:712–15.

27. Anderson, *St. Augustine and Being*, 19 and 23. In *The Middle English Mystics*, Riehle observes: "Apart from the term *essentia* or *esse* the concepts *natura* and *substantia* are frequently used in Latin theology for expressing the divine essence" (195n.102). Although the vocabulary of the German mystics includes such terminology, Riehle finds Julian of Norwich to be the first Middle English writer to introduce the cognates *substance* and *grounde*; however, since few of the German texts were available in Middle English during Julian's lifetime, it is difficult to identify her specific source. See Riehle's discussion of the influence of Scholasticism on Julian's use of these terms, 156–57; and Héribert Fischer, "Fond de l'ame," *Dictionnaire de spiritualité ascétique et mystique*, 5:650–62.

28. Augustine, *The City of God* 12.2, trans. M. Dods with G. Wilson and J. J. Smith, in *Basic Writings of Saint Augustine*, ed. Whitney J. Oates, 2 vols. (New York: Random House, 1948), 2:180; for the Latin text, see Dombart and Kalb, 14.2, 357.

29. Augustine, *The Trinity* 11.5.8, in McKenna, 327–28; Mountain and Glorie, 16.1, 344.

30. C. H. Dodd, *The Interpretation of the Fourth Gospel* (Cambridge: Cambridge University Press, 1953), 263–85, discusses these two denotations of the Greek word *logos* in relationship to the Prologue to John's Gospel and the Wisdom tradition.

31. Bell, *The Image and Likeness*, 36, discusses this distinction made in *Quaestiones in heptateuchum* 5.4; Pelikan attests the continuity of the distinction in the high Middle Ages, in *The Christian Tradition*, 3:146.

32. Augustine, *Eighty-Three Different Questions*, in Mosher, 50; Mutzenbecher, 28; see also Anderson, *St. Augustine and Being*, chapter 5.

33. Bell, *The Image and Likeness*, 49.

34. Ritamary Bradley points out the influence of the Wisdom tradition on Julian's conception, in "The Motherhood Theme in Julian of Norwich," *Fourteenth-Century English Mystics Newsletter* 2 (1976): 25–30; in "Patristic Back-

ground of the Motherhood Similitude in Julian of Norwich," *Christian Scholar's Review* 8 (1978): 101–13; and in "Mysticism in the Motherhood Similitude of Julian of Norwich," *Studia Mystica* 8 (1985): 4–14. For briefer discussions of the Wisdom tradition in relation to Julian, see Lagorio, "Variations on the Theme of God's Motherhood," 19–21; and Bynum, *Jesus as Mother*, 151.

35. Pelikan, *The Christian Tradition*, 1:186–93. For the similarities between John 1:1–14 and the Wisdom literature, see Dodd, *The Fourth Gospel*, 274–75. Gerhard Von Rad, *Wisdom in Israel* (Nashville, Tenn.: Abingdon Press, 1972), 144–76, analyzes the exemplarist theology implicit in the Wisdom literature of the Old Testament. Sister Mary Frances Smith, S.S.N.D., provides evidence of the popularity of the identification of Christ as Wisdom in the early English vernacular literature, in her Ph.D. dissertation, "Wisdom and Personification of Wisdom Occurring in Middle English Literature before 1500" (Catholic University of America, 1935), 134–45.

36. Peter Dronke, ed., *Bernardus Silvestris' Cosmographia* (Leiden: E. J. Brill, 1978), note iii 17–18, 165. Barbara Newman, "Some Mediaeval Theologians and the Sophia Tradition," *Downside Review* 108 (1990): 111–30, is the best available study of medieval interpretations of Wisdom.

37. Barbara Newman, *Sister of Wisdom: St. Hildegard's Theology of the Feminine* (Berkeley and Los Angeles: University of California Press, 1987), 45.

38. Translated by Bradley, "The Motherhood Theme," 27, from Alberti Magni, *Postilla super Isaiam* 49.15, ed. Ferdinand Siepmann, in *Opera omnia*, vol. 19 (Aschendorff: Monasterii Westfalorum, 1952), 491.

39. *The Works of Bonaventure*, 5:301–2; S. Bonaventurae, *Opera omnia*, 5:426. This example is cited by Bradley, "The Motherhood Theme," 28.

40. Sermon 40 in *Meister Eckhart: Teacher and Preacher*, ed. Bernard McGinn with Frank Tobin and Elvira Borgstadt, Classics of Western Spirituality (New York: Paulist Press, 1986), 302. As the editors comment: "The Son's (motherly) passivity in his relationship to the Father consists in his *being born*. The Son is also the 'place' in the Trinity where the (distinct) images of created beings, their exemplary causes, exist" (303–4n.13). Eckhart's association of exemplary cosmology with sapiential theology is also apparent in the selections from *The Commentary on the Book of Wisdom*, *The Sermons and Lectures on Ecclesiasticus* and *The Commentary on John* translated in this edition.

41. Thomas Aquinas, *Summa theologiae* 2a2ae.26, 10, Blackfriars ed., vol. 34, ed. and trans. R. J. Batten, O.P. (New York: McGraw-Hill, 1975), 149; for Latin text, see Sancti Thomae Aquinatis, *Opera omnia iussu impensaque*, 8:220. See discussions of the medieval conception of sexual difference in Vern L. Bullough, "Medieval Medical and Scientific Views of Women," *Viator* 4 (1973): 487–93; Kari Elisabeth Børresen, *Subordination and Equivalence: The Nature and Role of Woman in Augustine and Thomas Aquinas*, trans. Charles H. Talbot (1968; Washington, D.C.: University Press of America, 1981), 192–96;

Eleanor McLaughlin, "Equality of Souls, Inequality of Sexes: Woman in Medieval Thought," in *Religion and Sexism: Images of Woman in the Jewish and Christian Traditions*, ed. Rosemary R. Ruether (New York: Simon and Schuster, 1974), 215–19; Thomas Laqueur, *Making Sex: Body and Gender from the Greeks to Freud* (Cambridge: Harvard University Press, 1990), chapter 2. Distinguishing between the father as active and the son/mother as passive, Eckhart alludes to this same Aristotelian model in his statement about the motherhood of Wisdom cited above.

42. Newman, *Sister of Wisdom*, 63.

43. Philo, *On the Account of the World's Creation Given by Moses* (*De opificio mundi*) 49, in *Philo*, trans. F. H. Colson and G. H. Whitaker, Loeb Classical Library, 11 vols. (1929; reprint, Cambridge: Harvard University Press, 1949), 1:131.

44. McGinn, "The Human Person as Image of God, II: Western Christianity," 328. See also Rosemary Ruether, "Misogynism and Virginal Feminism in the Fathers of the Church," in *Religion and Sexism: Images of Woman in the Jewish and Christian Traditions*, ed. Rosemary Ruether (New York: Simon and Schuster, 1974), 150–83; Marie-Thérèse d'Alverny, "Comment les théologiens et les philosophes voient la femme," in *La Femme dans les civilisations des Xe–XIIIe siècles: Actes du Colloque tenu à Poitiers les 23–25 Septembre 1976*, Publications du Centre d'Études Supérieures de Civilisation Médiévale (Poitiers: Université de Poitiers, 1977), 15–39. The persistence to this day of the association of women with the body is clear in the writings of the French feminists.

45. R. Howard Bloch, *Medieval Misogyny and the Invention of Western Romantic Love* (Chicago: University of Chicago Press, 1991), chapter 1. For evidence of the complexity of medieval attitudes toward the body, see Caroline Walker Bynum, "Bodily Miracles and the Resurrection of the Body in the High Middle Ages," in *Belief in History*, ed. Thomas Kselman (South Bend, Ind.: University of Notre Dame Press, 1990), 68–106.

46. Børresen, *Subordination and Equivalence*, provides ample evidence from Augustine and Aquinas to document this tension in the medieval construction of woman; see also McLaughlin, "Equality of Souls, Inequality of Sexes." As Caroline Walker Bynum astutely observes in *Holy Feast and Holy Fast: The Religious Significance of Food to Medieval Women* (Berkeley and Los Angeles: University of California Press, 1987), medieval holy women often used this tension between the literal and the symbolic to empower themselves; see especially chapters 9 and 10.

47. Augustine, *The Trinity* 12.14.22, in McKenna, 363; Mountain and Glorie, 16.1, 375. Although the vocabulary varies somewhat during the later Middle Ages, this hierarchical and gendered division of the soul remains constant; see Javelet, *Image et ressemblance*, 1:179–80.

48. Augustine, *The Trinity* 12.3.3, in McKenna, 345; Mountain and Glorie, 16.1, 358.

49. Augustine, *The Trinity* 12.4.4, in McKenna, 346; Mountain and Glorie, 16.1, 358.

50. Augustine, *The Trinity* 12.7.10, in McKenna, 352; Mountain and Glorie, 16.1, 364.

51. Augustine, *The Trinity* 12.8.13, in McKenna, 355; Mountain and Glorie, 16.1, 367.

52. Augustine, *The Trinity* 12.7.12, in McKenna, 354; Mountain and Glorie, 16.1, 366–67.

53. Identifying the serpent as the body and the woman as the lower reason, Augustine congratulates himself on according Eve a higher stature than had previous allegorical commentators like Philo who "spoke of the man as the mind, but the woman as the sense of the body" (*The Trinity* 12.13.20, in McKenna, 361; Mountain and Glorie, 16.1, 373). In practice, though, his distinction between the literal and metaphoric uses of *woman* serves the same purpose in legitimizing medieval misogyny, for there is little difference between Philo's allegoresis of Eve as the body and Augustine's of Eve as the lower reason mediating between the body and the higher reason. More than a thousand years later, Milton, in *Paradise Lost*, continues the tradition of literalizing Augustine's metaphoric distinction between the higher and lower reason into an ontological difference between the two sexes:

> Not equal, as thir sex not equal seemd;
> For contemplation hee and valour formed,
> For softness shee and sweet attractive Grace,
> Hee for God only, shee for God in him.

(4.296–99)

54. Javelet, *Image et ressemblance*, 1:236–45, provides evidence of the influence of Augustine's ambivalence toward women throughout the Middle Ages. For a more positive attitude toward the lower reason and the affective capacities of the soul on the part of male writers in the mystical tradition, see chapters 3 and 4 on Bernard of Clairvaux and Richard Rolle in Astell, *The Song of Songs in the Middle Ages*.

55. *The Works of William of St. Thierry*, vol. 4, *The Golden Epistle: A Letter to the Brethren at Mont Dieu* 2.4, trans. Theodore Berkeley, O.C.S.O., Cistercian Fathers Series 12 (Spencer, Mass.: Cistercian Publications, 1971), 79; for the Latin text, see Migne, *PL* 184.340. Commenting on the androcentric dualism of William's anthropology, in "William of Saint-Thierry on the Myth of the Fall: A Phenomenology of *Animus* and *Anima*," *Recherches de théologie ancienne et médiévale* 46 (1979), Thomas Michael Tomasic writes:

> The interesting distinction between *animus* and *anima*, and the nostalgic wish for their reintegration, mythologically accentuates the primacy of the hermaphroditic or androgynous state as the original, paradisiacal situation of the self. The thought occurs that, if the unified self, i.e., the accomplished syzygy of *animus*

and *anima*, is the image of God, then the Divine Exemplar must also be understood to be androgynous. Unfortunately, nowhere does William develop this concept. . . . In any event, the androgynous structure of the image serves to articulate the phenomenon of the Fall, which consists in the alienation of the masculine and feminine correlates of the self. (27)

Although I question Colledge and Walsh's assertion that Julian of Norwich was influenced by William of St. Thierry, Tomasic's observation that a conception of an androgynous deity is the logical conclusion to the Augustinian model of the gendered *mens* nonetheless reveals Julian's astuteness in developing her analogy of Jesus as Mother.

56. Hilton, *The Scale of Perfection*, 213–14. Tarjei Park, "Reflecting Christ: The Role of the Flesh in Walter Hilton and Julian of Norwich," in *The Medieval Mystical Tradition in England: Exeter Symposium 5*, ed. Marion Glasscoe (Cambridge: D. S. Brewer, 1992), 32, also recognizes the similarity between what Hilton refers to as the lower reason and Julian's conception of the sensuality. Although Julian was probably not familiar with his writings, Meister Eckhart provides further evidence of the ubiquitousness of the gendered model of the soul in the late Middle Ages. In sermon 40, the same sermon cited earlier in which he refers to the Son as Wisdom, a mother, Eckhart continues: "I have often said that there are two powers in the soul: One is the man and one is the woman. . . . The power in the soul that one calls the man is the highest power of the soul in which God shines bare; for into this power nothing enters but God, and this power is continually in God" (*Meister Eckhart: Teacher and Preacher*, 302).

57. Kurath, Kuhn, and Lewis, *Middle English Dictionary*, s.v. "sensualite." From the examples cited under the first definition of *sensualite* as the "natural capacity for receiving physical sensation understood as an inferior power of the soul concerned with the body," it is clear that this term is the Middle English equivalent for the Augustinian lower reason; the quotations from Rolle and Chaucer are particularly relevant. Rolle states in his commentary on Ps. 6:6, "The nether party of my saule . . . is cald the sensualite"; see Richard Rolle, *The Psalter or Psalms of David and Certain Canticles with a Translation and Exposition in English by Richard Rolle of Hampole*, ed. Henry Bramley (Oxford: Clarendon Press, 1884), 23. Chaucer writes in the *Parson's Tale*, lines 260–61, "For it is sooth that God, and resoun, and sensualitee, and the body of man been so ordeyned that everich of thise foure thynges sholde have lordshipe over that oother, as thus: God sholde have lordshipe over resoun, and resoun over sensualitee, and sensualitee over the body of man"; see *The Riverside Chaucer*, ed. Larry Benson, 3d ed. (Boston: Houghton Mifflin, 1987), 294.

58. In "The Female Body and Religious Practice," in *Fragmentation and Redemption*, 222–38, Bynum demonstrates that "a concept of the person as soul *and* body (or, in modern parlance, a psychosomatic unity) undergirds scholastic discussions of such topics as bodily resurrection, miracles, embryol-

ogy, asceticism, Christology and the Immaculate Conception" (223). Bynum argues that not only the Thomists influenced by Aristotle but also the Platonic, Augustinian, and Franciscan thinkers recognized that the body was integral to personal specificity. See also the next essay in this collection, "Material Continuity, Personal Survival and the Resurrection of the Body: A Scholastic Discussion in Its Medieval and Modern Contexts," 239–97. The inception of this concept of psychosomatic unity can be traced back to the influence of the Greco-Arabic thinkers on twelfth-century Cistercians and Victorines; see Gerhart Ladner, *Ad Imaginem Dei: The Image of Man in Medieval Art*, Wimmer Lecture, 1962 (Latrobe, Penn.: The Archabbey Press, 1965), 53–64; and Coleman, *Ancient and Medieval Memories*, chapter 12. For the influence of Aristotle on Aquinas's conception of the body, see Roger Trigg, *Ideas of Human Nature: An Historical Introduction* (Oxford: Basil Blackwell, 1988), 38–53.

59. *The Middle English Mystics*, 148, 131–32, but Riehle attributes the metaphor of the soul as a city to Luke 10:38 and cites many examples comparing the soul to a castle rather than a city. Colledge and Walsh, *A Book of Showings*, 2:640, compare Julian's metaphor to Mechtild of Hackeborn's "city of the heart," based on Apoc. 17:14 and Ezechiel 40. See also Maria R. Lichtmann, "'I desyrede a bodylye syght': Julian of Norwich and the Body," *Mystics Quarterly* 17 (1991): 12–19.

60. Bynum points out the uniqueness of Julian's ideas about this second maternity in *Holy Feast and Holy Fast*, 266–67.

61. Julian's positive attitude toward the body is also indicated by her silence about ascetic discipline despite its centrality in the anchoritic literature. For a discussion of the prevalence of a literal *imitatio Christi* among other holy women of this period, see ibid., 208–18. In chapter 11 of *The Sociology of Religion*, trans. Ephraim Fischoff (1922; Boston: Beacon Press, 1963), Max Weber makes an important distinction between the ascetic's rejection of the world and the mystic's flight from the world. See also Bynum's reevaluation of Weber's categories in "The Mysticism and Asceticism of Medieval Women," in *Fragmentation and Redemption*, 53–78.

62. Julian perhaps uses the phrase *forth spredyng* to translate *diffusa* in Rom. 5:5: "The charity of God is poured forth in our hearts, by the Holy Ghost who is given to us." This entire chapter of Romans is significant for Julian's conclusion to her theodicy in chapters 61 through 63.

63. For surveys of similar references to Jesus as Mother in devotional texts and their scriptural sources, see Eleanor McLaughlin, "'Christ My Mother': Feminine Naming and Metaphor in Medieval Spirituality," *Nashotah Review* 15 (1975): 228–48; Lagorio, "Variations on the Theme of God's Motherhood"; and Heimmel, "*God Is Our Mother*," chapters 1 and 2. Bynum contrasts the references to Jesus as Mother made by men with those made by women as they reveal differences in their conceptions of gender, in "Jesus as Mother and

Abbot as Mother: Some Themes in Twelfth-Century Cistercian Writing,"
chapter 4 of *Jesus as Mother*, and in "'. . . And Woman His Humanity': Female
Imagery in the Religious Writing of the Later Middle Ages," in *Gender and
Religion: On the Complexity of Symbols*, ed. Caroline Walker Bynum, Steven
Harrell, and Paula Richman (Boston: Beacon Press, 1986), 257–88.

64. I discuss the differences between Julian's references to Jesus as Mother
and those in Aelred of Rievaulx's *De institutione inclusarum* and in the *Ancrene
Riwle*, in "Julian of Norwich and Anchoritic Literature," *Mystics Quarterly* 19
(1993): 148–60.

CHAPTER 6
RE-VISIONS AND *A BOOK OF SHOWINGS*

1. Watson presents the evidence of these constraints as part of his argument for dating the composition of the short text between 1382 and 1388, and
that of the long text in the early fifteenth century, perhaps as late as 1415, in
"The Composition of Julian of Norwich's *Revelation of Love*," 642–57.

2. Moore, "Mystical Experience, Mystical Doctrine, Mystical Technique,"
108.

3. Moore, "Christian Mysticism and Interpretation," 164. B. A. Windeatt
also comments on the layering resulting from Julian's transformation of the
short text into the long in "'Privytes to us': Knowing and Re-vision in Julian
of Norwich," in *Chaucer to Shakespeare: Essays in Honour of Shinsuke Ando*,
ed. Toshiyuki Takamiya and Richard Beadle (Woodbridge, Suffolk:
D. S. Brewer, 1992), 87–98. However, as Watson demonstrates in "The Trinitarian Hermeneutic in Julian of Norwich's *Revelation of Love*," it is not always
possible or necessary to distinguish between these different interpretive moments in Julian's texts.

4. Pelphrey, *Love Was His Meaning*, 80–83, identifies in the long text a
different threefold thematic structure associated with three manners of charity.

5. Colledge and Walsh, "Introduction," *A Book of Showings*, 1:66.

6. Moore, "Mystical Experience, Mystical Doctrine, Mystical Technique,"
111.

7. B. A. Windeatt, "The Art of Mystical Loving: Julian of Norwich,"
in *The Medieval Mystical Tradition in England: Papers Read at the Exeter Symposium, July 1980*, ed. Marion Glasscoe (Exeter: University of Exeter, 1980),
60.

8. See the discussion of meditation in Jean Leclercq, O.S.B., *The Love of
Learning and the Desire for God: A Study of Monastic Culture*, trans. Catharine
Misrahi (1957; New York: Fordham University Press, 1961), 73–77. The mem-
orization of Scripture fostered by such *meditatio* accounts for Julian's frequent
allusions to or memorial citations of biblical verses identified by Colledge and

Walsh, "Introduction," *A Book of Showings*, 1:45–47, and the footnotes throughout. In *The Book of Memory: A Study of Memory in Medieval Culture*, Cambridge Studies in Medieval Literature 10 (Cambridge: Cambridge University Press, 1990), Mary Carruthers documents the memorial practices of medieval culture that account for Julian's ability in this regard.

9. Colledge and Walsh, "Introduction," *A Book of Showings*, 1:21.

10. Windeatt, "Julian of Norwich and Her Audience," 7; he demonstrates Julian's greater assurance in the long text, in "'Privytes to us,'" 87–98. Lynn Staley Johnson also contrasts Julian's presentation of herself in the short and long texts, in "The Trope of the Scribe and the Question of Literary Authority in the Works of Julian of Norwich and Margery Kempe," *Speculum* 66 (1991): 820–38. Most critics who appreciate the literariness of *A Book of Showings* concentrate on Julian's rhetoric; see Robert Karl Stone, *Middle English Prose Style: Margery Kempe and Julian of Norwich* (The Hague: Mouton, 1970); and Colledge and Walsh, "Introduction," *A Book of Showings*, 1:47–52, and "Appendix: Rhetorical Figures Employed by Julian," 2:734–48.

11. Colledge and Walsh, "Introduction," *A Book of Showings*, 1:59.

12. Ibid., 20; the short-text chapters corresponding to the inception of a showing in the long text are viii = III.11, x = VIII.16, xiii = X.24, xix = XIV.41.

13. The division of the whole into distinct parts and the analysis of the interrelations among these parts are, of course, characteristic of scholastic treatises. For discussions of the scholastic interest in the structure (*ordinatio* or *forma tractatus*) of a text, see M. B. Parkes, "The Influence of the Concepts of *Ordinatio* and *Compilatio* on the Development of the Book," in *Medieval Learning and Literature: Essays Presented to Richard William Hunt*, ed. J.J.G. Alexander and M. T. Gibson (Oxford: Clarendon Press, 1976), 115–41; and A. J. Minnis, *Medieval Theory of Authorship: Scholastic Literary Attitudes in the Later Middle Ages*, 2d ed. (1984; Philadelphia: University of Pennsylvania Press, 1988), 145–59.

14. Gillespie and Ross, "The Apophatic Image," 58–69, examine the semantic and syntactical procedures of Revelation One in detail in order to demonstrate how Julian counteracts the referentiality of language that threatens her account of an apophatic experience.

15. Windeatt, "Julian of Norwich and Her Audience," 7; for the three other instances of such dislocation, see College and Walsh, "Introduction," *A Book of Showings*, 1:21–24.

16. Although it is impossible to ascertain when this amplification occurred, the table of contents does not mention the motifs of lord and servant or Jesus as Mother in Revelation Fourteen that these additions prefigure. It is likely, therefore, that Julian incorporated this new material during the second phase of her revision of the long text at the same time that she added chapters 51 through 63. See Colledge and Walsh, "Introduction," *A Book of Showings*, 1:24–25.

17. Ibid., 83 and 81. Gillespie and Ross present a detailed analysis of Revelation Two in "The Apophatic Image," 69–72.

18. Molinari draws parallels between chapters 10 and 43, in *Julian of Norwich*, 104–17.

19. Julian's conjunction of her vision of the face of Christ with this paradox of simultaneous *seeing* and *seeking* perhaps indicates her familiarity, either directly or indirectly, with Augustine's interpretation of Ps. 104:3–4 in bk. 15 of *De trinitate*:

> "Let the heart of those rejoice who seek the Lord; seek the Lord, and be strengthened; seek his face evermore." . . .
>
> If, therefore, He who is sought can be found, why was it said: "Seek his face evermore"? Or is He perhaps still to be sought even when He is found? . . . Why, then, does he so seek it if he comprehends that what he seeks is incomprehensible, unless because he knows that he must not cease as long as he is making progress in the search itself of incomprehensible things, and is becoming better and better by seeking so great a good, which is sought in order to be found, and is found in order to be sought? For it is sought in order that it may be found sweeter, and is found in order that it may be sought more eagerly.

See McKenna, 452; Mountain and Glorie, 460–61.

20. For discussions of similar structuring in works of medieval literature, especially romances, see F. Douglas Kelly, *Sens and conjointure in the Chevalier de la Charrette* (The Hague: Mouton, 1966), 166–84; Dale B. J. Randall, "A Note on Structure in *Sir Gawain and the Green Knight*," *Modern Language Notes* 72 (1959): 161–63; Larry Benson, *Malory's Morte Darthur* (Cambridge: Harvard University Press, 1976), 34–35; and Lee Patterson, "'For the Wyves love of Bath': Feminine Rhetoric and Poetic Resolution in the *Roman de la Rose* and the *Canterbury Tales*," *Speculum* 58 (1983): 669–74. Although there are classical antecedents for such structuring, the most influential during the Middle Ages was Ovid's *Metamorphoses*; see Brooks Otis, *Ovid as an Epic Poet* (Cambridge: Cambridge University Press, 1966), 78–90. I do not wish to imply that Julian of Norwich was familiar with these particular texts, but only that *emboîtement* was a common structural technique in medieval literature.

21. Julian has been compared to these literary authors, especially Langland, by A.V.C. Schmidt, "Langland and the Mystical Tradition," in *The Medieval Mystical Tradition in England: Papers Read at the Exeter Symposium, July 1980*, ed. Marion Glasscoe (Exeter: University of Exeter, 1980), 17–38; and Windeatt, "The Art of Mystical Loving."

22. These characteristics of fourteenth-century narrative poetry are identified by J. A. Burrow, *Ricardian Poetry: Chaucer, Gower, Langland, and the Gawain Poet* (New Haven: Yale University Press, 1971), 57–69; the structural patterning that I have identified in *A Book of Showings* is, however, more complicated than the circularity that Burrow finds characteristic of this poetry.

Conclusion

1. Upjohn gives an account of the publishing history of *A Book of Showings*, in *In Search of Julian of Norwich*, chapter 1.

2. Thomas Merton, "The English Mystics," in *Mystics and Zen Masters* (New York: Dell, 1961), 140–41.

3. Hick, *Evil and the God of Love*, 292; I am also indebted to Hick for the term "soul-making" and for his survey of this type of theodicy.

4. Ibid., 226–28 and 269–72.

5. Elizabeth Robertson applies Virginia Woolf's phrase to the anchorhold in *Early English Devotional Prose and the Female Audience* (Knoxville: University of Tennessee Press, 1990).

❋ *Works Cited* ❋

Abelard, Peter. *Opera theologica*. Vol. 1, *Commentaria in epistolam Pauli ad Romanos*. Edited by Eligius M. Buytaert, O.F.M. Corpus christianorum, Continuatio mediaevalis 11. Turnhout: Brepols, 1969.

Adams, Marilyn McCord. *William Ockham II*. Publications in Medieval Studies 26. Notre Dame, Ind.: University of Notre Dame Press, 1987.

Aelred of Rievaulx. *Aelred of Rievaulx's De institutione inclusarum: Two English Versions*. Edited by John Ayto and Alexandra Barratt. Early English Text Society, o.s., 287. London: Oxford University Press, 1984.

———. *Opera omnia*. Vol. 1, *Opera ascetica*. Edited by A. Hoste, O.S.B., and C. H. Talbot. Corpus christianorum, Continuatio mediaevalis 1. Turnhout: Brepols, 1971.

Albertus Magnus. *Postilla super Isaiam*. Edited by Ferdinand Siepmann. In *Opera omnia*, vol. 19. Aschendorff: Monasterii Westfalorum, 1952.

Allen, Hope Emily. *Writings Ascribed to Richard Rolle, Hermit of Hampole*. The Modern Language Association Monograph Series. New York: D. C. Heath, 1927.

Alverny, Marie-Thérèse d'. "Comment les théologiens et les philosophes voient la femme." In *La Femme dans les civilisations des Xe–XIIIe siècles: Actes du Colloque tenu à Poitiers les 23–25 Septembre 1976*. Publications du Centre d'Études Supérieures de Civilisation Médiévale. Poitiers: Université de Poitiers, 1977.

Anderson, James F. *St. Augustine and Being: A Metaphysical Essay*. The Hague: Martinus Nijhoff, 1965.

Anselm. *Opera omnia*. Edited by Francis Schmitt, O.S.B. 6 vols. Edinburgh: Thomas Nelson and Sons, 1938–1961.

———. *The Prayers and Meditations of St. Anselm with the Proslogion*. Translated by Sister Benedicta Ward, S.L.G. London: Penguin Books, 1973.

———. *Why God Became Man*. In *A Scholastic Miscellany: Anselm to Ockham*, edited and translated by Eugene Fairweather. Library of Christian Classics 10. Philadelphia: Westminster Press, 1956.

Aquinas, Thomas. *Opera omnia iussu impensaque, Leonis XIII P. M. edita*. Rome: Ex typographia polyglotta s. c. de propaganda fide, 1882–1919.

———. *Summa theologiae*. Blackfriars edition. 60 vols. New York: McGraw-Hill, 1964–.

Astell, Ann. *The Song of Songs in the Middle Ages*. Ithaca: Cornell University Press, 1990.

Atkinson, Clarissa. *Mystic and Pilgrim: The Book and the World of Margery Kempe*. Ithaca: Cornell University Press, 1983.

Auerbach, Erich. *Literary Language and Its Public in Late Latin Antiquity and in the Middle Ages*. Translated by Ralph Manheim. Bollingen Series 74. 1958. Reprint. New York: Pantheon Books, 1965.

Augustine. *Admonition and Grace*. Translated by John Courtney Murray, S.J. In *The Writings of Saint Augustine*, vol. 4. The Fathers of the Church 2. Washington, D.C.: Catholic University of America Press, 1947.

———. *Augustine: Confessions and Enchiridion*. Edited and translated by Albert Outler. Library of Christian Classics 7. Philadelphia: Westminster Press, 1955.

———. *The City of God*. Translated by M. Dods with G. Wilson and J. J. Smith. In *Basic Writings of Saint Augustine*, edited by Whitney J. Oates. 2 vols. New York: Random House, 1948.

———. *Concerning the City of God against the Pagans*. Translated by Henry Bettenson. Harmondsworth, England: Penguin Books, 1972.

———. *Confessionum, Libri XIII*. Edited by Lucas Verheijen. *Sancti Augustini opera*. Corpus christianorum, Series latina 27. Turnhout: Brepols, 1981.

———. *De civitate Dei*. Edited by Bernard Dombart and Alphonsus Kalb. *Aurelii Augustini opera*, Part 14, 1 and 2. Corpus christianorum, Series latina 47 and 48. Turnhout: Brepols, 1955.

———. *De correptione et gratia*. In Migne, *PL* 44.915–46.

———. *De diversis quaestionibus octoginta tribus*. Edited by Almut Mutzenbecher. In *Aurelii Augustini opera*, Part 13, 2. Corpus christianorum, Series latina 44A. Turnhout: Brepols, 1975.

———. *De Genesi ad litteram, imperfectus liber*. In Migne, *PL* 34.219–46.

———. *De libero arbitrio*. Edited by W. M. Green. In *Aurelii Augustini opera*, Part 2, 2. Corpus christianorum, Series latina 29. Turnhout: Brepols, 1970.

———. *De natura boni*. In Migne, *PL* 42.551–72.

———. *De trinitate*. Edited by W. J. Mountain with Fr. Glorie. *Aurelii Augustini opera*, Part 16, 1 and 2. Corpus christianorum, Series latina 50 and 50A. Turnhout: Brepols, 1968.

———. *Eighty-Three Different Questions*. Translated by David Mosher. The Fathers of the Church 70. Washington, D.C.: Catholic University of America Press, 1982.

———. *The Nature of the Good*. In *Augustine: Earlier Writings*, translated by John H. S. Burleigh. Library of Christian Classics 6. Philadelphia: Westminster Press, 1953.

———. *On Free Will*. In *Augustine: Earlier Writings*, translated by John H. S. Burleigh. Library of Christian Classics 6. Philadelphia: Westminster Press, 1953.

———. *Saint Augustine On Genesis*. Translated by Roland J. Teske, S.J. The Fathers of the Church 84. Washington, D.C.: Catholic University of America Press, 1991.

———. *The Trinity*. Translated by Stephen McKenna, C.SS.R. The Fathers of the Church 45. Washington, D.C.: Catholic University of America Press, 1963.

Baker, Denise N. "Julian of Norwich and Anchoritic Literature." *Mystics Quarterly* 19 (1993): 148–60.

Bede. *Bede's Ecclesiastical History of the English People*. Edited by Bertram Colgrave and R.A.B. Mynors. Oxford: Clarendon Press, 1969.

Beer, Frances. *Women and Mystical Experience in the Middle Ages*. Woodbridge, Suffolk: The Boydell Press, 1992.

Bell, David. *The Image and Likeness: The Augustinian Spirituality of William of St. Thierry*. Cistercian Studies Series 78. Kalamazoo, Mich.: Cistercian Publications, 1984.

Bennett, J.A.W. "*Nosce te ipsum*: Some Medieval Interpretations." In *J.R.R. Tolkien, Scholar and Storyteller*, edited by Mary Salu and Robert T. Farrell. Ithaca: Cornell University Press, 1979.

———. *Poetry of the Passion: Studies in Twelve Centuries of English Verse*. Oxford: Clarendon Press, 1982.

Benson, Larry. *Malory's Morte Darthur*. Cambridge: Harvard University Press, 1976.

Bernard of Clairvaux. *Selected Works*. Translated by G. R. Evans. Classics of Western Spirituality. New York: Paulist Press, 1987.

———. *On the Song of Songs IV*. Translated by Irene Edmonds. Cistercian Fathers Series 40. Kalamazoo, Mich.: Cistercian Publications, 1980.

———. *Opera*. Vols. 1 and 2, *Sermones super Cantica Canticorum*. Edited by J. Leclercq, C. H. Talbot, and H. M. Rochais. Rome: Editiones Cistercienses, 1957–1958.

———. *Opera*. Vol. 3, *Tractatus et opuscula*. Edited by J. Leclercq and H. M. Rochais. Rome: Editiones Cistercienses, 1963.

———. *The Works of Bernard of Clairvaux*. Vol. 2, *Song of Songs I*. Translated by Kilian Walsh, O.C.S.O. Cistercian Fathers Series 4. Kalamazoo, Mich.: Cistercian Publications, 1981.

———. *The Works of Bernard of Clairvaux*. Vol. 3, *On the Song of Songs II*. Translated by Kilian Walsh, O.C.S.O. Cistercian Fathers Series 7. Kalamazoo, Mich.: Cistercian Publications, 1983.

———. *The Works of Bernard of Clairvaux*. Vol. 7, *Treatises III: On Grace and Free Choice*. Translated by Daniel O'Donovan, O.S.C.O., with an introduction by Bernard McGinn. Cistercian Fathers Series 19. Kalamazoo, Mich.: Cistercian Publications, 1977.

Bloch, R. Howard. *Medieval Misogyny and the Invention of Western Romantic Love*. Chicago: University of Chicago Press, 1991.

Boffey, Julia. "Women Authors and Women's Literacy in Fourteenth- and Fifteenth-Century England." In *Women and Literature in Britain, 1150–1500*, edited by Carol Meale. Cambridge Studies in Medieval Literature 17. Cambridge: Cambridge University Press, 1993.

Bonaventure. *Opera omnia*. Edited by studio et cura pp. Collegii a S. Bona-ventura. 10 vols. Florence: Ad Claras Aquas (Quarachhi) ex typographia Collegii S. Bonaventurae, 1882- 1902.

———. *The Works of Bonaventure*. Translated by José de Vinck. 5 vols. Patterson, N.J.: St. Anthony Guild Press, 1960–1970.

Børresen, Kari Elisabeth. *Subordination and Equivalence: The Nature and Role of Woman in Augustine and Thomas Aquinas*. Translated by Charles H. Talbot. 1968. Washington, D.C.: University Press of America, 1981.

Bradley, Ritamary. *Julian's Way: A Practical Commentary on Julian of Norwich*. London: HarperCollins*Religious*, 1992.

———. "The Motherhood Theme in Julian of Norwich." *Fourteenth-Century English Mystics Newsletter* 2 (1976): 25–30.

———. "Mysticism in the Motherhood Similitude of Julian of Norwich." *Studia Mystica* 8 (1985): 4–14.

———. "Patristic Background of the Motherhood Similitude in Julian of Norwich." *Christian Scholar's Review* 8 (1978): 101–13.

Bullough, Vern L. "Medieval Medical and Scientific Views of Women." *Viator* 4 (1973): 487–93.

Burrow, J. A. *Ricardian Poetry: Chaucer, Gower, Langland, and the Gawain Poet*. New Haven: Yale University Press, 1971.

Butler, Dom Cuthburt. *Western Mysticism*. 1922. 3d ed. Reprint. New York: Barnes & Noble, 1967.

Bynum, Caroline Walker. "'. . . And Woman His Humanity': Female Imagery in the Religious Writing of the Later Middle Ages." In *Gender and Religion: On the Complexity of Symbols*, edited by Caroline Walker Bynum, Steven Harrell, and Paula Richman. Boston: Beacon Press, 1986.

———. "Bodily Miracles and the Resurrection of the Body in the High Middle Ages." In *Belief in History*, edited by Thomas Kselman. South Bend, Ind.: University of Notre Dame Press, 1990.

———. *Fragmentation and Redemption: Essays on Gender and the Human Body in Medieval Religion*. New York: Zone Books, 1991.

———. *Holy Feast and Holy Fast: The Religious Significance of Food to Medieval Women*. Berkeley and Los Angeles: University of California Press, 1987.

———. *Jesus as Mother: Studies in the Spirituality of the High Middle Ages*. Berkeley and Los Angeles: University of California Press, 1982.

Carruthers, Mary. *The Book of Memory: A Study of Memory in Medieval Culture*. Cambridge Studies in Medieval Literature 10. Cambridge: Cambridge University Press, 1990.

Cayré, P. Fulbert. *La contemplation augustinienne*. 1927. Reprint. Paris: Desclée de Brouwer, 1954.

Chaucer, Geoffrey. *The Riverside Chaucer*. Edited by Larry Benson. 3d ed. Boston: Houghton Mifflin, 1987.

Clanchy, M. T. *From Memory to Written Record: England, 1066–1307*. Cambridge: Harvard University Press, 1979.

Clark, John P. H. "*Fiducia* in Julian of Norwich, II." *Downside Review* 99 (1981): 214–29.

———. "Late Fourteenth-Century Cambridge Theology and the English Contemplative Tradition." In *The Medieval Mystical Tradition in England: Exeter Symposium 5*, edited by Marion Glasscoe. Cambridge: D. S. Brewer, 1992.

Cockerell, Sydney. *The Gorleston Psalter*. London: Printed at the Chiswick Press, 1907.

Coleman, Janet. *Ancient and Medieval Memories: Studies in the Reconstruction of the Past*. Cambridge: Cambridge University Press, 1992.

Colledge, Edmund, O.S.A., and James Walsh, S.J. "Editing Julian of Norwich's *Revelations*: A Progress Report." *Mediaeval Studies* 38 (1976): 404–27.

Courcelle, Pierre. *Connais-toi toi-même de Socrate à Saint Bernard*. Paris: Études Augustiniennes, 1974.

———. "Tradition Neo-Platonicienne et traditions Chrétiennes de la 'region de dissemblance.'" *Archives d'histoire doctrinale et littéraire du moyen âge* 23 (1957): 5–33.

Courtenay, William. *Schools and Scholars in Fourteenth-Century England*. Princeton: Princeton University Press, 1987.

Cousins, Ewert. "Bonaventure's Mysticism of Language." In *Mysticism and Language*, edited by Steven Katz. New York: Oxford University Press, 1992.

———. "Francis of Assisi: Christian Mysticism at the Crossroads." In *Mysticism and Religious Traditions*, edited by Steven Katz. New York: Oxford University Press, 1983.

———. "The Humanity and the Passion of Christ." In *World Spirituality: An Encyclopedic History of the Religious Quest*. Vol. 17, *Christian Spirituality: High Middle Ages and Reformation*, edited by Jill Raitt with Bernard McGinn and John Meyendorff. New York: Crossroad, 1987.

Delumeau, Jean. *Sin and Fear: The Emergence of a Western Guilt Culture, Thirteenth–Eighteenth Centuries*. Translated by Eric Nicholson. 1983. New York: St. Martin's Press, 1990.

Dictionnaire de spiritualité ascétique et mystique, doctrine et histoire. Paris: Beauchesne, 1937–.

Dodd, C. H. *The Interpretation of the Fourth Gospel*. Cambridge: Cambridge University Press, 1953.

Dronke, Peter, ed. *Bernardus Silvestris' Cosmographia*. Leiden: E. J. Brill, 1978.

D.S.H. [A Benedictine of Stanbrook]. "English Spiritual Writers: XII. Dame Julian of Norwich." *Clergy Review*, n.s., 44 (December 1959): 705–20.

Duffy, Eamon. *The Stripping of the Altars: Traditional Religion in England c. 1400–c. 1500*. New Haven: Yale University Press, 1992.

Dutton, Marsha. "Christ Our Mother: Aelred's Iconography for Contemplative Union." In *Goad and Nail*, edited by E. Rozanne Elder. Studies in Medieval Cistercian History 10. Kalamazoo, Mich.: Cistercian Publications, 1985.

———. "The Cistercian Source: Aelred, Bonaventure, and Ignatius." In *Goad and Nail*, edited by E. Rozanne Elder. Studies in Medieval Cistercian History 10. Kalamazoo, Mich.: Cistercian Publications, 1985.

Eckhart, Meister. *Meister Eckhart: Teacher and Preacher*. Edited by Bernard McGinn with Frank Tobin and Elvira Borgstadt. Classics of Western Spirituality. New York: Paulist Press, 1986.

Evans, G. R. *Augustine on Evil*. Cambridge: Cambridge University Press, 1982.

Geertz, Clifford. "Religion as a Cultural System." In *Anthropological Approaches to the Study of Religion*, edited by Michael Banton. New York: Frederick A. Praeger, 1966.

Gibson, Gail M. *The Theater of Devotion: East Anglian Drama and Society in the Late Middle Ages*. Chicago: University of Chicago Press, 1989.

Gillespie, Vincent. "Strange Images of Death: The Passion in Later Medieval English Devotional and Mystical Writing." In *Zeit, Tod und Ewigkeit in der Renaissance Literatur*. 3 vols. Analecta Cartusiana 117. Salzburg: Institut für Anglistik und Amerikanistik, Universität Salzburg, 1987.

Gillespie, Vincent, and Maggie Ross. "The Apophatic Image: The Poetics of Effacement in Julian of Norwich." In *The Medieval Mystical Tradition in England: Exeter Symposium 5*, edited by Marion Glasscoe. Cambridge: D. S. Brewer, 1992.

Gilson, Etienne. *The Mystical Theology of Saint Bernard*. Translated by A.H.C. Downes. New York: Sheed and Ward, 1940.

———. "*Regio dissimilitudinis* de Platon à Saint Bernard de Clairvaux." *Mediaeval Studies* 9 (1947): 108–30.

———. *The Spirit of Mediaeval Philosophy*. Translated by A.H.C. Downes. 1936. New York: Charles Scribner's Sons, 1940.

Glasscoe, Marion. "Time of Passion: Latent Relationships between Liturgy and Meditation in Two Middle English Mystics." In *Langland, the Mystics, and the Medieval English Religious Tradition: Essays in Honour of S. S. Hussey*, edited by Helen Phillips. Cambridge: D. S. Brewer, 1990.

———. "Visions and Revisions: A Further Look at the Manuscripts of Julian of Norwich." *Studies in Bibliography* 42 (1989): 103–20.

Gordon, R. K., ed. and trans. *Anglo-Saxon Poetry*. Rev. ed. New York: Dutton, 1954.

Gradon, Pamela. *Form and Style in Early English Literature*. London: Methuen, 1971.

Heimmel, Jennifer. "*God Is Our Mother*": *Julian of Norwich and the Medieval Image of Christian Feminine Divinity*. Elizabethan & Renaissance Studies

92:5. Salzburg: Institut für Anglistik und Amerikanistik, Universität Salzburg, 1982.

Hick, John. *Evil and the God of Love*. New York: Harper & Row, 1966.

Hilton, Walter. *The Scale of Perfection*. Translated by John P. H. Clark and Rosemary Dorward. Classics of Western Spirituality. New York: Paulist Press, 1991.

Hughes, Jonathan. *Pastors and Visionaries: Religion and Secular Life in Late Medieval Yorkshire*. Woodbridge, Suffolk: The Boydell Press, 1988.

Jantzen, Grace. *Julian of Norwich: Mystic and Theologian*. New York: Paulist Press, 1988.

Javelet, Robert. *Image et ressemblance au douzième siècle de Saint Anselme à Alain de Lille*. 2 vols. Paris: Éditions Letouzey & Ané, 1967.

Johnson, Lynn Staley. "The Trope of the Scribe and the Question of Literary Authority in the Works of Julian of Norwich and Margery Kempe." *Speculum* 66 (1991): 820–38.

Jones, Catherine. "The English Mystic Julian of Norwich." In *Medieval Women Writers*, edited by Katharina M. Wilson. Athens: University of Georgia Press, 1984.

Julian of Norwich. *A Book of Showings to the Anchoress Julian of Norwich*. Edited by Edmund Colledge, O.S.A., and James Walsh, S.J. 2 vols. Studies and Texts 35. Toronto: Pontifical Institute of Mediaeval Studies, 1978.

———. *Showings*. Translated by Edmund Colledge, O.S.A., and James Walsh, S.J. Classics of Western Spirituality. New York: Paulist Press, 1978.

Kelly, F. Douglas. *Sens and conjointure in the Chevalier de la Charrette*. The Hague: Mouton, 1966.

Kempe, Margery. *The Book of Margery Kempe*. Edited by Sanford B. Meech and Hope Emily Allen. Early English Text Society, o.s., 212. London: Early English Text Society, 1940.

———. *The Book of Margery Kempe*. Translated by B. A. Windeatt. Harmondsworth, England: Penguin Books, 1985.

Kieckhefer, Richard. "Major Currents in Late Medieval Devotion." In *World Spirituality: An Encyclopedic History of the Religious Quest*. Vol. 17, *Christian Spirituality: High Middle Ages and Reformation*, edited by Jill Raitt with Bernard McGinn and John Meyendorff. New York: Crossroad, 1987.

———. "Meister Eckhart's Conception of Union with God." *Harvard Theological Review* 71 (1978): 203–35.

———. *Unquiet Souls: Fourteenth-Century Saints and Their Religious Milieu*. Chicago: University of Chicago Press, 1984.

Kristeva, Julia. *Tales of Love*. Translated by Leon S. Roudiez. New York: Columbia University Press, 1987.

Kurath, Hans, Sherman Kuhn, and Robert Lewis, eds. *Middle English Dictionary*. Ann Arbor: University of Michigan Press, 1954–.

Ladner, Gerhart. *Ad Imaginem Dei: The Image of Man in Medieval Art.* Wimmer Lecture, 1962. Latrobe, Penn.: The Archabbey Press, 1965.

Lagorio, Valerie. "Variations on the Theme of God's Motherhood in Medieval English Mystical and Devotional Writings." *Studia Mystica* 8 (1985): 15–37.

Langland, William. *Piers Plowman: The B Version.* Edited by George Kane and E. Talbot Donaldson. London: The Athlone Press, 1975.

Langmuir, Gavin. Review of *Sin and Fear: The Emergence of a Western Guilt Culture, Thirteenth–Eighteenth Centuries,* by Jean Delumeau. *Speculum* 67 (1992): 657–59.

Laqueur, Thomas. *Making Sex: Body and Gender from the Greeks to Freud.* Cambridge: Harvard University Press, 1990.

Lasko, P., and N. J. Morgan, eds. *Medieval Art in East Anglia 1300–1520.* London: Thames and Hudson in association with Jarrold & Sons, 1974.

Leclercq, Jean, O.S.B. *The Love of Learning and the Desire for God: A Study of Monastic Culture.* Translated by Catharine Misrahi. 1957. New York: Fordham University Press, 1961.

Leff, Gordon. *Gregory of Rimini: Tradition and Innovation in Fourteenth Century Thought.* Manchester, England: Manchester University Press, 1961.

Lesnick, Daniel R. *Preaching in Medieval Florence.* Athens: University of Georgia Press, 1989.

Lichtmann, Maria R. "'I desyrede a bodylye syght': Julian of Norwich and the Body." *Mystics Quarterly* 17 (1991): 12–19.

Lochrie, Karma. *Margery Kempe and Translations of the Flesh.* New Cultural Studies. Philadelphia: University of Pennsylvania Press, 1991.

Louth, Andrew. *The Origins of the Christian Mystical Tradition.* Oxford: Clarendon Press, 1981.

Love, Nicholas. *Nicholas Love's* Mirror of the Blessed Life of Jesus Christ: *A Critical Edition.* Edited by Michael G. Sargent. Garland Medieval Texts 18. New York: Garland Publishing, 1992.

McGinn, Bernard. "The Human Person as Image of God II: Western Christianity." In *World Spirituality: An Encyclopedic History of the Religious Quest.* Vol. 16, *Christian Spirituality: Origins to the Twelfth Century.* Edited by Bernard McGinn and John Meyendorff. New York: Crossroad, 1985.

———. "Love, Knowledge and *Unio Mystica* in the Western Christian Tradition." In *Mystical Union and Monotheistic Faith: An Ecumenical Dialogue,* edited by Moshe Idel and Bernard McGinn. New York: Macmillan, 1989.

McLaughlin, Eleanor. "'Christ My Mother': Feminine Naming and Metaphor in Medieval Spirituality." *Nashotah Review* 15 (1975): 228–48.

———. "Equality of Souls, Inequality of Sexes: Woman in Medieval Thought." In *Religion and Sexism: Images of Woman in the Jewish and Christian Traditions,* edited by Rosemary R. Ruether. New York: Simon and Schuster, 1974.

Mâle, Emile. *Religious Art in France: The Late Middle Ages.* Edited by Harry

Bober and translated by Marthiel Mathews from 5th ed. Bollingen series 90, 3. Princeton: Princeton University Press, 1986.

———. *Religious Art in France: The Thirteenth Century*. Translated by Marthiel Mathews from 9th ed. Bollingen Series 90, 2. Princeton: Princeton University Press, 1984.

Mandouze, M. André. "Où en est la question de la mystique augustinienne?" In *Augustinus Magister: Congrès international augustinien*, Paris, 21–24 September 1954. Paris: Études Augustiniennes, 1954. 3:103–63.

Marrow, James. *Passion Iconography in Northern European Art of the Late Middle Ages and Early Renaissance*. Ars Neerlandica 1. Kortrijk, Belgium: Van Ghemmert, 1979.

Matter, E. Ann. *The Voice of My Beloved: The Song of Songs in Western Medieval Christianity*. Philadelphia: University of Pennsylvania Press, 1990.

Meale, Carol. "'. . . alle the bokes that I haue of latyn, englisch, and frensch': Laywomen and Their Books in Late Medieval England." In *Women and Literature in Britain, 1150–1500*, edited by Carol Meale. Cambridge Studies in Medieval Literature 17. Cambridge: Cambridge University Press, 1993.

Meditations on the Life of Christ. Translated by Isa Ragusa and edited by Isa Ragusa and Rosalie Green. Princeton: Princeton University Press, 1961.

Merton, Thomas. *Mystics and Zen Masters*. New York: Dell, 1961.

Migne, J. P., ed. *Patrologia Graeca* (*PG*). 162 vols. Paris, 1857–1866.

———, ed. *Patrologia Latina* (*PL*). 221 vols. Paris, 1844–1864.

Millett, Bella. "Women in No Man's Land: English Recluses and the Development of Vernacular Literature in the Twelfth and Thirteenth Centuries." In *Women and Literature in Britain, 1150–1500*, edited by Carol Meale. Cambridge Studies in Medieval Literature 17. Cambridge: Cambridge University Press, 1993.

Minnis, A. J. *Medieval Theory of Authorship: Scholastic Literary Attitudes in the Later Middle Ages*. 1984. 2d ed. Philadelphia: University of Pennsylvania Press, 1988.

Molinari, Paul, S.J. *Julian of Norwich: The Teaching of a Fourteenth Century English Mystic*. 1958. Reprint. N.p.: The Arden Library, 1979.

Moore, Peter. "Christian Mysticism and Interpretation: Some Philosophical Issues Illustrated in the Study of the Medieval English Mystics." In *The Medieval Mystical Tradition in England: Exeter Symposium 4*, edited by Marion Glasscoe. Cambridge: D. S. Brewer, 1987.

———. "Mystical Experience, Mystical Doctrine, Mystical Technique." In *Mysticism and Philosophical Analysis*, edited by Steven T. Katz. London: Sheldon Press, 1978.

Morris, Colin. *The Discovery of the Individual 1050–1200*. Medieval Academy Reprints for Teaching 19. 1972. Reprint. Toronto: University of Toronto Press, 1987.

Murray, Alexander. *Reason and Society in the Middle Ages.* Oxford: Clarendon Press, 1978.

New Catholic Encyclopedia. New York: McGraw-Hill, 1967–1979.

Newman, Barbara. *Sister of Wisdom: St. Hildegard's Theology of the Feminine.* Berkeley and Los Angeles: University of California Press, 1987.

————. "Some Mediaeval Theologians and the Sophia Tradition." *Downside Review* 108 (1990): 111–30.

Nuth, Joan. *Wisdom's Daughter: The Theology of Julian of Norwich.* New York: Crossroad, 1991.

Orme, Nicholas. *Education and Society in Medieval and Renaissance England.* London: Hambledon Press, 1989.

————. *English Schools in the Middle Ages.* London: Methuen, 1973.

Otis, Brooks. *Ovid as an Epic Poet.* Cambridge: Cambridge University Press, 1966.

The Oxford Book of Medieval Latin Verse. Edited by F.J.E. Raby. 2d ed. Oxford: Clarendon Press, 1959.

Pagels, Elaine. *Adam, Eve, and the Serpent.* New York: Random House, 1988.

Park, Tarjei. "Reflecting Christ: The Role of the Flesh in Walter Hilton and Julian of Norwich." In *The Medieval Mystical Tradition in England: Exeter Symposium 5,* edited by Marion Glasscoe. Cambridge: D. S. Brewer, 1992.

Parkes, M. B. "The Influence of the Concepts of *Ordinatio* and *Compilatio* on the Development of the Book." In *Medieval Learning and Literature: Essays Presented to Richard William Hunt,* edited by J.J.G. Alexander and M. T. Gibson. Oxford: Clarendon Press, 1976.

Patterson, Lee. "'For the Wyves love of Bath': Feminine Rhetoric and Poetic Resolution in the *Roman de la Rose* and the *Canterbury Tales.*" *Speculum* 58 (1983): 656–95.

Pelikan, Jaroslav. *The Christian Tradition: A History of the Development of Doctrine.* Vol. 1, *The Emergence of the Catholic Tradition (100–600).* Vol. 3, *The Growth of Medieval Theology (600–1300).* Vol. 4, *Reformation of Church and Dogma (1300–1700).* Chicago: University of Chicago Press, 1971, 1978, 1984.

Pelphrey, Brant. *Christ Our Mother: Julian of Norwich.* The Way of the Christian Mystics 7. Wilmington, Del.: Michael Glazier, 1989.

————. *Love Was His Meaning: The Theology and Mysticism of Julian of Norwich.* Salzburg Studies in English Literature, Elizabethan & Renaissance Studies. Salzburg: Institut für Anglistik und Amerikanistik, Universität Salzburg, 1982.

Peter Lombard. *Commentarius in Psalmos Davidicos.* In Migne, *PL* 191.61–1296.

————. *In Epistolam ad Romanos.* In Migne, *PL* 191.1301–1534.

Petroff, Elizabeth Alvilda. *Medieval Women's Visionary Literature.* Oxford: Oxford University Press, 1986.

Philo. *Philo.* Translated by F. H. Colson and G. H. Whitaker. 11 vols. Loeb

Classical Library. 1929. Reprint. Cambridge: Harvard University Press, 1949.

Power, Eileen. *Medieval English Nunneries, c. 1275–1535.* 1922. Reprint. New York: Biblo and Tannen, 1964.

The Prickynge of Love. Edited by Harold Kane. 2 vols. Elizabethan & Renaissance Studies 92:10. Salzburg: Institut für Anglistik und Amerikanistik, Universität Salzburg, 1983.

"The Privity of the Passion: Bonaventura de mysteriis passionis Iesu Christi." In *Yorkshire Writers: Richard Rolle of Hampole and His Followers*, edited by C. Horstman. 2 vols. London: Swan Sonnenschein, 1895.

Pseudo-Dionysius. *The Complete Works.* Translated by Colm Luibheid. Classics of Western Spirituality. New York: Paulist Press, 1987.

Rad, Gerhard Von. *Wisdom in Israel.* Nashville, Tenn.: Abingdon Press, 1972.

Randall, Dale B. J. "A Note on Structure in *Sir Gawain and the Green Knight.*" *Modern Language Notes* 72 (1959): 161–63.

Réau, Louis. *Iconographie de l'art chrétien.* Vol. 1, *Iconographie de la Bible.* 1956. Reprint. Nendeln, Liechtenstein: Kraus Reprints, 1974.

Reynolds, Sister Anna Maria, C.P. "Some Literary Influences in the *Revelations* of Julian of Norwich (c. 1342–post-1416)." *Leeds Studies in English and Kindred Languages*, nos. 7 and 8 (1952): 18–28.

Richard of St. Victor. *The Twelve Patriarchs, The Mystical Ark, Book Three of The Trinity.* Translated by Grover A. Zinn. Classics of Western Spirituality. New York: Paulist Press, 1979.

Riddy, Felicity. "'Women talking about the things of God': A Late Medieval Sub-Culture." In *Women and Literature in Britain, 1150–1500*, edited by Carol Meale. Cambridge Studies in Medieval Literature 17. Cambridge: Cambridge University Press, 1993.

Riehle, Wolfgang. *The Middle English Mystics.* Translated by Bernard Standring. 1977. London: Routledge & Kegan Paul, 1981.

Ringbom, Sixten. *Icon to Narrative: The Rise of the Dramatic Close-Up in Fifteenth-Century Devotional Painting.* 1965. 2d ed. Doornspijk, The Netherlands: Davaco, 1984.

Robertson, Elizabeth. *Early English Devotional Prose and the Female Audience.* Knoxville: University of Tennessee Press, 1990.

Rolle, Richard. *The Fire of Love.* Translated by Clifton Wolters. London: Penguin Books, 1972.

———. *The Psalter or Psalms of David and Certain Canticles with a Translation and Exposition in English by Richard Rolle of Hampole.* Edited by Henry Bramley. Oxford: Clarendon Press, 1884.

———. *Richard Rolle: Prose and Verse.* Edited by S. J. Ogilvie-Thomson. Early English Text Society 293. Oxford: Oxford University Press, 1988.

Ruether, Rosemary. "Misogynism and Virginal Feminism in the Fathers of the Church." In *Religion and Sexism: Images of Woman in the Jewish and*

Christian Traditions, edited by Rosemary Ruether. New York: Simon and Schuster, 1974.

Russell, Jeffrey Burton. *Lucifer: The Devil in the Middle Ages*. Ithaca: Cornell University Press, 1984.

[Salter], Elizabeth Zeeman. "Continuity and Change in Middle English Versions of the *Meditationes vitae Christi.*" *Medium Aevum* 26 (1957): 25–31.

———. *Nicholas Love's "Myrrour of the Blessed Lyf of Jesu Christ."* Analecta Cartusiana 10. Salzburg: Institut für Englische Sprache und Literatur, Universität Salzburg, 1974.

Sandler, Lucy Freeman. *Gothic Manuscripts 1285–1385*. 2 vols. A Survey of Manuscripts Illuminated in the British Isles 5. London: Harvey Miller Publishers in conjunction with Oxford University Press, 1986.

Sargent, Michael. "Bonaventura English: A Survey of the Middle English Prose Translations of Early Franciscan Literature." In *Spätmittelalterliche Geistliche Literatur in der Nationalsprache*. 2 vols. Analecta Cartusiana 106. Salzburg: Institut für Anglistik und Amerikanistik, Universität Salzburg, 1984.

Sarum Missal. Edited by J. Wickham Legg. 1916. Reprint. Oxford: Clarendon Press, 1969.

Schiller, Gertrud. *Iconography of Christian Art*. Vol. 2, *The Passion of Jesus Christ*. Translated by Janet Seligman. 1968. Greenwich, Conn.: New York Graphic Society, 1972.

Schmidt, A.V.C. "Langland and the Mystical Tradition." In *The Medieval Mystical Tradition in England: Papers Read at the Exeter Symposium, July 1980*, edited by Marion Glasscoe. Exeter: University of Exeter, 1980.

Simons, W., and J. E. Ziegler. "Phenomenal Religion in the Thirteenth Century and Its Image: Elisabeth of Spalbeek and the Passion Cult." In *Women in the Church*, edited by W. J. Sheils and Diana Wood. Studies in Church History 27. Oxford: Basil Blackwell for The Ecclesiastical History Society, 1990.

Smith, Sister Mary Frances, S.S.N.D. "Wisdom and Personification of Wisdom Occurring in Middle English Literature before 1500." Ph.D. diss., Catholic University of America, 1935.

Southern, R. W. *The Making of the Middle Ages*. New Haven: Yale University Press, 1953.

Stoeber, Michael. *Evil and the Mystics' God*. Toronto: University of Toronto Press, 1992.

Stone, Robert Karl. *Middle English Prose Style: Margery Kempe and Julian of Norwich*. The Hague: Mouton, 1970.

Tanner, Norman P. *The Church in Late Medieval Norwich, 1370–1532*. Studies and Texts 66. Toronto: Pontifical Institute of Mediaeval Studies, 1984.

Tarvers, Josephine Koster. "'Thys ys my mystrys boke': English Women as Readers and Writers in Late Medieval England." In *The Uses of Manuscripts in Literary Studies: Essays in Memory of Judson Boyce Allen*, edited by Charlotte Morse, Penelope Doob, and Marjorie Woods. Studies in Medieval Culture 31. Kalamazoo, Mich.: Medieval Institute Publications, 1992.

Tentler, Thomas. *Sin and Confession on the Eve of the Reformation.* Princeton: Princeton University Press, 1977.

Tomasic, Thomas Michael. "William of Saint-Thierry on the Myth of the Fall: A Phenomenology of *Animus* and *Anima.*" *Recherches de théologie ancienne et médiévale* 46 (1979): 5–52.

Trigg, Roger. *Ideas of Human Nature: An Historical Introduction.* Oxford: Basil Blackwell, 1988.

Tristram, E. W. *English Medieval Wall Painting.* Vol. 2, *The Thirteenth Century*, with a Catalogue compiled in collaboration with Monica Bardswell. Oxford: Published on behalf of the Pilgrim Trust by Oxford University Press, 1950.

Upjohn, Sheila. *In Search of Julian of Norwich.* London: Darton, Longman and Todd, 1989.

Verbeke, Gérard. "Connaissance de soi et connaissance de Dieu chez saint Augustin." *Augustiniana* 4 (1954): 495–515.

[Ward], Sister Benedicta, S.L.G. "Julian the Solitary." In *Julian Reconsidered.* Fairacres, Oxford: SLG Press, 1988.

Watson, Nicholas. "'A Good Lord, How Myte Al Ben Wele?' Julian of Norwich's Self-Invention as a Theologian." Paper presented at conference, "The Roles of Women in the Middle Ages," Binghamton Center for Medieval and Early Renaissance Studies, October 1992.

———. "The Composition of Julian of Norwich's *Revelation of Love.*" *Speculum* 68 (1993): 637–83.

———. *Richard Rolle and the Invention of Authority.* Cambridge Studies in Medieval Literature 13. Cambridge: Cambridge University Press, 1991.

———. "The Trinitarian Hermeneutic in Julian of Norwich's *Revelation of Love.*" In *The Medieval Mystical Tradition in England, Exeter Symposium 5*, edited by Marion Glasscoe. Cambridge: D. S. Brewer, 1992.

Weber, Max. *The Sociology of Religion.* Translated by Ephraim Fischoff. 1922. Boston: Beacon Press, 1963.

William of St. Thierry. *De natura et dignitate amoris.* In Migne, *PL* 184.379–408.

———. *Epistola seu tractatus ad fratres de Monte Dei.* In Migne, *PL* 184.307–64.

———. *The Works of William of St. Thierry.* Vol. 4, *The Golden Epistle: A Letter to the Brethren at Mont Dieu.* Translated by Theodore Berkeley, O.C.S.O. Cistercian Fathers Series 12. Spencer, Mass.: Cistercian Publications, 1971.

Williams, Norman Powell. *The Ideas of the Fall and of Original Sin.* 1927. Reprint. London: Longmans, Green and Co., 1938.

Wilmart, André. "Eve et Goscelin (II)." *Revue Bénédictine* 50 (1930): 42–83.

Windeatt, B. A. "The Art of Mystical Loving: Julian of Norwich." In *The Medieval Mystical Tradition in England: Papers Read at the Exeter Symposium, July 1980*, edited by Marion Glasscoe. Exeter: University of Exeter, 1980.

————. "Julian of Norwich and Her Audience." *Review of English Studies*, n.s., 28 (1977): 1–17.

————. "'Privytes to us': Knowing and Re-vision in Julian of Norwich." In *Chaucer to Shakespeare: Essays in Honour of Shinsuke Ando*, edited by Toshiyuki Takamiya and Richard Beadle. Woodbridge, Suffolk: D. S. Brewer, 1992.

Woolf, Rosemary. *The English Religious Lyric in the Middle Ages*. Oxford: Clarendon Press, 1968.

————. "The Theme of Christ the Lover-Knight in Medieval English Literature." *Review of English Studies*, n.s., 13 (1962): 1–16. Reprinted in *Art and Doctrine: Essays on Medieval Literature*, edited by Heather O'Donoghue. London: The Hambledon Press, 1986.

Wormald, Francis. *Collected Writings*. Vol. 1, *Studies in Medieval Art from the Sixth to the Twelfth Centuries*. Edited by J.J.G. Alexander, T. J. Brown, and Joan Gibbs. London: Harvey Miller Publishers in conjunction with Oxford University Press, 1984.

Zum Brunn, Emilie. *St. Augustine: Being and Nothingness*. Translated by Ruth Namad. 1978. 2d ed. New York: Paragon House, 1988.